MONROE COLLEGE LIBRARY

WITHDRAWN from
Monroe College Library

3 7340 01075350 4

D0207680

PORTABLE PENSION PLANS
FOR CASUAL LABOR MARKETS

23,514

PORTABLE PENSION PLANS
FOR CASUAL LABOR MARKETS

Lessons from the
Operating Engineers
Central Pension Fund

Teresa Ghilarducci, Garth Mangum,
Jeffrey S. Petersen, Peter Philips

Foreword by Ray Marshall

MONROE COLLEGE LIBRARY
2468 Jerome Ave.
Bronx, NY 10468

Q

QUORUM BOOKS
Westport, Connecticut • London

HD
7116
.B92
U66
1995

Library of Congress Cataloging-in-Publication Data

Portable pension plans for casual labor markets : lessons from
    the operating engineers Central Pension Fund / Teresa Ghilarducci . . .
    [et al.] ; foreword by Ray Marshall.
        p.   cm.
    Includes bibliographical references (p.   ) and index.
    ISBN 0–89930–995–X (alk. paper)
    1. Construction workers—Pensions—United States.   2. Building-
service employees—Pensions—United States.   3. Mechanics
(Persons)—Pensions—United States.   4. Steam engineers—Pensions—
United States.   5. Pension trusts—United States.   6. International
Union of Operating Engineers.   I. Ghilarducci, Teresa.
HD7116.B92U63   1995
620'.0068'3—dc20   95–7960

British Library Cataloguing in Publication Data is available.

Copyright © 1995 by Teresa Ghilarducci, Garth Mangum,
Jeffrey S. Petersen, and Peter Philips

All rights reserved. No portion of this book may be
reproduced, by any process or technique, without
the express written consent of the publisher.

Library of Congress Catalog Card Number: 95–7960
ISBN: 0–89930–995–X

First published in 1995

Quorum Books, 88 Post Road West, Westport, CT 06881
An imprint of Greenwood Publishing Group, Inc.

Printed in the United States of America

The paper used in this book complies with the
Permanent Paper Standard issued by the National
Information Standards Organization (Z39.48–1984).

10 9 8 7 6 5 4 3 2 1

Contents

Contents

Tables and Figures

TABLES

FIGURES

Acronyms

ABC	Associated Building Contractors
AFL	American Federation of Labor
AFL-CIO	American Federation of Labor and Congress of Industrial Organizations
AGC	Association of General Contractors
CII	Council of Institutional Investors
COLAs	cost-of-living-allowances
CPF	Central Pension Fund of the International Union of Operating Engineers and Participating Employers
CSPF	Teamsters Central States Pension Fund
DOL	Department of Labor
EBRI	Employee Benefit Research Institute
EJPF	Engineers Joint Pension Fund
ERISA	Employee Retirement Income Security Act
ETIs	economically targeted investments
FSA	funding standard account
GNP	gross national product
HIT	Housing Investment Trust
IBEW	International Brotherhood of Electrical Workers
IBT	International Brotherhood of Teamsters
IRA	individual retirement account
IRS	Internal Revenue Service

IUOE	International Union of Operating Engineers
MICA	Mass Insurance Consultants and Administrators
MPPAA	Multiemployer Pension Plan Amendments Act
NLRA	National Labor Relations Act
NLRB	National Labor Relations Board
PBGC	Pension Benefit Guarantee Corporation
REA	Retirement Equity Act
S&P	Standard & Poor's
SEC	Securities and Exchange Commission
SSA	Social Security Act
UAW	United Auto Workers
UFOs	unidentified flying objects
UMWA	United Mineworkers of America

Foreword

This is a valuable book for a number of reasons. First, it deals with an extremely important subject, pension systems, that are not well enough understood by policymakers and the general public. With a value over $4 trillion, pension funds are the chief independent source of equity capital in the United States. How these funds are managed, therefore, has very important implications for the health of the American economy and financial markets, as well as the retirement security of American workers. As this study demonstrates, since union workers are twice as likely to have pensions as non-union workers, the declining incidence of unions in the private sector raises serious questions about the adequacy of retirement security for American workers.

Portable Pension Plans for Casual Labor Markets likewise provides important analytical and factual bases for U.S. pension policy, which needs strengthening to clarify such questions as: Who owns pension funds? Who should control them? What should trustees be allowed to do with the funds? The authors conclude, I think correctly, that pension funds are deferred wages and therefore should be jointly trusteed by workers and managers.

A second reason why this is a valuable book is that a complex subject is very competently and clearly handled by one of America's leading labor economists, Garth Mangum, who also tends to be thoroughly familiar with the International Union of Operating Engineers, and Teresa Ghilarducci, a labor economist who not only thoroughly understands pension funds, but also knows how to make this subject accessible to non-specialists. Peter Philips is rapidly coming to the forefront among younger labor economists, and Jeff Petersen, who drew his Ph.D. dissertation from the study, is a promising newcomer to the field. These authors have used the evolution of the Operating Engineers Central Pension Fund (CPF) to provide readers with an excellent primer on the theory, history, administration, and regulation of pension funds. In addition, they examine the relationships between pension funds, skill development, economic performance of companies and industries, union policies and strengths, and general economic conditions. Since the CPF represents relatively small employers, of increasingly skilled workers in a mix of casual and stable employment, it provides valuable insights into how pension funds can simultaneously provide for the retirement security of workers and meet company and union needs in these important and growing industry segments.

A third factor that makes this a valuable book is the insights it provides into the importance of labor-management cooperation in jointly trusteed pension funds. The CPF example makes it very clear that worker representatives can develop the skills needed to manage pension funds in a highly competent and sophisticated manner. Indeed, the CPF's trustees made judicious use of professional advisors and educated themselves sufficiently well in sophisticated portfolio management matters to outperform many, if not most, independent asset managers; to pioneer some techniques; and to develop others well before they became common practice. Indeed, the CPF has acquired a strong reputation for sophistication and competence among professional money managers, as well as in the multiemployer pension fund community. CPF trustees learned early that money management is not a science and that workers' trustees could learn these techniques if they had the opportunity and were willing to learn the fundamentals, to perfect their skills and knowledge from experience, develop competent staffs, to make effective use of consultants, and, most important, to be actively involved in making decisions about the funds.

The CPF clearly has had exceptional leadership, but there is general evidence that jointly trusteed funds are at least as well managed (and probably much better managed) as those controlled entirely by companies. There is absolutely no doubt that well-managed, jointly trusteed funds like the CPF provide much better, and more secure, benefits for workers and their families. The company-managed funds too often put company financial concerns ahead of the interests of beneficiaries, while the beneficiaries' welfare is the only concern of well-managed, jointly trusteed plans. The CPF case provides important insights into the kinds of things trustees must do to effectively meet their fiduciary responsibilities.

This, therefore, is a valuable book for industrial relations specialists, labor leaders, managers, policymakers, and anyone interested in this important subject.

Ray Marshall

Chapter 1

The Evolving Challenge

Jack Smith, Jill Jones, John Black, and Tony Chavez share the occupation of operating engineer, Jack and Jill as machine operators in the construction industry and John and Tony responsible for operating and maintaining the equipment that heats, cools, secures, and facilitates movement and communication within large buildings. Each day they, like the rest of us, are twenty-four hours closer to the inevitable retirement from which only early demise can save any of us. At that time, they will be dependent for subsistence income on their savings and investment from their working years, the forced savings of the Social Security system, support from their families, and if they have been wise or lucky enough in their career choice, pensions from their employers.

But these four also have something else in common. They are all employed in industries characterized by small firms and sporadic employment relationships. None of their employers has the economies of scale and probabilities of survival to dependably promise them a pension on retirement. Jack and Jill will likely work only a few months for any of dozens or even hundreds of employers in their working lifetimes. John and Tony have more stable employment but share it with only a handful of fellow employees. How in those settings can the pension contributions of numerous small employers be combined to ensure an adequate retirement income to skilled workers providing essential services under casual employment? That is the role of the Central Pension Fund of the International Union of Operating Engineers and Participating Employers, which we celebrate as an example of the efforts of a number of unions charged with the task of creating retirement security from a working career marked by employment insecurity.

This chapter sets the stage with an overview of the theory of union-management trusteed defined-benefit pension funds in the context of casual labor markets. We then review the challenges of establishment, growth, and maturity of the CPF played out within an atmosphere of rapid expansion and contraction of unionized employment.

PENSIONS IN SMALL OR CASUAL LABOR MARKETS

Because nearly a century ago the same motive power—the steam engine—that generated electricity and provided heat and lights individually to each major building in America's cities was also applied to the power shovels that excavated for the foundations and the hoists that lifted building materials in the construction of such buildings, a union was born in 1896, joining together the operating engineers involved in both activities. That union, which was originally known as the International Union of Steam Engineers and later—with the demise of steam as motive power—as the International Union of Operating Engineers (IUOE), would ever after have two major divisions: the stationary engineers, characterized by the immobility of their workplaces, and the hoisting and portable engineers, operating mobile construction equipment. Technological trends dictated that the stationary engineers would dominate the first half of the union's history to date and the hoisting and portable the second half, but with another reversal of the relative growth pace characterizing the end of the first century.

Pensions were not a major concern of the first half century of IUOE history. At the union's beginning, with the United States just emerging from its agrarian age, families were still large and extended, with each generation steeped in the tradition of supporting the previous one through its relatively brief non-working years. Within forty years of the union's founding, government would mark the decline of the extended family and the rise of the nuclear one, along with the diminished economic role of the aged in an industrial society, by guaranteeing a minimum retirement income through the Social Security Act of 1935. By 1949, the Supreme Court of the United States had concluded that a pension at retirement was such a critical "condition of work" that an employer could not refuse to bargain over it under the requirements of the National Labor Relations Act.

But the IUOE still had a problem. The Supreme Court's decision was handed down in a case involving the demand that the Inland Steel Company bargain with the United Steelworkers of America over a pension for employees who expected to spend their working lifetimes in the employ of a large, stable business firm. How was that to work for a handful of stationary engineers in the bowels of an office building, or individual equipment operators employed sporadically by a variety of relatively small contractors over an extended landscape? Asking as well as answering that question requires an understanding of the labor markets and circumstances in which operating engineers work.

As noted, the stationary engineers, who constitute 28 percent of the IUOE membership, operate and maintain the physical plant systems of office buildings, schools, factories, hospitals, and similar facilities. They work typically in small groups of five to twenty employees, sometimes as the only employees of the owner of a single building, sometimes the employees of a building management contractor, sometimes as an isolated unit of specialists within a larger employing entity such as a hospital. In the latter cases, the stationary engineers might be included in a *pension plan* covering the entire enterprise. But typically the employing unit is too small to mount and maintain its own pension plan. Neither does the employing unit ordinarily have the associational connections with the employers of other stationary engineer units that would make possible an employer-initiated multiemployer plan. If the stationary unit is unionized, the union could provide the initiative and binding force. However, stationary engineers' locals within the International Union of Operating Engineers are typically small. The average stationary local has 200 members, nowhere near enough to either administer or spread the risks of a pension plan.

Not only are the employing units of the construction industry typically small, but the employer-employee relationship is a casual one. Dependent on their ability to be the lowest bidder for a construction contract, few individual contractors can successfully predict their future volume of business and employment. Except for a few key personnel, employment is limited from project to project. Even within a particular project, employment fluctuates widely by craft. On a commercial or industrial building, for instance, operating engineers and teamsters are required to operate earth-moving equipment for site preparation and excavation. They then largely disappear in favor of carpenters, concrete finishers, iron workers, plumbers, pipefitters, and electricians, except for a reduced number of operating engineers to hoist building materials. On a highway project, a dam, or other primarily earth-moving projects, the operating engineer employment will be more continuous, although the types of equipment operated will fluctuate. But that continuity lasts only until project completion. A general contractor is responsible for an entire project and typically employs the five basic trades—carpenters, laborers, cement masons, operating engineers, and teamsters, subcontracting with specialty contractors for the other required skills. The specialty trades move even more frequently among projects, although they may remain for several projects in the employ of a single subcontractor. Whether for basic or specialty trades, any one project may last from a few weeks to a few years. A construction worker may have one or several employers in one construction season and upwards of one hundred or more employers over a working career.

Obtaining contracts by bid, a contractor cannot afford to keep on between projects, or between applications of a particular skill within a project, the full complement of skills required by each project. A casual labor market is the result. Both the employer and the employee may be permanently attached to the industry, but they are not ordinarily attached to each other. Weather adds an additional seasonal and sporadic factor to the employment relationship, differing by geographical section of the country. A fully employed construction worker, taking advantage of favorable weather, can rarely expect more than 1,500 annual hours of employment, including overtime. Weather vulnerability varies considerably by type of construction, the earth-moving activities of operating engineers being more vulnerable to weather-related time loss than the building activities of electricians or plumbers. Type of construction adds another geographical factor. Housing and commercial construction may be fairly continuous, although fluctuating in volume, in any one locality. Highway construction will be sporadic in any one locality but fairly continuous within a state. Heavy construction projects, such as dams and airports, and major industrial construction, such as power-generating plants, oil refineries, and factories occur rarely in any one locality. Commercial and housing contractors can therefore concentrate geographically, whereas industrial and heavy and highway contractors must maintain geographical mobility. Craft mobility must be equal to that of the contractors who employ them.

The industrial relations of the construction industry were shaped by these forces. Because the employers tended to be relatively small and tenuous, the various building and construction trades unions came to serve as the personnel arm of the industry in order to protect their members. With labor costs representing a relatively high portion of total production costs and contracts awarded by competitive bidding, workers had an interest in seeing that wages were not unduly driven down in the process. Hence the primary goal of construction unions—to take wages out of competition. Although any one contractor might find advantage in being able to break ranks and bid on the basis of lower wages in a particular instance, all had an interest in knowing that their competitors could not obtain skilled labor any more cheaply than they. Hence, there was not strong employer resistance to any uniformly enforced wage rate. Within reasonable limits, wages negotiated between a craft union and an association of all of the employers of that craft was an advantage to all within the industry—although not necessarily to the purchaser of construction services.

The training and recruitment functions were shaped by the same forces. Few construction industry employers are large enough and provide sufficient continuity of employment to afford to train their own employees. The costs must be imposed on the employees or the public education system, or spread over the entire industry. If a trainee is to have reasonable continuity of employment and exposure to all applications of the craft, there must be a mechanism for rotation among employers. A jointly negotiated and administered but union-driven apprentice system is the result. And if employers were to be free to release any unnecessary employees, yet be assured of access to competent skills when they were again needed, there had to be a multiemployer referral system. Because the priority interest was that of the employees, it was to be expected not only that the union would be the driving force in hiring hall operations, but also that employer cooperation would be essential to it.

If all of that is so, why has the construction industry, which was 70 percent union a generation ago, evolved to a 70 percent non-union system? First, the driving force in the "open shop movement" has been not the contractor-employers, but the large-scale purchasers of construction services, members of the Business Roundtable. Whereas contractors were concerned only for relative costs and not absolute costs, the purchaser of construction was paying the tab for all. Many of them insisted upon non-union construction and assisted in the foundation of the Associated Building Contractors (ABC) to facilitate that development. Second, there has been considerable slack and high unemployment in the industry for the past quarter century. Skilled workers were available and they had to accept employment where they could find it. If purchasers insisted on non-union conditions and workers had no alternatives, open shop contractors had no difficulty finding the needed skills.

What the future portends, with the open shop sector failing to train replacements, is a speculation for another treatise. Our purpose here is to explore the implications of a casual labor market for retirement systems.[1] An individual employed with cyclical interruptions by the same employer over a lifetime can have deferred wages set aside and paid out after retirement. An employee rotating among various employers within an industry can prepare for retirement only by either consistently saving a portion of earnings or by having each employer defer and deposit some portion of the individuals wages into some sort of industry or broader pool for payment after retirement. Any set of employers could agree to establish and administer some such system. But short of government intervention and absent labor organization, there is no force external to the individual employer to persuade and enforce participation and to provide continuous monitoring and administration. All employers in concert may recognize the advantage of a pension in maintaining a skilled labor pool, as well as feeling a sense of moral obligation to the industry workforce, but any one employer can perceive the short-term advantage of breaking ranks for a labor cost windfall. Once again, the choice is between a government agency or a union as the persuader and enforcer of a multiemployer pension system.

Here again the issue of geographical scope arises. As we have noted, wage bargains and training and recruitment systems have tended to take on the same geographical dimensions as the area over which employers bid against each other for contracts. As a substantial component of labor costs, pensions must of necessity be negotiated along with wages, suggesting decentralized pension administration. But as will be explored later, an essential element in pension administration, as in any insurance system, is the advantage of spreading risks and costs over large groups of people. A pension paid to a long-lived person is lessened in cost because some members of the same pension scheme die early. The smaller the pool of pensioners, the higher the risk and the costs. Some locals of the IUOE are as large as some international unions and operate over substantial geographical expanses—Local 3 with its 35,000 members spread over four large western states, for instance. But 112 IUOE locals have fewer than 1000 members, and 75 locals have fewer than 500 members. Then there is the pipeline industry, wherein one project may traverse the jurisdictions of many local unions. Similarly, there are the General Presidents' Contract Maintenance agreements, in which the presidents of several building and construction unions negotiate jointly with individual contractors engaged in the maintenance of industrial plants, oil refineries, or other facilities in a variety of localities. Should the locals or the international be responsible for pension administration? Must pension negotiation and pension administration have the same geographical scope? The answer to these questions has been the key to the historical emergence of the complex local/international pension relationship within the IUOE.

WHAT UNION-MANAGEMENT TRUSTEED DEFINED-BENEFIT PENSIONS DO

Employment-based, *defined-benefit pensions* should not be confused with employment-based individual savings for retirement such as 401Ks, or with other forms of individual retirement savings such as individual retirement accounts (IRAs), mutual fund holdings, or savings accounts. The basic reason for this is that defined-benefit pension funds are a form of wealth held in common, whereas individual savings vehicles, even in the employment context are a form of individual wealth. Defined contribution plans that are jointly administered but individually credited with benefits limited to earnings on the contributions credited to specific individuals are also individual rather than group wealth.

Group wealth can do three things that individual wealth precludes. First, group wealth can insure participants within the group against unforeseen circumstances, such as disabling injuries or unexpected longevity. Second, wealth held in common can be redistributed within the group to reward certain behaviors, such as institutional loyalty, or to meet some notions of group fairness. Finally, because group wealth is not individual wealth, individuals can be restricted from having access to this wealth prior to retirement, death, or disability. Thus, the rules of the group force the individual to save until retirement.

The terminology "labor-management trusteed" or "jointly trusteed" refers to the requirement imposed by the Taft-Hartley Act of 1947 that any pension plan administered by a labor union be governed by a board of trustees representing both union and management. The CPF and most other jointly trusteed pension funds within the construction industry are defined-benefit pension programs. To the extent that non-union contractors in construction offer any pension benefits at all, they are typically defined-contribution, 401K pension plans rather than defined-benefit plans. Thus, the major alternative to jointly trusteed, defined-benefit pensions within construction is a system of individual savings for retirement.[2] Because it is important to understand the unique aspects of common-wealth, defined-benefit pension funds, we explain these three functions in some detail.

Employment-based, defined-benefit pensions provide a form of insurance that individual savings accounts cannot provide. Employer contributions to a pension fund go into a common pool of savings and investment. From this common pool of wealth, workers are paid retirement benefits, typically for the rest of their lives and often for the rest of their spouses' lives. Some workers live a long time in retirement, whereas others die sooner. The common pool of wealth in pension funds insures each worker against outliving their retirement income. Workers who live into their nineties continue to receive retirement income that comes from the monies contributed into the fund on behalf of workers who died prematurely after retirement. Pension funds like the CPF therefore redistribute benefits from their short-lived to their long-lived participants. Often, employment-based pension funds also insure their participants against becoming disabled on the job. Like insuring against living too long, disability insurance is also a form of redistribution, in this case from the healthy to the disabled. Individual savings accounts do not form a pool of collectively owned wealth and therefore cannot insure against longevity or disability through redistribution.

The money in these defined benefit pension funds is not only a form of group wealth that allows for insurance against the unforeseen, it is also a form of deferred wages. In a capitalized, defined-benefit pension program, the employer has agreed to save and invest money today on behalf of a set of workers to create the wealth needed to provide income to those workers when they have retired.

In general, wages serve as an incentive structure inducing work from workers. For instance, by setting current wages in an occupation higher than what is easily available from similar jobs, an employer can induce workers to work harder today. By setting the structure of wages so that wages rise with seniority within the firm, the employer can induce workers to remain and develop long-term loyalty to the company.

Like wages that are paid at the end of each pay period, deferred wages can be used by employers to structure work incentives. By setting vesting rules, rules for breaks in service and benefit formulas to reward long-term service to the company, employers can use deferred wages like current wages as an incentive structure to generate firm attachment and loyalty.

Collectively bargained pension rules and benefits reflect the interests and intentions of unions as well as management. As collective bargaining agents, unions inevitably have to weigh the relative interests of distinct groups within their membership when bargaining for both current and future wages. Pension benefits, along with health, schooling, and other benefits are part of an overall wage package the union negotiates. In the context of multiple trade-offs, union negotiators must keep in mind the politics of contract approval, union elections, and institutional interest as they pursue the collective interests of their members. Union negotiators must weigh the relative merits of training, current wages, and improved health benefits along with pensions in negotiating a wage package. In this, negotiators must consider the interests of skilled and unskilled workers, younger and older workers, workers and retirees, workers with and without families, and other distinct interest groups.

Along with interest groups within the union, labor negotiators also must think of the union as an institution. Like many firms, the union often has an interest in worker attachment to the union. Thus, the union may wish to structure pension rules and benefits to reward continuous attachment to the union. Thus, extended vesting rules and break-in-service rules may be designed to discourage workers from seeking non-union work. The union may also join management in touting pension promises as bigger than they actually are. In difficult negotiations, it may become politic to agree to a pension benefit that looks like it promises much in the future but in fact has a limited current cost to the company or the jointly managed pension fund. This may sweeten the deal for contract approval without costing the company much now, or allow for greater company concessions in another area of the contract. Unions may also negotiate pension benefits for small but politically powerful groups within the union that cost the company little and promise the majority of union members nothing. Thus, not only do defined-benefit pension funds insure against the unforeseen, they also redistribute wealth in order to reward certain behaviors such as institutional loyalty, and they can sometimes seem to promise more than they eventually deliver.

Employment-based pension funds are also a form of forced savings. Both employer-initiated and collectively bargained defined-benefit pensions alter the relationship between the worker and a surrounding consumer society which promotes consumer debt rather than savings. The pressure to consume in the U.S. economy is intense and the institutions providing consumer loans are widespread. It is commonplace for workers to borrow to finance vacations, Christmas gifts, home improvements, consumer appliances, automobiles, and many other items. In the case of borrowing to buy a house, typically the house remains and is usable after it is paid for. Thus, paying off a debt-financed house prior to retirement is both a form of current consumption and savings for the future. However, no other major consumer purchase is as durable as a house. In most other cases, the consumer item typically is used up around the time the debt that financed its purchase is extinguished. Thus, debt-based purchases usually constrain the worker's ability to save for retirement by adding debt maintenance to needed expenditures prior to putting away any residual savings. Furthermore, advertisements and the consumer culture they promote push immediate needs to the forefront and drive retirement needs out of mind.

In the case of workers who are seasonally or cyclically employed or who must migrate to work, what savings there are typically must go to cover consumption during layoffs or while on the move. For these workers, saving for the distant future of retirement is all the harder. Pensions force consumers to save despite the press of current needs and the exigencies of layoffs and job search. In contrast to IRAs and 401Ks, defined-benefit pension contributions are not voluntary and cannot be withdrawn prematurely. This is because these pension contributions are not current wages put into savings. They are future wage promises vouchsafed by a common wealth created by these contributions.

In sum, individual retirement savings plans are not group forms of wealth. Therefore, they cannot insure against the unforeseen, they cannot share wealth either fairly or unfairly through redistribution, and they cannot insulate the individual from the periodic crises of current consumption needs. IRAs, 401Ks, mutual fund holdings, and other forms of individual wealth are atomistic efforts at achieving consumption after a person's work life has ended. Defined-benefit pension funds are a collective strategy for achieving the same goal. Defined-contribution plans are groups in their insurance aspect but individualized in their payout. In the past, the family has formed a wealth-sharing collective by which income was redistributed across generations and among the sexes. Employment-based pension funds have assumed a similar role in redistributing income and accumulated wealth among older and younger workers, between married and unmarried workers, and between disabled and healthy workers.

Viewed as insurance, pension funds redistribute among participants based on unforeseen events that happen to some but not to others. Viewed as deferred wages, pension funds redistribute among participants based on accomplishments some achieve but others do not. Viewed as a supplement to the extended family, pension funds force individuals to save, manage the consequent collective wealth for the good of the group and distribute income among participants based partly on institutional norms of right and wrong.

PREVIEW OF PORTABLE PENSIONS FOR CASUAL LABOR MARKETS

Chapter 2 details the struggles, failures, and eventual successes of unions and union employers to provide benefit programs to their members. The number of workers covered by collectively bargained pension plans grew rapidly after World War II. This growth was partly in response to the fact that Social Security benefits had failed to keep pace with inflation through the 1940s. But wage-price controls during and immediately following World War II also discouraged wage increases and allowed for increases in overall compensation through an increase in benefit payments. Furthermore, health and pension demands snowballed through the union community after John L. Lewis, president of the United Mineworkers, won the establishment of $100 a month pensions for retired mine workers. This achievement in 1946 came after a nationally visible strike and posed a challenge to all strong labor leaders to obtain the same or better benefit.

Like Social Security, the Mineworkers' pension plan was a pay-as-you-go program in which each year's pension obligations were paid for from that year's mine production revenues. Walter Reuther, president of the United Auto Workers, upped the ante among labor negotiators by obtaining a fully capitalized pension program in 1950. The Auto Workers' plan called for the establishment of a capital fund that would finance pension benefits from accrued savings. This pension form gave the pension program relative independence from year-to-year changes in the business fortunes of the auto industry. In the case of the auto workers, each car company established its own corporate pension plan through a collectively bargained agreement with the United Auto Workers. The capital fund established by the collectively bargained contract was under the management and control of each company.

Union-management trusteed pension funds in mining, trucking and construction also grew rapidly after World War II. By 1959, over 3 million workers in these industries were covered by union-management trusteed pension funds that were jointly managed by an equal number of union and management trustees. Prior to the 1930s, some unions had occasionally run their own benefits programs covering death, disability, pensions, and sometimes health. These early benefits programs were financed out of union dues and were typically on a pay-as-you-go basis. But the jointly trusteed health and pension programs that emerged after World War II were financed from the wage packet negotiated with employers. And as a rule, these plans were capitalized programs in which the funds collected by the pension program accumulated over time. Thus, these joint trustee boards became responsible for the management and investment of an ever increasing pool of money. The various capital funds tended to grow because these new pension programs were young, with a high proportion of currently employed workers relative to retirees receiving benefits. So, in the beginning, these new funds took in a lot more money than they paid out in benefits. Consequently, capital funds grew and needed to be managed.

In both single-employer management-trusteed funds and multiemployer, jointly trusteed funds, the growth of invested capital posed problems as well as benefits. The most common problem was simply how to invest these monies prudently and profitably. Union trustees in jointly managed funds were often cautious investors, wanting the growing pool of money to be put in low-risk rock-solid investments that yielded very limited returns. A common problem of single-employer, company-managed pensions was the tendency to underfund the capital needed to meet future commitments. A dilemma faced by all jointly trusteed pension programs was deciding the extent to which pension investment policies would be made compatible with union bargaining goals and philosophies. Often, this merely meant refraining from investing in overseas ventures and avoiding investments in blatantly anti-union companies. However, jointly trusteed funds on occasion would succumb to the temptation to invest in schemes promoted by individuals close to some union or management trustee.

The problem of corruption and malfeasance in capitalized pension programs went in quite opposite directions, depending on whether it was a single-employer company-managed program or a multiemployer jointly managed program. In the company-managed pension plans, corruption focused on shorting contributions into the pension fund and diverting these monies for other corporate or executive purposes. In the multiemployer pension programs, the money had to be contributed to the plan before it could be misdirected, mismanaged, or stolen. In the single-employer context, mismanagement and corruption often showed up years after the fact when it became apparent that there were insufficient funds to pay retirement benefits, or the company was in bankruptcy, effectively voiding its commitments to retirees. In the multiemployer context, it was much less common to find pensioners without pensions simply because it was unlikely that all of the multiplicity of employers would dodge their obligations by declaring bankruptcy. Corruption and mismanagement tended to show up in "brother-in-law" investments that had gone sour or poor investment decisions that were rooted more in a desire to promote union business, or protect employer interests, than in promoting prudent, profitable returns.

The most notorious case of corruption in the multiemployer, jointly-trusteed context was the Central States Pension Fund (CSPF) of the International Brotherhood of Teamsters.[3] After the expulsion of the Teamsters from the American Federation of Labor and Congress of Industrial Organizations (AFL-CIO), Teamster President Jimmy Hoffa aggressively promoted pension benefits at the bargaining table. In 1961, Hoffa claimed the highest monthly benefit at the earliest retirement age of any union in the country, although a close reading of vesting requirements and benefit payouts would show that few union members would qualify for monthly benefits and that these benefits would only last until Social Security payments kicked in at age sixty-five.

The Central Pension Fund of the International Union of Operating Engineers and Participating Employers emerged in this environment. It was shaped by the problems and prospects of the casual but booming labor market in construction. It was stimulated by the growth of union competition over providing workers with decent health and retirement benefits when it was becoming increasingly clear that Social Security was not going to do the entire job by itself. The CPF was also chastened by the specter of corruption in the Central States Pension Fund of the Teamsters and, to a lesser extent, by the problems of ineptitude and nepotism occasionally visible elsewhere among union-management trusteed pension programs.

Chapter 3 documents the beginnings of the CPF. Several locals within the IUOE had established pension funds in the 1950s. Most of the IUOE locals that established pension funds were construction locals, simply because stationary locals tended to be small and could not afford the administrative costs associated with putting together a pension plan for a few hundred workers. Along with most stationary locals, the smaller hoisting and portable locals within the IUOE had not established pension plans by the late 1950s. In 1959, the International began looking into the possibility of establishing a central pension fund that would serve those locals unable or not desiring to undertake their own pensions.

Such a centralized pension program would have the added advantage for construction workers within the union of providing coverage across locals for workers who traveled from area to area in search of work. At the time, local pension programs did not have legally binding reciprocal agreements with each other to handle traveling workers. Consequently, workers coming into an area would have benefits paid into a local pension fund on their behalf but these workers would have very little probability of accumulating enough work in the area to qualify for benefits from the local's pension program. A centralized pension program would solve this problem for transient workers who moved among locals within the central pension fund. This would also begin to present a solution to the problem of operating engineers who worked on pipeline construction and typically moved across local jurisdictions throughout their work lives.

Workers within the IUOE are a relatively homogeneous lot compared to industrial union workers. There are the two divisions of hoisting and portable engineers and stationary engineers. Within each division, the work skills are similar and the work lives are similar. Thus until recent years, when some locals have aggressively organized a wide range of workers, the membership of any one local in one area would consist of a relatively homogeneous group of similarly skilled engineers facing similar job prospects and working roughly similar hours over the year. However, a centralized pension fund faced two problems of diversity that local funds did not face. First, unlike almost all local pension funds, a centralized pension fund would have to harmonize the divergent work lives of stationary and portable engineers. Construction workers tend to work fewer annual hours but engineers in the construction industry, at least in the 1950s and 1960s, were typically paid a higher hourly wage. A centralized pension fund had to address the fact that half its participants would not work 2,000 hours per year, whereas the other half would. How much work per year would qualify a worker for one year of service credit toward vesting?

The second problem a centralized pension faced yet local pension programs could dodge was the fact that wages for both portable and stationary engineers varied widely across the country. Bargaining for pension contributions (except for the pipeline contract), the subject of Chapter 4, was always at a local level. Stronger regions had stronger contracts and could put more money into a pension program. A centralized pension fund had to include members with weak contracts and minimal pension contributions, as well as these stronger ones. Thus, establishing a centralized pension fund had the advantage of offering economies of scale to smaller locals and the ability to vest traveling workers, but it also had to overcome the obstacles of differences between stationary and construction engineers and between strong and weak locals.

These differences among workers and locals were harmonized by adopting a hybrid benefits formula, that offered a defined benefit but based that benefit on a percentage of the contributions put into the CPF on behalf of any one worker. This allowed pension benefits to be graded based on both the wages and hours of specific individual participants, and thus this formula mitigated the inherent differences among fund participants and their locals.

Most large locals within the IUOE, however, remained outside the CPF. Although the CPF offered the advantages of economies of scale and portability, strong locals with thousands of members and hundreds of employers did not need the administrative economies the CPF could offer. The International Union of Operating Engineers had traditionally been a highly decentralized organization with strong local leaders. There were both political and service advantages associated with operating a local pension fund. Politically, the operations of a successful local pension fund made a clear and strong statement that the local union and its leaders had brought this benefit to their members. At the level of participant services, some local pension funds were joined to local health and welfare funds. Economies of scale could be achieved by operating health and pension funds out of the same offices. Other local pension funds were administered by third parties that administered other construction union funds from the same area. This allowed for coordination within the region and a sharing of administrative costs.

On the other hand, local pension funds were jointly trusteed by union and management representatives who met each other not only at the trustees table but occasionally at the bargaining table. This overlap of functions, for better or worse, tends to bring closer together the issues of bargaining and pension administration. This may help explain why the CPF trustees have a long history of non-conflictual, consensus decision making across union and management lines. Drawn from around the country, CPF union and management trustees rarely meet again as union and management negotiators. Thus, they do not bring a past adversarial relationship into the trustees meeting. The institutional distance of CPF trustees from local bargaining issues may also help explain why the CPF trustees, relative to some local pension fund trustees, are not particularly drawn to using pension fund investments to promote job creation efforts for local union contractors. True, the CPF eventually developed a building investment policy that attempts to direct its real estate investments into structures built within the jurisdiction of its locals. The CPF restricts its real estate investments to buildings that were built and/or are staffed by union members. However, this is a relatively limited set of social targets for investments compared to some local pension funds within and outside the IUOE.

In an effort to jump-start the CPF in the 1960s, the Fund's trustees chose to provide retirement credits to long-standing union members for past service within the union. In effect, this gave older workers rights to some pension benefits even though they had only been contributing into a pension fund in their last few years before retirement. Because locals only entered the CPF after a majority vote, this offering of past service credits to older workers sweetened the deal for older workers and encouraged their support. Without past service credits, the CPF had little to offer workers who were near retirement at its onset. It was obvious to everyone, however, that these past service credits were going to be paid by the contributions of younger workers to the Fund. Chapter 5 addresses these redistributive issues. Fund organizers justified this redistribution from the young to the old in local membership meetings by recalling that the older workers in the 1960s were the ones who made the sacrifices in the 1930s needed to build the union and make contemporary union wages and benefits possible. Both the philosophy of ''one hand washes the other'' and the fact of redistribution among participants are essential elements of union-negotiated, defined-benefit pension programs. The hybrid formula of the CPF, which tied the defined benefit of a participant to the contributions paid into the Fund on his or her behalf, limited the scope for redistribution within the CPF. Past service credits offered to older workers as locals joined the Fund in the 1960s and 1970s, however, are one example of the collective and redistributive attitudes and decisions made by the Fund's trustees and agreed on by the local union members.

When the CPF began in 1960, it hired outside, third-party administrators to administer both the collection of pension contributions and the disbursement of pension benefits. The CPF also hired financial consultants to invest the accumulating capital in the Fund's possession. As the Fund grew, however, the trustees explored the possibilities of hiring their own administrators and staff to do most of the day-to-day activities needed to run a growing pension fund. The CPF trustees felt that the outside administrators were slow to understand the specific needs of a central fund within a decentralized union of operating engineers. They felt that communication between the dispersed locals and the CPF would be enhanced if the Fund administrators were fully involved in running the CPF and not dividing their attention between the several funds administered by a third-party service company. The move to self-administration also reflected an underlying belief among the trustees that a hands-on policy led to better service.

In 1970, the CPF began to administer its own affairs by buying a building in Washington, D.C. It is significant that the Fund did not choose to move into the headquarters building of the IUOE. Although the CPF trustees have promoted a hands-on approach to Fund administration, they have also sought an arm's-length relationship with the international union. The creation of a separate Fund headquarters in Washington reflects both philosophies at once.

The Fund continued to grow through the 1970s, partly because of the continued addition of new locals but primarily because the Fund was still young and contributions from active members still outpaced payouts to retirees. With growth came more economies of scale, which allowed the Fund to vigorously pursue its hands-on philosophy. The fund's assistant administrator began to develop a financial expertise that allowed an in-house staff person to oversee and evaluate the performance of various financial service providers who were investing the Funds accumulating capital. By 1978, with the assistance of an outside financial consultant, the trustees and the staff had developed the Fund's first long-range, over-arching financial investment policy, which would guide the Fund over the long run. Chapter 6 details the evolution of CPF's investment policy. Eventually, economies of scale and a commitment to a hands-on administration would lead the Fund to bring in-house financial, legal, and computing expertise in an effort to improve the efficiency of administration and the profitability of investment. Both day-to-day investment activity and actuarial services continue to be provided by independent service companies. Relative to most pension funds within the construction industry, however, the CPF has an unusual degree of its administrative functions done in house. As the CPF has assumed greater control over its own administrative and investment destiny, it has learned more about its own activities and performance and has sought to use this knowledge to enhance communication with local unions and Fund participants.

Although the CPF has consciously assumed greater responsibility for the operation of the pension fund, its arm's-length relationship to both the international union and to local union affairs has reinforced a philosophy among the trustees and the administrators within the Fund that fostering growth in union membership is not a responsibility the Fund should directly assume. Trustees and administrators within the CPF believe that the Fund should provide the highest possible retirement benefits consistent with prudent investments and contribution rates established by collectively bargained agreements. Achieving this goal should indirectly support union organizing efforts. Most Fund trustees are wary about taking on any greater responsibility for union membership growth through job creation schemes, socially targeted investment, or corporate activism both for economic and legal reasons. Recent declines in union membership in the United States, however, pose a challenge to all union-based pension funds, including the CPF.

Just as the CPF was gaining greater mastery over its own internal operations and the fate of its investments was proving fortunate, the destiny of the CPF was altered by the decline in union membership, over which the Fund had no direct control. Starting in the 1970s, annual growth rates for the U.S. economy slowed down considerably, real wages stagnated, employment shifted from the manufacturing to the service sector, and the political climate turned increasingly hostile toward unions. Not surprisingly, the percentage of American workers in unions declined and by the mid-1980s the absolute number of union members began to fall as well. The completion of the interstate highway system in the late 1970s cut into the membership of hoisting and portable locals within the IUOE. In contrast, the growth of the service economy fostered a building boom in the 1980s that supported membership within stationary engineer locals. The slow growth in stationary local membership, however, was more than offset by the decline of membership within the construction locals of the IUOE. The CPF was established to serve smaller locals within the IUOE. Because many of these locals were stationary locals, the CPF has benefitted from the relative health of this section of the union. Because most of the construction locals within the CPF were also smaller locals, however, this section has been hurt the most during union decline of the 1980s. The CPF's size and diversity of locals gives it stability especially compared to retirement funds based in smaller construction locals, but continued union decline poses serious problems for the CPF.

Although the number of participants within the CPF has been falling since the 1980s, the average age of participants and the ratio of retirees to active participants have been rising. Nonetheless, the financial size of the CPF measured as the value of its investments continues to grow. This is because the stock market boom of the 1980s and early 1990s has offset, in the short run, the decline in contributions associated with a decline in union membership and a rise in payouts associated with an increased percentage of retired participants.

There is a distinct irony here. The same political and economic forces that hurt unionization in the 1980s—a pro-business climate, the globalization of markets, a decline in real wages—helped make the stock market boom. The same forces that hurt labor and helped capital also helped labor's capital, pension funds like the CPF.

In the long run, the fate of the CPF is tied to the fate of the union. As the age of fund participants rises and the number of fund participants falls, CPF administrative costs rise. This is partly because retiring and retired participants are more expensive to administer than actively working participants. It is also because as fund participation declines, the Fund loses the economies of scale it gained during its growth period. Chapter 7 addresses the issues of declining participation, the changes in the composition of CPF participants, and their impact on the administrative process. It may be that the computer revolution will provide labor-saving economies to offset the demographic pressures on administrative costs. Without growth and rejuvenation of the IUOE membership, however, the CPF must husband its resources to ensure that all participants' retirements are properly vouchsafed. Fortunately, IUOE membership ended its decline and returned to modest growth in the late 1980s and early 1990s but it is too soon to judge whether this is a permanent reversal of trends.[4] Whether the prudent use of funds and careful offering of benefits includes the raising of benefits to make union membership more attractive or the social targeting of investment to make collective bargaining more viable are difficult questions the CPF trustees will continue to face.

The concluding chapter, Chapter 8, summarizes the accomplishments of those involved with the CPF over its thirty-four year history. In addition, Chapter 8 summarizes the lessons that can be learned from the CPF and the model of union-management trusteed pension funds. Those lessons are crucial. Income support during one's declining years has traditionally been described as a three-legged stool resting on a combination of personal savings, private pensions, and public pensions. But at the present, each of those legs is tottering. Declining real wages threatens personal savings as indicated by the historical low of savings in the national income accounts. Downsizing, mergers and acquisitions, interest rate fluctuations, and intensifying international competition, among other developments, threaten both the incidence and survivability of pensions from private employers. Looking at the age structure of the population, young workers are currently more willing to believe in the reality of unidentified flying objects (UFOs) than in their future receipt of social security pensions. The CPF experience carries potent advice for shoring up that wobbly stool.

American employers are changing their relationship with workers, perhaps forever. Long service in specialized jobs with narrow lines of promotion is rapidly declining in Americas' high-performance firms.[5] Global competition and shakier profit margins pressure corporations to shed risk and off-load health insurance, pension, and other risks to workers. Defined benefit plans that reward long service workers are out, defined contribution and 401K plans are in. Loyalty to customers, craft, and flexibility, rather than to employers are the new slogans for the new workforce.

In 1978 and again in 1994, in the context of these workplace changes, the labor movement pushed hard for labor law reform to expand workers' participation and protection. A dissident voice from labor reformers emerged—it was female, minority, and working poor.[6] These reformers warned that labor law reform had to address the new reality of peripetic workers, part time status, intermittent work. They argued that labor law based on industrial workforce model with strict lines of promotion and hierarchical structure will miss the new workers' needs.

ERISA, the Employee Retirement Income Security Act of 1974, addressed primarily the needs of workers in defined-benefit plans who expected fulfillment of their employers' pension promises. Instead, it appears that the explosion of defined contribution and 401K plans—often nothing more than savings accounts—will replace pension plans that reward long service.

But, in some pockets of the American workforce, long service contracts never existed. This book is about the remarkable construction of good pensions for people who worked for small employers or in casual labor markets. It is a book about a pension scheme that grew up to fit a workforce that looks very much like the emerging workforce.

The struggles of the International Union of Operating Engineers to create its pension fund can serve as a model for the rising millions of workers without secure jobs and attractive fringe benefits. One lesson it teaches is workers, through their unions, can create a security base, even when employers and the government are unwilling or unable to do so. The operating engineers, along with many other workers and similar unions, created supplemental income to skilled workers under insecure circumstances. The Central Pension Fund of the International Union of Operating Engineers and Participating Employers is a prototype example of an innovative worker institution that employee organizations, in cooperation with their employers, can create to adapt to constantly changing realities.

NOTES

1. Whereas our interest here is in the casual labor markets of the construction industry, it is useful to note that most of the same forces are at work in a number of other industries—particularly major components of transportation such as longshore and maritime, and, to a lesser degree, trucking.

2. Some stationary engineers employed by government, large hotel chains, or other large corporations have the alternative of a single-employer defined-benefit pension.

3. Ralph and Estelle James, *Hoffa and the Teamsters: A Study of Union Power* (Princeton, N.J.: D. Van Nostrand Company, 1965).

4. Garth L. Mangum and John Walsh, *Union Resilience in Troubled Times: The Story of the Operating Engineers, AFL-CIO, 1960–1993* (New York: M.E. Sharpe, 1994).

5. Eileen Appelbaum and Rosemary Batt, *The New American Workplace* (Armonk, N.Y.: M.E. Sharpe, 1994) and the U.S. Department of Labor, *High Performance Firms* (Washington, D.C.: Government Printing Office, 1994).

6. Dorothy Sue Cobble, "Labor Law Reform," *Dissent* (Summer 1994), and Howard Wial, "Labor Law Reform and Secondary Workers," *Yale Law Review* 1993.

Chapter 2

A Century of Union Pension Funds

The urge among working people to organize in pursuit of their own economic well-being preceded the emergence of employer-employee relationships. Economic security needed to extend from cradle to grave for workers and their families. Once agrarianism gave way to industrialization and the extended family to the nuclear one, however, support for the aged became an issue of social concern. The options were for the older to retire on their own savings, for the children to reciprocate by supporting in old age those who supported them during childhood, for employers to retain earnings to support their retired workers, for organizations of workers to support their predecessors, or for governments to impose the responsibility on the succeeding generations. None of this was automatic. The trial-and-error fluctuations between labor organizations, employers, and governments as sources of support during old age are the subject of this chapter, leading to the emergence of the CPF in the chapter that follows.

THE END OF AGRARIANISM AND ITS EFFECT ON CARE OF THE ELDERLY

For those engaged in agriculture, control of or attachment to the land, the economic value of the accumulated knowledge of the elderly, and the ability of senior citizens to continue to produce at gradually declining rates provided at least the likelihood of reasonable security to the aged. That, however, pertained to land owners, not slaves or tenant farmers. It also assumed a subsequent generation, ready to take over and gradually assume support of the declining aged, but the United States from the beginning was a society of high mobility; that next generation might be somewhere beyond the frontier. Still, sale of the land might provide sustenance for the remaining life span. Ownership of a handicraft shop represented capital accumulation. The aging owner could arrange with a successor for both gradually declining involvement and continuance of sustenance throughout old age.

The employee had no such resort. There came an age of declining productivity, which the employer was not prepared to support. Gaston Rimlinger states that with the breakdown of agrarianism, "Workers became dependent on the wage of the family breadwinner; any interruption of the ability to work or of the availability of a job spelled dire want. Having left the land, the family was no longer a production unit. The aged and the children became a greater burden."[1] Unless there were earnings beyond subsistence and the self-discipline and good fortune to be able to save them, economic well-being for the no longer employable could emerge only from the gratuities of children supporting three generations, sharing among members of a labor organization, forced savings by employers, or the largesse of taxpayers. With diminishing numbers of children, increasing geographical mobility and the rise of cyclical unemployment, the first was bound to decline in dependability. With the decline of agrarianism, care of the elderly was no longer embedded within the framework of society. Initially, close-knit communities paid for the boarding out of the indigent aged as well and others.[2] As communities expanded in size and the competitive market prevailed, that personalization disappeared. For a while, many aged workers who became "too old to work but too young to die" were forced into poor houses along with the disabled, the insane, and orphaned, but this was not acceptable for long.

The end of agrarianism came at a precarious time for the elderly. Improved medical technology was extending human life expectancy, and the population of the United States over age sixty-five was growing rapidly. The increase in numbers was nothing like it would be a century later, but the proportionate increase was far greater. Figure 2.1[3] shows that from 1860 to 1910 the percentage of the population over sixty-five increased 59 percent, and from 1860 to 1930 there was a doubling. Thus, care of the aged was becoming an increasingly important task at the same time it was becoming a more difficult one. Social welfare would not be considered a responsibility of the federal government for at least another half century and states were not yet ready to assume the role, even to the extent of taking over the burden of poor houses from the local communities. The initial attempt was to retain care of the elderly as the responsibility of the family. By 1870, every state had a law that adult members were required to take care of all needy family members: "The scope of this obligation ran the gamut from New York's law which imposed reciprocal responsibility on adult children and their parents, to the California example, in which all members of the family—including brothers and sisters—in a direct line from grandparents to grandchildren were liable for each other's support."[4]

Figure 2.1
The number of elderly persons in the United States from 1860 to 1930

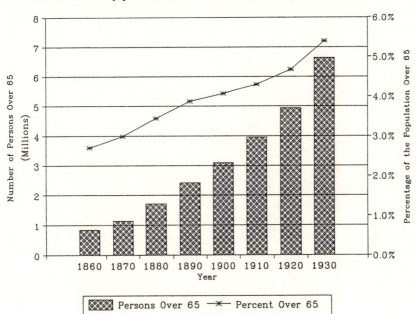

Few families, however, really had the economic means to adequately provide for their aged and passing a law did not make it so.

TRADE UNION OLD AGE PENSIONS: AN INTERNATIONAL PERSPECTIVE

Unlike the United States, the other leading industrial powers, Germany and England, enacted government legislation for providing old age assistance in the late nineteenth and early twentieth centuries. Agrarianism lasted forty years longer in the United States, which may explain the U.S. government's reluctance to begin a simultaneous old age assistance program; it simply was not yet as necessary as in those other countries. Another prominent reason is that the English and German governments faced mounting pressure from trade unions to begin social insurance programs. American labor unions have traditionally followed the doctrine of business unionism rather than the political unionism practiced by British and German unions. The choice was a pragmatic one. European unions had political power; American unions—at least those of the skilled— had some economic power but none politically. This business unionist ideology led American labor unions to seek to solve the problem of aging by themselves, rather than to look to the government as German and English unions did. By examining trade union involvement in pension plans internationally, one can understand the beginnings of American labor union pensions more thoroughly.

German trade unions did not want government involvement in the administration of their social insurance programs, whereas English unions did. German unions wanted the government to contribute to their programs but believed that the administration of the plans should be left to the individual unions. This was partially due to the ideology of autonomy and not wanting government interference in union matters, and partially because the German unions could not get the support of their allies in government for such programs. The Social Democrats in the Reichstag would not support social insurance of this manner because "they thought that such schemes did not constitute true social reform but were merely an improvement of the poor relief system which, furthermore, was used only as a device to distract the workers from the right course."[5] Initially, the government stayed entirely out of the process. In 1864, trade unions were able to extend the Employer Liabilities Act to include voluntary contributions from workers and employers to the development of a pension system. "This scheme was to pay out funds to a worker when he reached a certain age; the worker was free to choose whether or not he wished to contribute to the scheme and the employer was to feel morally obliged to assume part of the costs of the contributions."[6]

In 1881, the German government attempted to take control of all German social welfare programs in order to quell the rising socialist tide resulting when the "German Reich enacted legislation introducing social insurance to an extent unknown up to that time."[7] This movement was led by Bismarck, who "felt that with mere police measures the problem [blocking trade union and socialist power] cannot be solved."[8] His solution to neutralize the trade union and socialist movement was to tie workers to the state. This would appeal to their sense of loyalty and downplay any revolutionary tendencies. Bismarck's fears of revolution were real in the context of the Paris Commune of 1871, the growing International Workingmen's Association formed by Karl Marx, and the Social Democrats gaining twelve seats in the Reichstag in 1877. Bismarck knew that repression was not the answer; he needed to co-opt the working class into the state. He proclaimed that the state must "plunge into the socialist movement and 'achieve that which seems legitimate in the socialist demands' within the existing social and political framework."[9] Bismarck had two routes to follow in order to accomplish his goals. He could enact factory and labor legislation to improve the plight of the working class, or enact social insurance schemes. He opted for the latter:

Labor legislation of the kind that would increase trade union security and would strengthen collective bargaining did not seem suited to his aims. Social insurance, in his belief, offered the best possibilities for the kind of human management that would bind the laboring classes to the state.[10]

Bismarck was able to get the Kaiser to address the Reichstag on the issues of social insurance on November 17, 1881. The Kaiser proposed that workman's compensation be instated, along with general health insurance for workers. In addition, the Kaiser proposed: "those who are disabled in consequence of old age . . . possess a well founded claim to a more ample relief on the part of the State than they have hitherto enjoyed."[11] However, Bismarck never fully realized his goal in regards to pensions. Unions continued to administer the programs, with one third of contributions coming from workers, one third from employers, and one third from the government.[12]

The repeal of the Poor and Corn Laws[13] in 1834 ushered in England's reign as the hegemonic capitalist state. The ideology, which David Ricardo[14] developed in 1814, finally saw its practical conclusion with these repeals. The main issue in regards to the repeal of the Poor Laws was to develop a perfectly elastic supply of labor so capitalists would be uninhibited in their employment decisions. Any type of social insurance was blocking this process. Pensions, for example, would enable the elderly to refuse to supply their labor time at going market wage rates. This type of rampant individualism was constantly being fought by those most harmed by it and eventually broke down.[15]

Ironically, as the English government rolled back its laissez-faire economic structure, the first social insurance to be reinstated was old age assistance. The Old Age Pension Act of 1908 was financed through taxation and simply granted a pension to anyone over seventy years of age whose means did not exceed a certain amount.[16] The Pension Act came as a result of trade union pressure for the government to take care of the elderly. English unions were already doing a relatively good job of providing pensions for their members, with 38 of the 100 principle unions paying benefits in 1901.[17] However, unions believed that without government in old age pensions the majority of their members would never be covered. The drive for old age assistance began in 1899, with the formation of the National Committee of Organized Labor for the Promotion of Old Age Pensions. When the Liberal Party won the election of 1906, trade unions acquired friends in government and their influence resulted in the 1908 Act.[18]

THE BEGINNINGS OF EMPLOYER SPONSORED PENSION FUNDS

In the United States, unions began pursuing various kinds of benefit programs, but a few employers started pension schemes before unions were strong enough to demand them. Since the inception of industrial society, employers have been responsible for the payment of labor services in the form of wages. Also, since the inception of industrial society, employers and employees have fought over how much and in what form the payment for labor services would be. When a worker or his or her dependents fall prey to sickness or injury, is it the responsibility of the employer to see that hospital bills are paid, or is it the employees' responsibility to set aside part of their wages for such a crisis situation? In the case of old age, does the employer owe an income to a former employee who is no longer productive for the company? In 1935, Don Lescohier addressed the attitude of American employers towards their employees once an employee was no longer a productive member of the company:

It has long been urged that the modern industrialist has a definite responsibility toward the aged worker and his dependents; that having used him during his active years, industry owes him, and his wife, life long support rather than merely hour to hour wages. The old age pension and insurance legislation enacted in many foreign countries has recognized this responsibility and required employers to contribute to pension funds for the industrial population. . . . [However] American employers as a whole had not conceded down to 1935 that they owed this responsibility to the workers as a whole or even to their own employees, but a large number of individual concerns and governmental bodies had set up pension plans for their own employees.[19]

Although most employers did not feel pensions were a necessary feature of employment, the company that put forward the following statement reflects the attitude of several employers who saw benefits in having a pension plan:

Believing that those who have served this company faithfully for a long period of years deserve the special consideration of the company, particularly when retirement from active service is apt to work a hardship upon those who have depended for their support upon earnings no longer available, the company has established a system of retirement pensions for employees who have earned or who may earn an honorable retirement on account of age or disability. The plan is an evidence of the company's appreciation of the fidelity, efficiency and loyalty of employees who have given to its service the most productive years of their lives. The pensions granted have no relation whatever to the determination of the amount of wages or salaries paid or to be paid the company. They are granted as a voluntary reward for fidelity and persistency of service, and in the hope that the existence of this pension system may encourage permanently such efficiency and persistency of service among the employees of the company.[20]

In the late nineteenth and early twentieth centuries, company pension plans were mainly confined to the railroad industry, public utilities, iron and steel, banks, and the oil industry. The first company-sponsored pension plan in the United States was established by the American Express Company in 1875. It was a noncontributory plan, with the employer paying all of the costs. The Grand Trunk Railway of Canada preceded the American Express Company with a contributory plan organized on October 1, 1874, and the Baltimore and Ohio Railroad followed with a contributory plan on May 1, 1880, but these were complete failures because the employees would not contribute to the funds. In 1901 the manufacturing field saw its first enduring plan, from the Carnegie Steel Company. Standard Oil started a pension in 1903. Mines and mercantile establishments began pension plans between 1901 and 1905.[21] However, Lescohier states:

there was little reason to believe that the number of company pension plans in existence in 1932 would be sufficiently increased within a reasonable period to constitute a satisfactory coverage of the American industrial population. Apparently it has been impossible to interest only a small minority of employers in setting up voluntarily such things as pensions, group insurance, and profit sharing. There has been nothing in the history of private industrial pension plans, either in the United States, Canada, or European countries, to indicate that the movement was apt to extend over industry generally. In 1927, about 83 percent of the employees in the railroad industry were working for railroads which had pension plans. There was no other type of industry, unless it was the public utilities, in which private plans promised an important coverage of the wage earners.[22]

Because employers did not feel it necessary to provide old age assistance, working people who were fortunate enough to belong to a labor union looked to their union leadership to provide pension plans.

AMERICAN LABOR UNION PENSION FUNDS

American labor unions, although generally beginning later than their European counterparts, sought to add benefits beyond wages to improve the well-being of their members. Lacking the means and the leverage to provide pensions, they at first had to settle for paying a death benefit to cover funeral expenses. The aged worker had to work until he dropped or depend on his children. The widows of fallen union members were usually left to the mercy of their children or the county poorhouse, or to struggle on at the lowest rungs of the labor force. Attempts of unions to provide pension plans experienced limited success until they became strong enough to prevail on their employers through collective bargaining to pay for them.

American labor unions began benefit programs for their members as early as the 1850s. The movement toward accident, death, and retirement benefit funds, however, did not gain much strength until the 1890s (Table 2.1).[23] The establishment of these funds represented a dramatic break in the old ideology that insurance programs were more of a burden to unions than an advantage. In 1860, the reason union officials were not in favor of instituting insurance schemes was that union dues would have to be raised to administer the programs and this would inhibit organizing. Kennedy writes:

The establishment of local benefits conflicted with the success of the national organizations. A local union was usually forced to impose certain restrictions upon claimants of benefits, either an initiation fee or a requisite term of membership, in order to protect its funds. Such limitations on the full participation of all members in the benefits of membership militated severely against the carrying out of the prime function of the national unions—the nationalization of membership. The leaders in the trade-union movement of

Table 2.1
The first unions to establish benefit systems

Name of Organization	Established Benefit System	Established National Organization
Cigar Makers Union	1867	1864
Iron Molders' Union	1870	1859
Granite Cutters	1877	1877
Carpenters and Joiners, Brotherhood	1882	1881
Typographia, Deutsch-Amerikanishen	1884	1873
Hatters Association	1887	1853
Painters' Brotherhood	1887	1887
Tailors Union	1890	1884
Metal Polishers' Union	1890	1890
Wood Workers	1890	1890
Typographical Union	1891	1850
Glass Bottle Blowers	1891	1857
Stone Cutters' Association	1892	1853
Machinists' Association	1893	1889
Barbers' Union	1895	1887
Pattern Makers' League	1898	1887
Tobacco Workers' Union	1898	1895
Boot and Shoe Workers' Union	1898	1895
Leather Workers on Horse Goods	1898	1896
Piano and Organ Workers	1898	1898
United Metal Workers	1900	1900
Garment Workers' Union	1902	1891
Iron, Steel, and Tin Workers	1903	1876
Plumbers' Association	1903	1889

this period were interested chiefly in strengthening the relations of the local unions. They saw, therefore, in the local benefits a hindrance to the accomplishments of their aims. By 1860 it had become a fairly well accepted doctrine that a trade union should not attempt to develop beneficiary functions.[24]

By 1880, however, the ideology had changed. Unions recognized that benefit funds strengthened the union because they bolstered their treasuries. The funds were not subject to a great deal of regulation by the government, and thus the union could invest the money as it wished or dip into the treasury in an emergency situation, such as a strike. Also, allegiance to the union was strengthened, reducing scabbing. Death benefits or pensions could only be obtained if the worker remained with the union throughout his career. When the economy took a downturn and employers tried to cut costs by cutting wages through hiring non-union workers, such future benefits were a factor in convincing union members not to scab in order to avoid the loss of this future income.[25] For example, during the depression of 1893- 97, the Cigar Makers Union, which had established benefit programs, lost only 1.5 percent its membership, whereas the Brotherhood of Carpenters, which did not have benefit programs, lost 50 percent of its membership. The president of the Cigar Makers said the reason the union survived the depression unscathed was to be "attributed to the beneficiary system which held the membership in good standing."[26]

The first union-sponsored benefit funds were not collectively bargained for and were administered solely by the unions. In almost all unions, the administration of benefit funds was "carried on by the officers who maintained the general affairs of the union."[27] The exceptions to this rule were the Brotherhood of Locomotive Engineers and the National Association of Letter Carriers, which "maintained a mutual benefit department administered by separate officers."[28] The success of these funds in paying out benefits was limited mainly to death benefits. In 1907, sixty-three unions paid a death benefit, six paid a benefit to wives of members who passed away, twenty-four unions paid a sick benefit, eight paid a traveling benefit, and six paid out-of-work benefits.[29]

The initial leader in retirement benefits was the Typographical Workers Union. In 1857, the union established a home for aged printers in Philadelphia, and in 1889 a similar home was opened in Colorado Springs.[30] Twenty-two people inhabited the home in Colorado Springs in 1893, and by 1907 it housed 143 persons. However, "about 1904 an agitation began to be carried on in the union for making more adequate provisions for the maintenance of aged members. The establishment of the home had made provision only for those incapacitated members who were willing to leave their families and live in an institution."[31] This agitation resulted in the Typographical Workers becoming the first union to provide a monthly pension benefit in 1908. They were followed by the Brotherhood of Locomotive Engineers in 1912; the Bricklayers, Masons, and Plasterers in 1915; the Railway Conductors in 1917; the Bridge and Structural Iron Workers in 1918; the Locomotive Firemen and Enginemen in 1920; the Railroad Trainmen in 1923; the Printing Pressmen in 1924; and the Brotherhood of Electrical Workers in 1928.[32]

The benefits of these pensions were not solely confined to the unions and their members. Employers shared in the rewards. Union pensions, once a few became available, provided employers with an "orderly system for removing older workers whose efficiency has been impaired."[33] Also, recruitment of higher-grade employees was made easier, and most employers who initiated pension plans got higher productivity from their workers by improving morale. Union pension programs "removed one of the basic insecurities plaguing workers [a source of income in their old age]."[34]

The American Federation of Labor's Response

Facing the limitations of employer and union-provided plans, a nationwide movement for publicly provided pensions began in the 1920s, during which time eight states began pension programs. These bills were aggressive in nature, trying to mandate statewide coverage. Prior to this time, individual counties within a state could opt not to provide old-age assistance. However, in 1931, with the onset of the depression, the trend was moving toward compulsory coverage at the statewide level. Nearly 100 bills were introduced in state legislatures requiring old-age assistance.[35] The American Federation of Labor's (AFL) response to this push for statewide pension plans was surprisingly optimistic. Rimlinger writes: "The AFL decided in 1932 to reverse its traditional opposition to insurance. For the first time in history, it declared itself officially in favor of a compulsory insurance system."[36] Prior to this time, the organization denounced any government intervention in providing for workers in their old age. The only government pension plan the AFL would endorse was for widowed mothers because it would mean women and their children would not enter the labor market and bid down the wages of male workers. The AFL leadership viewed social insurance as simply another tool of government to invade the lives of the working class. In a fiery speech in 1886, Samuel Gompers, the first president of the AFL, proclaimed:

Social insurance can not even undertake to remove or prevent poverty. It is not fundamental and does not get at the causes of social injustice. The only agency that does get at the cause of poverty is the organized labor movement. I would rather help in the inauguration of a revolution against compulsory insurance . . . than submit. As long as there is one spark of life in me . . . I will help in crystallizing the spirit and sentiment of our workers against the attempt to enslave them by well-meaning siren songs of philosophers, statisticians, and politicians.[37]

Teresa Ghilarducci concurs with Rimlinger "Gompers . . . was strongly opposed to government pension schemes and employer pensions. He saw both as a means of reducing worker and union autonomy. While firms were establishing pension plans, unions formed their own mutual aid societies—a course of individualism and self help approved of by the president of the largest and most powerful U.S. union."[38] As noted, however, the AFL position was not written in stone. If unions wanted to keep the government completely out of the social insurance business, they would be fighting a battle they could not win. The Great Depression highlighted the need for government involvement, and the sweeping legislation of the Social Security Act was just around the corner.

UNION PENSION PLANS DECIMATED BY THE GREAT DEPRESSION

By the time the Great Depression began, pension plans covered a higher percentage of union members than nonunion corporate employees. Twenty percent of union members were in pension plans whereas only 15 percent of corporate employees were covered. The period 1890–1930 saw eighteen unions

Table 2.2
Union pension funds in existence after the Depression

Union	Number of Pensioners	Monthly Benefit
Carpenters	12,000	$15.00
Typographical Workers	7,200	48.00
Electrical Workers, IBEW	3,000	50.00
Printing Press	1,800	12.00
Iron Workers	600	15.00

establish funds, with about twelve actually paying benefits,[39] but this initial prosperity was to be short-lived. With the onset of the Depression, pensions gave way to more urgent union goals. As pension contributions were suspended, the funds deteriorated at a rapid pace. These benefit programs were established on a pay-as-you-go basis. This meant that promises made for future benefits were not secured by present investments. To receive a pension, workers had to hope that when they were eligible, other members were paying into the fund to generate their benefit. Thus, when unemployment soared, the majority of funds went bankrupt. Sass writes: "The typical union plan had but two to three years' current benefits put away at the end of the 1920s, and contributions were roughly ten percent of the amount needed to fund the programme properly."[40]

THE SOCIAL SECURITY ACT OF 1935

The enactment of old age assistance under the Social Security Act of 1935 (SSA) ended the need for unions to provide pensions for their members for the time being. Without the SSA unions may have fought harder to maintain their pension plans, but, as shown by Table 2.2,[41] only five of the strongest unions preserved theirs. Trade unions began pension plans to relieve the typical destitution of their members when their working lives ended. The government had now assumed that role. The SSA not only provided for old age assistance, but it also covered federal and state public assistance and unemployment compensation, disability benefits, and child welfare. Other federal programs provided maternal and child health services, services for crippled children, and vocational rehabilitation services. By 1938, all jurisdictions in the United States were making old age assistance payments under the SSA.[42]

Retirement payments from Social Security, however, did not keep pace with inflation during the 1940s, and unions felt increased pressure from their mem-

Figure 2.2
Index of Social Security payments

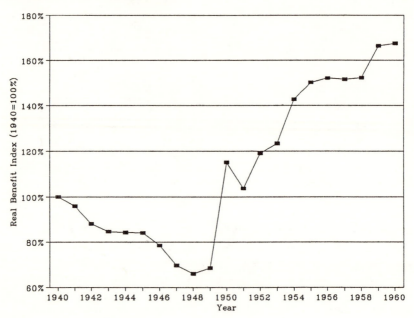

bership to reenact old age pensions. From 1940 to 1949 the average monthly Social Security payments increased from $23.17 to $26.92 in nominal terms. Figure 2.2[43] shows that in real terms this represented a decrease of 32 percent. In 1950, the average monthly benefit moved substantially upward as the nominal payment jumped to $45.67, representing a real 46 percent increase in one year and pushing the real monthly amount above its 1940 level for the first time in a decade.

Social Security was never intended to be the complete retirement package. It was simply supposed to serve as the foundation on which a retirement income was built. This foundation, however, was declining rapidly and retired union members had seen their standard of living eroded for ten years. The increase in payments of 1950 and subsequent increases throughout the 1950s were probably a case of "too little too late." The push for union pensions was back in full swing.

Labor's agenda in the area of pension funds was bolstered by the Wagner Act of 1935, which granted workers substantial rights in the area of organization and collective bargaining. These new legislative rights set the stage for a newly emerging group of powerful labor leaders to instill old age security for their membership following World War II.

UNION PENSION PLANS DURING AND AFTER WORLD WAR II

Following World War II, pension programs emerged as an integral objective of American unionism. Chronologically, the first factors contributing to the growth of union-negotiated pension plans were the wage stabilization and taxation policies enacted during the war, which extended into the postwar period. The economic boom fostered a favorable climate at the collective bargaining table for union negotiators. Their ability to bargain for increased wages, however, was checked by government wage controls. Thus, compensation had to be diverted into other areas besides their members' pocketbooks. Taxation laws favored a shift from wages because employer contributions toward employee insurance were tax deductible. Also, employees did not have their pension contributions taxed as income. The Internal Revenue Service decided to tax pensions only upon their receipt and not their accumulation. The result was an increase in the number of health insurance and pension programs within unions. A U.S. Department of Labor report, published in 1953, tells the story:

Interest in pension plans was stimulated during the war and immediate postwar periods by a number of factors. Among these were the Government's wage stabilization and taxation policies which made such programs feasible and less expensive to employers. Wage stabilization regulations limited the amount of wage increases which employers could grant, but, at the same time, permitted the adoption of reasonable employee insurance and pension benefits. Under Federal tax regulations employers were permitted to deduct, with specified limits, contributions to pension plans when computing their tax returns.[44]

Additionally, Social Security payments had not changed during the 1940s.[45] In 1949, the Steel Industry Fact-Finding Board's Reports and Recommendations stated: "Social insurance and pensions should be considered a part of normal business costs to take care of temporary and permanent depreciation in the human 'machine,' in much the same way as provision is made for the depreciation and insurance of plant and machinery. This obligation should be among the first charges on revenues. . . . So long as Government fails to provide an adequate amount, industry should take up the slack."[46] Thus as inflation, mild as it was, eroded retirement income, unions and employers felt an increased obligation to subsidize their members. A problem confronting many AFL unions was that trade union employment was characterized by a combination of small employers and casual employment. Thus, pensions could only be offered on a multiemployer basis. Ironically, an industrial union that had vacillated between the CIO and AFL,[47] the United Mineworkers of America (UMWA), made the first breakthrough in solving this problem in 1946, by establishing a multiemployer pension fund. The UMWA was subsequently followed by AFL unions, most notably the Teamsters.

The UMWA fund took contributions directly from employers and promised a $100 monthly benefit on retirement. Academics, along with labor leaders, see John L. Lewis as a groundbreaker in the area of union pension plans. Estelle and Ralph James summarize the extent of Lewis' accomplishment:

The mushrooming of union-negotiated pension plans began at the close of World War II. The garment trades set off this new development in 1944–1945 and were quickly followed by the IBEW. The really big impetus, though, came from John L. Lewis. Lewis brought the coal industry to a halt in 1946, and precipitated government seizure, over his demand for a combined health, welfare, and retirement plan. After a complicated series of legal and collective bargaining maneuvers, he victoriously announced a $100 monthly pension at age 62, after 20 years' service, for his miners. . . . His achievement posed a challenge, . . . and Walter Reuther, Philip Murray, and James Carey immediately set ''$100 pensions'' as primary goals.[48]

The pension amendments to the Taft-Hartley Act of 1947 were a direct response to Lewis' success and his perceived ''war chest.'' The act was a response to the National Labor Relations Act (NLRA) of 1935, which bolstered the power of organized labor. Management and the conservative members of government sought to even the playing field, or tip it in the direction of employers, with the passage of Taft-Hartley. Its authors trusted employers, but not unions, to unilaterally administer pension funds. In the case of union-negotiated pension funds, a requirement for management representation was designed to prevent the union from using pension fund money to foster union goals. Although management was given the right to serve on all union pension plans, Taft-Hartley did not mandate union representation on all pension funds that covered union members. The condition of union representation only extended to multiemployer plans. Single-employer plans, such as the General Motors pension, which covers members of the United Auto Workers, can be run exclusively by the employer. Subsection 302(c)(5)(b) of Taft-Hartley mandated that the multiemployer union pension funds must be governed by an equal number of employer and union trustees. Generally, the union trustees were to be appointed by the president of the union in the case of a nationwide fund, or appointed by the chief administrative officer of a local union in the case of a local fund. Employer trustees were to be elected by the participating employers. Employer trustees leaving a board might also name their successor.

From 1948 to 1959, multiemployer pension plans grew 2000 percent, union members covered by pensions increased from 750,000 to more than 3 million (see Figure 2.3).[49] In addition to the failure of retirement payments from Social Security to keep pace with inflation as noted above, two other important developments explain part of this exponential growth in the number of multiemployer pension plans.

Most important for all unions, the National Labor Relations Board (NLRB) ruled in 1948 that pension and insurance benefits were included in the term

Figure 2.3
Multiemployer pension funds: 1943–1959

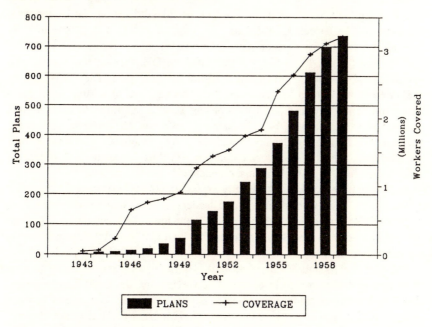

"wages," which meant that pensions and group insurance were mandatory subjects of collective bargaining. This decision came after a Chicago local of the United Steelworkers took the Inland Steel Company to court on the issue of employee benefits. Ghilarducci summarizes the action:

Since 1930, the Inland Steel Company of Chicago had a pension plan covering employees earning more than $3,000 per year. It expanded coverage to all employees in 1943. The original plan mandated retirement at age sixty-five, a rule that was dropped during World War II. In 1946, Inland reinstated the compulsory retirement age, and the steel workers objected, demanding that this move be the subject of collective bargaining. Inland refused to bargain, but the NLRB ruled against the company. The Supreme Court upheld the NLRB decision in April, 1949.[50]

The effort of the Chicago local was a turning point in the history of unions' struggles for benefit programs. Because employers now had to bargain "in good faith" over such benefits, although they did not have to grant them, health insurance and pensions became an integral part of any compensation package.

Even prior to the Inland Steel decision, however, when John L. Lewis began the UMWA pension fund in 1946 and instilled a new level of confidence among labor leaders that they could begin benefit plans. "You said to yourself if John L. Lewis could do it, I can do it. And, you did it," said Walter Carlough when asked why his father began a pension plan for the Sheetmetal workers during that time period.[51]

Following both the Lewis-led strike and the Inland decision, the United Auto Workers (UAW) struck Chrysler for 104 days in 1950 on the issue of fully funding the employees pension plan.[52] During the strike, Joe Glazer wrote the classic song "Too Old To Work Too Young To Die." Lewis had settled on a pay-as-you-go method of financing the Mineworkers' plan. The UAW, led by Walter Reuther, wanted full financing with the payment of normal costs and a maximum of thirty-year amortization of past service liabilities. General Motors had agreed to such a pact, but Chrysler was resisting. The 1950 strike was the result of the bargaining deadlock, and the UAW emerged victorious. A new standard was set in collectively bargained pensions—contributions from employers and full funding of promised benefits.[53]

The effect of the strike may partially explain the UAW's success in bargaining for pensions. They were definitely the leaders in providing for their members in the postwar period. From 1949 to 1954, "the union had negotiated more than 200 distinct pension plans—a larger number than that in which any other union has been involved."[54]

Although Lewis and Reuther had broken ground with employers by forcing them to ensure that members of the Mineworkers and the UAW received pensions, another labor leader was going to challenge conventional use of pension money. Jimmy Hoffa attempted to use the Teamsters Central States Pension Fund (CSPF) to foster his unions' goals in any manner he saw fit. His actions did not go unnoticed. In fact, Hoffa's actions may have forever tarnished public opinion of labor union pension plans.

JIMMY HOFFA AND THE TEAMSTERS CENTRAL STATES PENSION FUND

After Lewis and Reuther's accomplishments, Jimmy Hoffa stepped into the ring of union pension funds with the intention of becoming the undisputed champion of pension benefits. Prior to becoming the president of the International Brotherhood of Teamsters (IBT), Hoffa had, in 1955, negotiated the first IBT pension plan for workers in midwestern and southern freight companies.[55] Following the IBT's expulsion from the AFL-CIO in 1957, Hoffa went on a mission to provide his union members with the highest pension benefit in the labor movement. The year after the Operating Engineers Central Pension Fund came into existence, 1960, was the year Hoffa achieved his goal. In 1961, the Teamsters Central States Pension Fund offered retirees the highest monthly benefit—$200 a month. This $200 monthly benefit, available at age sixty for participants with twenty years of service, however, was designed to provide only interim support. Its payments were provided only until the pensioner was able to begin collecting Social Security. Not only was the Teamsters' pension only transitional, but the union's financial administration raised the ire of the congressional McClellan Committee and tainted the image of union participants in pension management.[56] Hoffa, although the most visible, however, was not the only person in the pension business engaged in suspect practices relating to the administration and investment of pension fund money. Company pensions were failing to deliver promised benefits, and jointly trusteed public funds were engaged in imprudent activities with the participants' money. Employers were unilaterally promising pensions they could not deliver or improperly investing and managing funds. These problems of the early 1960s sparked a decade-long debate over how to reform the pension industry. The result of this debate was the Employee Retirement Income Security Act (ERISA) of 1974.

ERISA

ERISA did not require the provision of pensions, but it did establish a set of principles and governing rules to ensure that whatever pensions were provided could be depended on to fulfill their promises. The act was comprehensive and complex, covering every type of pension, but focusing its regulations on defined-benefit plans because they were the ones that made promises that were most subject to disappointment. Collectively bargained plans were not the special focus of the law, but they were included within the legislation. Single-employer union pension funds were targeted heavily, whereas multiemployer funds were not subject to such stringent rules.[57] In general, the six important areas ERISA affected were (1) funding requirements, (2) vesting rules, (3) required payments to the Pension Benefit Guarantee Corporation (PBGC), (4) reporting and disclosure, (5) investment, and (6) audited financial statements.[58]

ERISA did not require labor union–management trusteed pension funds be fully funded. A ceiling was imposed that stated the assets to liabilities ratio may not exceed 150 percent. The upper limit was established to impose restrictions on boards of trustees, who often wanted to enlarge the size of the pension plan without ever granting benefit increases to the participants. The ceiling also served to limit tax evasion by single-employer plans.

Vesting rules established by ERISA sought to end practices of malfeasant behavior by boards of trustees who established lucrative pension benefits but made it difficult to qualify for them. As mentioned earlier in the chapter, the Teamsters' CSPF was probably the most notable example of this practice. ERISA imposed a maximum vesting requirement of ten years of service for jointly trusteed funds and five years of service for unilateral funds. There is room for unions to decide what constitutes a year of service, but the law requires that it be no more than 1,000 hours.

The government bodies responsible for enforcing ERISA's rules are the Internal Revenue Service (IRS) and the Department of Labor (DOL). If either of these two governing bodies discovers a fund is not acting in accordance with ERISA, it may terminate the plan's qualified status. A disqualified plan loses its tax-exempt status, which means employer contributions and fund income will be taxed during the years in which the plan is disqualified.[59]

The reasoning behind regulating single-employer union pension plans more stringently than multiemployer funds was that Congress believed multiemployer funds were more financially stable. For instance, employers who withdrew from participating in multiemployer funds would incur only withdrawal liability if the plan terminated within five years of their withdrawal. The industries that had multiemployer plans were economically strong at the time of ERISA's passage. Losing an employer or two from a pension plan was not regarded as anything serious. In the years following, however, the industries that established multiemployer funds began to experience decline. As a result, Congress became concerned with the financial viability of these funds, since the federal government, through the PBGC, was now responsible for seeing that pension promises would still be delivered if the union and participating employers were no longer able to pay. Congress feared an exodus of employers from multiemployer plans would occur in declining industries.[60] The House Ways and Means Committee summarized their concerns in a report delivered to congress:

A key problem of ongoing multiemployer plans, especially in declining industries, is the problem of employer withdrawal. Employer withdrawals reduce a plan's contribution base. This pushes the contribution rate for remaining employers to higher and higher levels in order to fund past service liabilities, including liabilities generated by employers no longer participating in the plan, so called inherited liabilities. The rising costs may encourage—or force—further withdrawals, thereby increasing the inherited liabilities to be funded by an ever-decreasing contribution base. This vicious downward spiral may continue until it is no longer reasonable or possible for the pension plan to continue.[61]

To remedy this foreseen problem of employers fleeing and destroying multiemployer funds, Congress passed the Multiemployer Pension Plan Amendments Act of 1980 (MPPAA).

MPPAA

Under the MPPAA, an employer participating in a overfunded union-management trusteed pension fund may withdraw at will. Employers participating in an underfunded plan, however, can only withdraw if they pay their share of the unfunded liability. An employer's unfunded liability amounts to a proportionate share of the plan's unfunded vested benefits for twenty years. Calculation of this payment is complex, and is undertaken on a case-by-case basis. Needless to say, the obligation is substantial, and it is quite often the case that an employer worth only $1 million can have an $800,000 withdrawal liability. Thus, a key issue between employer and union trustees is maintaining a plan of assets-to-liabilities ratio above 100 percent. Multiemployer plans situated in thriving industries are likely to be above 100 percent to attract new employers, whereas plans situated in declining industries are apt to let the assets-to-liabilities ratio slip below 100 percent to discourage employers from leaving. The International Union of Bricklayers, for example, has seen hard times in recent years, and it is reflected in their pension fund, which currently has unfunded liability. Frank Stupar, the former administrator of the Bricklayers Central Fund, explains why the pension fund is not fully funded:

"We're not fully funded. And do you know why you don't want to be funded? Because as long as there is withdrawal liability, the employer will stick with you. When they get fully funded then they decide why don't we just annuitize everybody and get rid of the fund."[62]

Two Examples of MPPAA Applications

Two examples will illustrate the significance of MPPAA enforcement. The first illustrates employer withdrawal regulations. In 1975, the trustees of IUOE Local 12's pension plan attempted to reclassify their fund from a defined-benefit to a defined-contribution fund. This would exempt them from payments to the PBGC. The trustees staked their claim based on the manner in which benefits are calculated. Retiring Local 12 members receive a certain percentage, established by the trustees, of all the contributions made on their behalf from the employers who participate in the fund (the CPF also uses this formula, see Chapters 3 and 5). Thus, when employers contribute to the fund they are in effect paying for their employees/participants' pensions. According to Local 12's trustees, this entitles the pension fund to be labeled a defined-contribution plan.[63]

Initially, a district court in southern California ruled in the trustees' favor, but a circuit court overturned the decision and sent the matter to a three-judge court for final adjudication. During the litigation, Congress passed the MPPAA. The trustees subsequently amended their complaint to exempt participating employers from withdrawal liability.

The three-judge court ruled in favor of the PBGC, stating that the manner in which benefits were calculated did not remove the fund from the spectrum of governmental regulation under ERISA and MPPAA. Local 12's pension fund was forced to continue payments to the PBGC, and employers would incur withdrawal liability if they suspended contributions during a period in which the plan was underfunded.

Some labor unions in recent years have brought pressure on recalcitrant employers by threatening to withdraw union funds from banks supporting these companies. MPPAA inhibited union-management trusteed pension plans from undertaking such corporate campaigning by regulating how a pension fund may vote its shares of stock in a company. Most union-management trusteed funds simply hand over the process of voting shares to its money managers with guidelines on how they wished them to vote. This piece of MPPAA legislation took corporate campaigning out of the hands of union-management trusteed pension funds and placed it in the trust of financial professionals, who were less likely to pressure companies to undertake specific actions of reform. Some unions' pension funds, however, do vote all of their shares and aggressively undertake corporate campaigning. The Brotherhood of Carpenters, for example, has a state-of-the-art computer network that tracks the equity holdings of many different union pension plans. When a company undertakes unfriendly actions toward unions or union busting, the pension funds that hold shares of stock in the company are contacted and instructed to be present at the next shareholders meeting to denounce the practice. The old strategy of "do not invest in non-union companies" has been replaced by a "purchase and reform" from within strategy. In these and other examples, a union can usually do what it considers to be in the best interest of its membership, but it has to learn to do so within the framework provided by ERISA.

CONCLUSION

In the 100 years American labor unions have sought to provide retirement benefits to their members, they have had to work within a framework of economic change, legislative reform, and an evolving government attitude toward the problem of old age. Each decade of the twentieth century changed the manner in which unions could provide pensions to their members. Economic conditions from 1900 to 1940 dominated the manner in which unions organized their pension plans. From 1940 to the present, a mixture of legislative change and the economic climate have set the tone for collectively bargained pensions. During this time, the persistence and perseverance of union leaders along with their members insisting that labor unions should provide for their members after the working years are over, cannot be understated.

The ideology of looking out after one's own, whether it is the bond of the family, a friendship, or belonging to the same trade union, is embedded within and will likely remain a permanent characteristic of the supposedly individualistic free-market society. Trade unions have always highlighted the need for workers to bond together to improve their working lives. In the current era, as many professional economists speculate on the coming crises in Social Security retirement payments, union-management trusteed pension funds may play an increasingly important role for their members as they become "too old to work too young to die."

This story now examines how one particular union-management trusteed pension fund, the Central Pension Fund of the International Union of Operating Engineers and Participating Employers, went about the task of providing retirement payments to its participants. As shall be seen, the CPF, in the same manner as other union-management trusteed pension plans, has had to roll with the punches of a changing economic climate and legal system in order to deliver a promised retirement income. The history of how those involved in the CPF went about the task of establishing and delivering pensions to members of the IUOE is deserving of a rigorous study as an illustration of the economic and social role of such plans and their struggles to meet their obligations. The coming chapters detail how the CPF was built, how legal and economic conditions have framed its actions, and what the future can be expected to hold for the plan's administrators and beneficiaries.

NOTES

1. Gaston Rimlinger, *Welfare Policy and Industrialization in Europe, America, and Russia* (New York: John Wiley & Sons, Inc., 1971), 8.

2. Merrit Ierley, *With Charity for All: Welfare and Society, Ancient Times to the Present* (New York: Praeger, 1984), 39–86, and Robert Morris, *Rethinking Social Welfare: Why Care for the Stranger?* (New York and London: Longman, Inc., 1986), 145–62.

3. U.S. Committee on Economic Security, *Social Security in America: The Factual Background of the Social Security Act as Summarized from Staff Reports to the Committee on Economic Security* (Washington, D.C.: Government Printing Office, 1937).

4. Hace Tischler, *Self Reliance and Social Security: 1870–1917* (Port Washington, N.Y.: National University Publications, 1971), 5.

5. Peter Kohler, *The Evolution of Social Insurance 1881–1981: Studies of Germany, France, Great Britain, Austria, and Switzerland* (London: Frances Pinter, 1982), 12.

6. Ibid.

7. Ibid., vii.

8. Rimlinger, *Welfare Policy and Industrialization*, 112.

9. Ibid.

10. Ibid., 116–17.

11. Quoted in ibid., 114.

12. Kohler, *The Evolution of Social Insurance*, 26.

13. The Corn Laws regulated the price at which foreign agricultural produce entered English markets.

14. David Ricardo, *The Principles of Political Economy and Taxation* (London: Dent, 1962).

15. For a description of the breakdown of the laissez-faire capitalism in England see Karl Polanyi, *The Great Transformation: The Political and Economic Origins of Our Time* (Boston: Beacon Press, 1944).

16. Kohler, *The Evolution of Social Insurance*, 153.

17. James B. Kennedy, *Beneficiary Features of American Trade Unions* (Baltimore: Johns Hopkins Press, 1908), 100.

18. Kohler, *The Evolution of Social Insurance*, 177–78.

19. Don D. Lescohier, "Old Age Pensions, Private Plans," *History of Labor in the United States, 1896–1932* (New York: The Macmillan Company, 1935), 386.

20. Quoted in ibid., 393.

21. Ibid.

22. Ibid.

23. Kennedy, *Beneficiary Features of American Trade Unions*, 12.

24. Ibid., 10.

25. Ibid., 10–12.

26. Quoted in ibid., 13.

27. Ibid., 106.

28. Ibid.

29. Ibid., 17.

30. Ibid., 103–104.

31. Ibid., 104.

32. Robert Bartell, *Pension Funds of Multiemployer Industrial Groups, Unions and Nonprofit Organizations* (New York: National Bureau of Economic Research, 1968), 2.

33. Norman A. Somers and Louis Schwartz, "Pension and Welfare Plans: Gratuities or Compensation?" *Industrial and Labor Relations Review* (October 1950): 81.

34. Ibid.

35. Rimlinger, *Welfare Policy and Industrialization*, 208.

36. Ibid., 214.

37. Ibid., 83.

38. Teresa Ghilarducci, *Labor's Capital: The Economics and Politics of Private Pensions* (Cambridge, Mass.: M.I.T. Press, 1992), 17.

39. U.S. Department of Labor, *National Union Benefit Plans 1947–1967.* (Washington, D.C.: Government Printing Office, 1970), 31–32.

40. Steven Sass, "Pension Bargains: The Heyday of U.S. Collectively Bargained Pension Arrangements," *Workers Versus Pensioners: Intergenerational Justice in an Ageing World* (Manchester: Manchester University Press, 1989), 94.

41. U.S. Department of Labor, *National Union Benefit Plans 1947–1967*, 31–32.

42. Gerald D. Nash, *Social Security: The First Half Century* (Albuquerque: University of New Mexico Press, 1988), 313–14.

43. U.S. Bureau of the Census, *Historical Statistics of the United States: Colonial Times to the Present* (New York: Basic Book Publishers, 1975), 351.

44. U.S. Department of Labor, *Pension Plans Under Collective Bargaining* (Washington, D.C.: Government Printing Office, 1953), v.

45. Ibid.

46. Quoted in Arthur Ross, "The New Industrial Pensions," *The Review of Economics and Statistics* (May 1950): 133–38.

47. In 1943 the UMWA broke from the CIO and joined the AFL in 1945. They eventually withdrew from the AFL in 1947.

48. Ralph and Estelle James, *Hoffa and the Teamsters: A Study of Union Power* (Princeton, N.J.: D. Van Nostrand Company, 1965), 215.

49. U.S. Bureau of Labor Statistics, *Multiemployer Pension Plans Under Collective Bargaining* (Washington, D.C.: Government Printing Office, 1960).

50. Ghilarducci, *Labor's Capital*, 38–39.

51. Walter Carlough, interview by authors, tape recording, Alexandria, Va., 17 September 1992.

52. Ghilarducci, *Labor's Capital*, 30.

53. Sass, "Pension Bargains," 103.

54. U.S. Department of Labor, *Monthly Labor Review* (Washington, D.C.: Government Printing Office, January, 1954), 13.

55. Ghilarducci, *Labor's Capital*, 46.

56. James and James, *Hoffa and the Teamsters*, 361.

57. Warren Ogden and Gerard Gasperini, "Avoiding MPPAA Liability via Continued Participation or Total Participation" *Labor Law Journal* (April 1985): 239.

58. Richard Steinberg, et al., *Pensions and Other Employee Benefits: A Financial Reporting and ERISA Compliance Guide* (New York: John Wiley & Sons, 1993), 4–5.

59. Ibid., 73–74.

60. Ogden and Gasperini, "Avoiding MPPAA Liability," 240.

61. Quoted in ibid.

62. Frank Stupar, interview by authors, tape recording, Washington, D.C., 17 September 1992.

63. *Connolly vs. PBGC*, 106 S. Ct. 1018.

Chapter 3

Building the Central Pension Fund

Although growing rapidly in membership and bargaining power during the 1940s and 1950s, the IUOE remained largely decentralized, its economic and political power resting with its local unions who bargained primarily with numerous localized and regionalized employers. These local unions ranged widely in size, in the prosperity of their local economies, and in their relationships with employers. Confronted by the same member needs and interests as all unions, the larger and stronger locals began in the early 1950s to add the negotiation of pensions to their bargaining demands. Those possessing bargaining power sufficient to persuade the employers, and membership large enough to provide the essential economies of scale to mount a workable pension scheme—most but not all of them hoisting and portable—soon had their own union-management trusteed plans. The first IUOE local to start a pension fund was New York Local 137 in 1953, it was followed by New Jersey Local 825 in 1955, Washington Local 302 in 1957, and Northern California's Local 3 in 1958. However, the smaller construction locals, and all the stationary locals except Northern California Local 39, Southern California Local 501, New Jersey Local 68, and New York Local 30 were on the outside looking in.

Along with the local membership, the business managers and staffs of the powerful locals had their own coverage. The international office had introduced at the 1956 convention a General Pension Fund covering employees of local unions. That only increased the pressure on those local unions not yet able to negotiate and mount their own plans. To a large extent the CPF is the result of one of the strongest of the stationary locals, Southern California Local 501, opting for this national program.

The establishment of the CPF in 1960 solved the problems that the small local unions within the IUOE were facing. By pooling the resources of local unions throughout the country, the economies of scale associated with a small membership base that made it practically impossible for all but the largest locals to start a pension were overcome. Prudent administration and investment advice are expensive. Local union labor leaders who had no experience in the pension arena would have to rely heavily on outside counsel for the successful operation of a pension plan. Also, a small membership pool means a small resource pool, which leads to inadequate diversification of revenue sources in potentially volatile markets.

The larger local unions that chose to enter the CPF did so mainly as a matter of convenience. As stated, local labor leaders in the IUOE had very little experience with administering pension plans. By joining the CPF, large local unions saved themselves the headaches associated with running a pension. They were "piggybacking" on the professionalism of the CPF. This chapter details the many and varied reasons why IUOE locals chose to participate in the CPF, as well as the origins of the fund.

THE GENESIS OF THE CENTRAL PENSION FUND

As noted, one of the foremost reasons the CPF was started was that the IUOE had established a pension plan for the employees of local unions. Business managers of IUOE local unions now had pensions, but their members did not. Those local unions without the membership base to start a pension on their own began to flood IUOE headquarters with inquiries about the feasibility of the International solving their pension problem. In 1959, IUOE General President Joe Delaney addressed the IUOE Executive Board on the issue of pension coverage for all members of the union. The following is a summary of Delaneys' speech, as reported in the *International Operating Engineer* (the publication of the IUOE):

General President Delaney reported that numerous inquiries had been received by the general office from local unions seeking information on the possibility of developing a pension plan which would cover the members of local unions whose membership is scattered throughout the jurisdiction of the International Union. The problem which these small local unions face is the prohibitive cost in securing adequate coverage for their small membership. In addition these small local unions are unable to secure for their membership many of the fringe benefits which are enjoyed by the larger local unions. The result of this has been that many small local unions have lost membership or have been faced with severe road blocks in their organizing programs.[1]

Two local labor leaders who were exemplary in the push for a central pension fund, as described by Delaney, were Ray Tucker and Ralph Crammer. Crammer was the international representative assigned to Ohio under Regional Director

Frank Converse. Crammer's full-time job was to service the twenty-nine stationary local unions in Ohio. The total stationary membership in his area was around 3,000 persons, so the locals were very small. Crammer was concerned that in the absence of a suitable pension fund for stationary engineers, they would ultimately wind up abandoning the IUOE for the Bakers, the Brewery Workers, or the Teamsters, who could offer them pensions.

On April 2, 1958, Crammer wrote to Hunter Wharton, then IUOE secretary-treasurer, regarding pension coverage for his members. He told Wharton of the problem of economies of scale associated with small stationary locals. Their small membership base made it impossible for the local unions in his area to start a pension plan. It was quite common for companies to employ stationary members in groups of four to fifteen workers in Ohio's jurisdiction. Some companies placed these stationary engineers into the company pension plan, but most of the membership in Ohio did not have any coverage. To highlight the problem, Crammer told Wharton that two companies, Linde Air Products and Fairmont Foods, recently terminated their stationary engineers, during company cutbacks, and also terminated their pensions. These workers were in their fifties, which made relocating difficult and made the possibility of generating a decent pension before they retired practically non-existent.[2]

Wharton advised Crammer that he begin a correspondence with Lane Kirkland, who, as good fortune would have it, had recently transferred from the Social Security branch of the AFL-CIO to become the research and education director of the IUOE. After writing to each other, Kirkland and Crammer decided to sit down with some large insurance companies to try to find a solution to pension coverage for the smaller IUOE local unions who could not start a pension on their own.[3] These meetings with insurers proved fruitless. There were no insurance companies who could offer a plan to meet the needs of these various locals. Kirkland and Crammer advised Delaney that the problem would have to be solved from within the union. There was no external solution available.

Another IUOE labor leader who was writing to Delaney on a regular basis about pension problems was Ray Tucker. Tucker was business manager of Southern California Stationary Local 501, which already had pension contributions in escrow in excess of $750,000. Tucker told Delaney he was willing to bring his local union into a central fund if the IUOE would decide to have one. He comments, "I thought to myself, now I have a good pension but what does the average member have? He ain't got nothing and if the IUOE could get a pension going it would be a way of organizing the un-organized. You have got more to sell them. Our local was big enough to have its own fund, but I felt we needed to pool our resources with other locals. It would be good for our local members and the rest of our IUOE brothers."[4] With Local 501's resources, the IUOE now had the capital base it needed to look seriously at starting a central pension fund.

Tucker's commitment to transfer his funds to a central plan spurred Lane

Kirkland to begin intensively researching the topic of a pension for the IUOE. His expertise in retirement programs was to prove a crucial factor in the successful start of the CPF. He took the lead in meeting with actuarial and administrative firms and investment counselors. In addition, Kirkland was in charge of seeking interested employer representatives for the formulation of the initial board of trustees. He wrote to George Kall of Beatrice Food Company, Richard Dennis of Dennis Trucking Co., and James Egan of Ward Banking Company requesting their participation in the CPF as management trustees, which they all accepted.[5]

In April 1960, at the twenty-sixth convention of the IUOE, Kirkland addressed the convention about the development of a central fund. Kirkland was speaking directly to the leaders of the smaller locals to allay their fears that pension coverage would continue to be impossible for their membership:

As many of you know, the International right now has been, and for some time has been, in the process of developing a new program by which the local unions might provide pension benefits for their members by negotiating employer contributions into a central pool pension fund. By bringing together the resources of many local unions, this would make possible a better level of benefits than would otherwise be available. It would make it possible for many locals that could not establish pension plans at all to set up such a plan.[6]

In September 1960, Kirkland and Crammer, along with the initial union trustees of the CPF—S. A. Boston, John Possehl, and Ray Tucker (hereafter Kirkland et al.)—appeared before the executive board of the IUOE and gave a detailed report of their initial study of the feasibility of an IUOE Central Pension Fund. Kirkland et al. felt the time was right to begin a fund and requested a loan from the International to cover the start-up costs. The board was impressed with their report and voted unanimously to give these men a $10,000 loan to start the CPF.[7]

The money from Local 501's pension plan provided the initial capital to "pump-prime" the CPF. There were heavy prices to pay to move Local 501's pension out of a guaranteed investment contract with New York Life. The company charged them 5 percent of the total to get the money transferred to the CPF. Also, Tucker had to fight a battle at home to convince his membership this was the right move. Only a strong business manager could sway the membership to abandon their local pension fund and send the money to Chicago, where the CPF was housed until 1970, to be administered by someone other than Local 501 representatives. Even Robert Fox, a subsequent trustee of the CPF and business manager of Local 501 from 1965 to 1993, admits he hassled Tucker about wanting to move Local 501's pension plan from their home territory to Chicago.[8] However, Tucker was able to convince the membership by appealing to their sense of brotherhood with other operating engineers and by describing the possibilities for growth and large benefits that a central fund would have.[9]

The team of Kirkland et al. realized that greater benefits could be provided if the cost of administration was kept at a minimum. The initial CPF board of trustees voted unanimously to accept the recommendation of Kirkland et al. that the plan permit each local union to negotiate for employer contributions to the centrally administered commingled fund in order to spread risks and to keep administrative expenses as low as possible. Another advantage was the fact that members could maintain their pension rights while moving between jobs or from one local area to another. The plan was also designed to accommodate any amount of contributions that locals may negotiate with their employers above a five cent per hour minimum. These advantages are built in to the benefit formula. The CPF's benefit formula is a hybrid, which combines both aspects of a defined-contribution and defined-benefit pension plan, and was developed by Kirkland et al. in conjuncture with Jim Higgins of Marsh and McLellan, the CPF's initial actuary. The benefit formula stated that retirees would get a fixed percentage per month based on the amount contributed on their behalf by the participating employers. Thus, it is a defined-contribution plan in the sense that each member has an individual record, but it is a defined-benefit plan when it actually comes time to pay benefits to a retiree.[10]

In addition to hiring Marsh and McClellan as the actuarial firm, the board of trustees appointed Bloomquist and Reeves as the plan administrator and Chase Manhattan Bank as the investment advisor. With everything in place—union and management trustees, administration, and professional advice on money management—the CPF was ready to begin servicing the pension needs of IUOE local unions and their membership who chose to sign up with the fledgling fund.

Kirkland attended the first two meetings of the CPF's board of trustees and then departed from the operation, leaving matters to the board. Ralph Crammer returned to his duties in Ohio after the CPF was up and running, and Ray Tucker served only on the board until 1965. Thus, those who bore the main responsibility for starting the CPF ended their affiliation with the Fund relatively soon after its inception. In the early and middle 1960s, following the exit of these individuals, a new leadership core was established that would define the course the fund would take to the present.

THE CPF'S LEADERSHIP CORE

Between the years of 1961 and 1976, key individuals were added to the CPF that would define the character of the Fund. Three groups of representatives are the decision makers. The union trustees were initially led by Ray Tucker, who was later superseded by Reese Hammond and Robert Fox. Management trustees have followed the lead of Hailey Roberts and Jack Cullerton (see the Appendix for a list of all the trustees appointed to the CPF). The professionals with the most direct input to the board of trustees throughout the history of the fund are Bill Riehl, Frank Gould, and Jack Johnson.

The Union Trustees

In September 1961, IUOE General President Hunter Wharton appointed Reese Hammond to serve as a trustee on the CPF. Hammond was born on November 17, 1928, in Holyoke, Massachusetts. After serving in the U.S. Army, he went to work as a mechanic and welder in 1948. Hammond became a labor organizer for the AFL in 1953, working with the American Federation of State, County, and Municipal Employees until 1958. He was serving as the director of Research and Education for the IUOE when he was appointed as a trustee to the CPF. Following the unexpected death in December 1961 of S. A. Boston, the first secretary of the CPF, Hammond was voted secretary of the CPF and served in that position until 1991. His continual presence was to prove a crucial factor in the recruitment of locals into the CPF, and together with Tucker he set the tone for the character and actions of the CPF Trustees. Richard Ennis, the CPF's investment consultant, says: "The CPF is an exemplar, a paragon. It has to do with the men who brought it into existence and the way they conducted their affairs and a lot had to do with Reese Hammond . . . he is a classic old school trade unionist in the best social sense of that. . . . He is a very well educated man, an intellectual."[11] In regard to the CPF's early investment decisions and Hammonds' influence, Ennis states:

What I think is special about the CPF was the sense of mission and trust that has existed within the International Union that this is a special thing and it won't be corrupted. Just like the law says it [the CPF] exists for the exclusive benefit of the participants. While there is natural pride in the fund and a close association with the interest of the inter-national union and all of its locals, the board of trustees has always been very inde-pendent. By independent, I don't mean cussed or ornery. Just independent given the duty of loyalty to run the best fund that they could. Reese has been the leading light in that regard and has always protected the Fund. He has always been very sensitive to any rumblings anywhere in the International or any place else.[12]

In 1965, Ray Tucker was appointed to the position of director of region 8 in the IUOE and resigned from the board of trustees of the CPF. His replacement was Robert Fox, who had become the business manager of Local 501. Fox, like Tucker, had developed an antiestablishment mentality during an earlier era in which Local 501 had been taken under supervision by the International union. In the late 1940s and early 1950s, Fox was an aggressive supporter of Tucker's bid to become the business manager and end 501's supervision status. Fox says:

I was one of the rebels while the local was under supervision. Tucker was running things as a secretary hired by the International. When there was a contract dispute in the hotel industry, the International tried to get Tucker to force a lousy contract down the membership's throat and Tucker refused. Instead of firing him, the International took his job away as secretary and made him a business agent. Boy did they make a big mistake. Tucker was in the field all day talking to the men about the dictatorial structure of the International. When we finally got to have an election Tucker was voted in as business manager.[13]

After becoming the business manager, Tucker asked Fox to be an agent. Working together, the two actively campaigned for 501 to have local autonomy. The local was granted in 1951, but it did not take effect until Tucker became the business manager in 1957. The fact that Tucker and Fox became key CPF trustees with this particular history of struggle with the international was one of the factors that led to the CPF's policy of being at arm's length from the international union—a distinct position among many union trusteed pension plans. That relative autonomy would not have occurred without the positive encouragement of international officers, however. Both Delaney and his successor, Hunter Wharton, had been critics of the proclivity of their predecessors to impose and retain supervision over local unions. In part because of the unfavorable publicity given this practice by the senatorial McClellan Committee during the 1950s, Wharton, who replaced Delaney as general president in 1962, in fact insisted on CPF autonomy.[14]

The Management Trustees

In 1966, Richard Gump of the Pipe Line Contractors' Association resigned from the board because of the press of other business. Pipeliners were an essential part of the beginning of the CPF, as these workers significantly increased the participant base. Pipeline work requires members to move around a great deal and work in several different locals' jurisdictions. Without a central institution to control reciprocity agreements, few pipeline workers would ever qualify for a pension benefit. Reese Hammond recounts the move of the Pipeline workers into the CPF:

The IUOE had a pipeline agreement with the main pipeline contractors association for a number of years and by 1963 it was the determination by both management and labor that it was time to have a pension fund for the pipeliners who are boomers and move around quite a bit. They move all over the country and pipeline work by definition crosses many local union borders. So the ground was set for some kind of a nationwide pension fund for the pipeline industry and in 1963 the logical place to turn was the Central Pension Fund.[15]

Gump suggested Hailey Roberts, an attorney for the Pipeline Contractors' Association, as his replacement. At the next board meeting Roberts was confirmed and has served on the board up to the present. He is well respected among administrators of union-management trusteed funds and serves on several boards. Frank Gould, administrator of the CPF from 1963 to 1994, says of

Roberts, "Very, very strong trustee. Was asked many, many times to be chairman but never wanted to be chairman. . . . Hailey has a very quick mind, an
unbelievably quick mind."[16] When controversy arose over difficult decisions,
Roberts would serve as leader of the management trustees and would bargain
with Hammond. The two of them were always able to reach an agreement.
"Basically, Hailey on the employer side and Reese on the union side would
serve that purpose [leadership]."[17]

Union-management trusteed funds have a difficult time attracting top-notch
management people, and Hailey Roberts was the type of individual many funds
would want. The ability to add Roberts can be attributed to the existing trustees:
"The leaders set a tone. Reese has always set a tone . . . that makes it more
attractive for other trustees to serve. Getting top-notch management in particular
is one of the challenges you always have for these funds. And the top labor
people set the tone on who they can attract as the top management person in
terms of position, integrity, character, commitment."[18] The ability of the CPF
to attract quality people to management is also attributable to its nationwide
status. Union trustees on local funds frequently bring collective bargaining issues
to board meetings, making uncomfortable situations for the management trustees. Heated arguments often follow. In the case of the CPF, having trustees
from around the country encourages collective bargaining issues to be left at
home. Bob McCormick, a management trustee of the CPF since 1982 and a
trustee on several jointly trusteed local funds, confirms this reasoning: "The
funds on a national basis tend to be more equal in terms of the relationships
between the trustees, on a local fund the collective bargaining relationships are
so ingrained that you have a hard time differentiating between the C-B table
and your role as a trustee. On a national basis I feel a lot more comfortable and
it results in an equal partnership to work towards the benefits of the pensioners."[19]

Another first-rate management trustee attracted by the CPF was John Cullerton from the Hilton Hotel Corporation in 1976. Cullerton holds credentials in
all aspects of understanding union-management trusteed benefit funds. He comes
from a union background that began at the University of Illinois when he was
studying economics. He wrote an article about the unification of the AFL and
CIO and was subsequently asked to become the secretary for a political action
committee supporting a candidate for mayor of Chicago. After holding several
union-organizing positions with different unions in the Chicago area and serving
as the director of labor for Illinois, he moved over to the management side in
1969 as the executive vice president of the Greater Chicago Hotel and Motel
Multiemployer organization. Cullerton's move to management was facilitated
by his familiar relationship with the relevant employers during his twelve years
as a union representative. In 1970, Cullerton began studying the professional
side of pension fund administration as an officer at Mass Insurance Consultants
and Administrators (MICA). The following year Cullerton was hired by the
Hilton Corporation as a senior officer of employee relations. In 1976, he joined

the CPF and was elected chairman following the death of Al MacIntyre in 1981. He has remained in that position until the present. Cullerton's experience with the union, professional managers, and employers makes him a valuable asset to the CPF's leadership.

The Professionals

In 1961, Bill Riehl of Marsh and McLellan was assigned the actuarial duties for the CPF. This position has been unusually influential. The CPF has never granted a benefit increase that the actuary did not approve, accepting implicitly judgments based on complicated calculations. Riehl had a unique relationship with the board. He says, "I always felt like one of the trustees, not a paid gun like Reese Hammond liked to call me." How did the trustees decide they could afford a plan improvement when Riehl was the actuary? They would look to Riehl who would say, "I am comfortable with that," if he believed the action was fiduciarily sound. The trustees never voted against one of Riehl's recommendations.[20]

In 1963, the fund switched from Bloomquist and Reeves as a third-party administrator to MICA. The trustees felt that Bloomquist and Reeves' performance was subpar and that it was time for a new administrator. The person MICA assigned to do the "everyday" types of administration for the CPF was Frank Gould. Gould was fresh out of college and began an apprenticeship in the administration of union-management trusteed pension plans. The trustees were impressed with his performance and eventually, within the MICA operation, he began to devote all of his time to administrative duties for the CPF, a role he held until his retirement in late 1994. Gould has always been a third party to the CPF:

The trustees have always felt very strongly that this is a jointly administered fund and the role of the third party administrator, in my case self-administrator later on, was a very important role in order to have balance to represent the Fund. By philosophy I have never been a member of the union. I have been asked to join on a regular or honorary basis, but I have never done that because it was in the best interest of the Fund that I not be affiliated with the union. Obviously I work very closely with the union, but I have never been a member and will not become one.[21]

The other side of the management team is Jack Johnson, who came to work at the CPF in 1970. The hiring of Johnson was one of the first moves made by the board of trustees after the Fund moved to self-administration, as is discussed later in this chapter. Initially, Johnson was hired to be the assistant administrator, but through his own initiative he evolved into the director of finance beginning in 1977. "My background is in economics and I had been doing a lot of studying of finance, so it seemed natural for me to move into this role,"[22] Johnson asserts.

Table 3.1
The largest stationary locals in the IUOE

	Membership in 1975	Established Local Pension Fund or Joined the CPF
1. Local 501 (California)	5,601	Joined CPF in 1961
2. Local 39 (California)	4,239	1955
3. Local 399 (Illinois)	4,136	Joined CPF in 1961
4. Local 547 (Michigan)	3,529	Joined CPF in 1962
5. Local 94 (New York)	3,320	Joined CPF in 1961
6. Local 68 (New Jersey)	3,149	1954
7. Local 2 (Missouri)	2,926	Joined CPF in 1969
8. Local 30 (New York)	2,920	1954
9. Local 347 (Texas)	2,752	Joined CPF in N.A.
10. Local 286 (Washington)	2,691	Joined CPF in 1962

An in house investment expert like Johnson is rare among union-management trusteed funds, which usually rely on outside counsel for investment advice.

Thus, these key players: Hammond, Tucker, and Fox, representing the union; Roberts and Cullerton, representing the participating employers; and Riehl, Gould, and Johnson, representing professionals of the fund, established a continuity of leadership. The culture of how decisions would be made was solidified in the 1960s and 1970s by these individuals and has remained to the present.

RECRUITING LOCALS

The growth of the CPF came primarily from the entrance of existing union locals into the Fund and secondarily from the growth of local membership during the 1960s and 1970s. Reese Hammond and Frank Gould had the main responsibility for recruiting locals into the Fund. Hammond did the leg work—that is, the face-to-face organizing—and Gould handled the administrative process. Along with smaller locals, the CPF sought to enlist larger locals that did not have pension plans. All but one of the larger construction locals, however, declined their invitation.

Table 3.1[23] lists the membership numbers of the largest stationary locals in the IUOE and whether those locals joined the CPF or had a pension plan of their own. As the table shows, seven of the ten largest stationary locals joined the CPF. Local 501, as noted earlier, already had pension contributions in escrow and transferred their funds into the CPF. The other business managers of the large locals were quite content with their previously established pension funds. Art Viat, business manager of Local 39 since 1965, says, "By the time the CPF started we were too well established. Our trustees did not want to have anything

Table 3.2
The largest hoisting and portable locals in the IUOE

	Membership in 1975	Established Local Pension Fund or Joined the CPF
1. Local 3 (California)	35,765	1958
2. Local 12 (California)	25,326	1960
3. Local 18 (Ohio)	15,817	1964
4. Local 324 (Michigan)	13,812	1958
5. Local 49 (Minnesota)	12,875	Joined CPF in 1967
6. Local 150 (Illinois)	12,591	1963
7. Local 302 (Washington)	10,547	1957
8. Local 115 (Brit Columbia)	9,155	N.A.
9. Local 825 (New Jersey)	8,447	1955
10. Local 542 (Pennsylvania)	7,056	1960
11. Local 793 (Ontario)	6,997	N.A.
12. Local 428 (Arizona)	6,492	N.A.
13. Local 701 (Oregon)	6,141	1960
14. Local 9 (Colorado)	5,904	Joined CPF in 1968
15. Local 139 (Wisconsin)	5,689	Joined CPF in 1967
16. Local 181 (Kentucky)	4,829	Joined CPF in 1965
17. Local 450 (Texas)	4,496	Joined CPF in 1966
18. Local 406 (Louisiana)	4,417	Joined CPF in 1966
19. Local 513 (Missouri)	4,367	1963
20. Local 955 (Alberta)	3,836	N.A.

to do with it."[24] The CPF did not actively recruit Stationary Locals 39, 68, or 30 for this very reason. It would simply have been a waste of CPF expenses to send representatives to these locals.

The CPF also did not pursue the larger construction locals with existing pension funds. Tom Stapleton, business manager of Local 3, responded in a similar manner to Viat when he was asked why Local 3 would not consider joining the CPF, "We did not need them. That was our attitude; still is. Our territory is so large and we have enough members to provide a pension on our own."[25] As Table 3.2[26] shows, seven of the fifteen largest IUOE construction locals did not have pension plans. These seven were Ohio Local 18, Minnesota Local 49, and Illinois Local 150 with memberships over 10,000 persons, and Colorado Local 9, Wisconsin Local 139, Kentucky Local 181, and Texas Local 450 with memberships in excess of 4,000 persons. The CPF made attempts to bring all of these locals on board. Their large membership numbers would significantly increase the contribution base of the CPF.

Locals 9, 139, 181, and 450 all chose to join the CPF. It was a mutually beneficial situation. These locals were borderline on the ability to have a fund of their own, so they chose to take advantage of the economies of scale associated with a large nationwide fund. The CPF was able to hire highly regarded administration, actuarial, and money management firms to advise the board of trustees on allocating the participants contributions. Thus, these locals could be assured that their membership's money would be well taken care of while avoiding the hassle of managing a pension fund of their own. In return, the CPF acquired some rather large local unions, which helped the fund to grow substantially in its formative years.

"They Wanted to Stomp Their Own Snakes"

Illinois Local 150 and Ohio Local 18 chose to form their own pension funds. Reese Hammond explains the reason why: *"They wanted to stomp their own snakes.* We made presentations to the locals because they expressed an interest in coming on board, but in the end they wanted to maintain autonomy over their pension fund money."[27] For a while it looked as though the Ohio local would join. John Possehl, president of Local 18 in 1960, was one of the initial trustees appointed to the CPF under the assumption the local was coming in:

Possehl was named a trustee with the idea that Local 18 would be coming into the CPF; that this should be their fund and they should not have one of their own. He was desirous of that. It turned out that it would not happen because of a person named Frank Converse [a long-time general vice president and retired Local 18 business manager] who was a very strong person within the International and in charge of Local 18 at the time. We went and made a presentation to Local 18 about the CPF, and Converse said that while the CPF does pay out good benefits, we are not going to join because we want to stomp our own snakes.[28]

Minnesota Local 49 was the largest construction local that chose to come aboard the CPF rather than having its own pension fund. The fact that Local 49 is easily large enough to have its own plan has led to a long-standing debate among CPF trustees as to whether Local 49 would have been better off remaining outside the Fund. Relative pros and cons for the Minnesota local joining the CPF are difficult to determine. As the only large local in the IUOE not to have a pension program as late as 1967, joining the CPF undoubtedly seemed like a quick and convenient way to redress this problem at the time.

Recruiting Techniques

Recruitment of locals into the CPF was not only a function of size and local control, but also of the recruiting techniques of Reese Hammond. Skills he developed while working as an organizer for the international and other unions were important in determining whether or not a local would join the CPF. For instance, on a trip through Montana Hammond used a domino strategy:

The business managers, three or four, and I were together as we went from one local to another. Initially we had Billings saying they wanted in, so we had their OK going for us in Great Falls, and when they said OK in Great Falls, we had Billings and Great Falls going for us when we got to Kalispell. So when we got to Butte or Helena it didn't make too much difference because everyone else in Montana said we want the Central Pension Fund.[29]

In addition to Hammond's skills, the CPF benefit formula included a system of rewarding past service credits to new entrants into the fund. This was very attractive to the older retiring members. The system for calculating past service was based on years of service prior to a worker becoming covered by the CPF. Therefore, when a local would join the CPF the members who were about to retire would still receive a pension benefit even though they had very little money contributed on their behalf by the participating employers. Hammond describes how the system worked:

The past service credits was the feature that the guys liked most of all, especially because they got money put in on their behalf. If they worked 2,000 hours, they got 2,000 times a dime. If they worked 1,200 hours, they got 1,200 times a dime in other words $120 bucks [a month]. A number of funds in those days were paying on a year of service. I recall up in Chicago they started out with ten years of past service but each active year knocked out one year of past service. So within ten years up in Chicago they had gotten rid of any past service obligation. We still carry some past service obligation because a lot of people that came in have not yet retired.[30]

However, the CPF did not offer past service credits to lure locals into the fund. These credits were a reward to the older members who had built the union and made a pension fund possible. "Even the younger guys understood the essential fairness of the past service credits,"[31] Hammond said.

Louisiana Construction Local 406 joined the CPF for many reasons, including Hammond's recruiting skills and the advantage of the past service credits. The leader of the local at the time, Peter Babin, Jr., was also an advocate of IUOE locals pooling their resources so that diversification would prevent a local union from going bankrupt if the local economy failed. Peter Babin, Jr.'s story and Local 406's entrance into the CPF are detailed in the following.

Local 406 Enters the CPF in 1966

During the 1950s and 1960s real wages for Local 406 members were increasing rapidly, and the local instituted a health and welfare program. This made it easier to convince the membership to forgo money now in return for a pension later. It was still a very difficult task, however, to convince the membership that joining the CPF was in their best interest. The entrance of Local 406 into the CPF is largely due to the actions of one man, Peter Babin, Jr., father of Peter

Babin III, who is currently the business manager of the local and a vice president of the International Union.

Babin, Jr.'s father was a construction worker in Louisiana during the nonunion era. Eventually Babin, Sr., became a state construction inspector. At sixty-seven he suffered a heart attack and was never again able to work. Having no union retirement or Social Security, the wages he earned prior to his heart attack were his last source of income until his death two years later. His son relates:

When my dad got his heart attack, he got his last pay check. In those days, [state construction inspectors] never had Social Security. My dad died two and a half years later. And, he did not receive even a penny from anybody. Fortunately, after I left the ship yard, I went to work for a construction company as an operator. And, between my sister and I, we had to pay for rent, food, and other things for our mother and our dad. My sister and I supported my mother after my dad died. And, I think, she got $82 a month from the state of Louisiana as they called it "old age aids" or something like that. But, we took care of her. And my son when he bought his house, he built a little nice apartment in the back of his house and my mother lived there for the rest of her life.[32]

This hard-scrabble ending of his father's life left a deep impression on Peter Babin, Jr. He subsequently committed his life to improving the living conditions of operating engineers and other construction workers in Louisiana. He never wanted another construction worker to have to suffer through what his father and family had to endure.

Babin, Jr., was born on April 20, 1911, in New Orleans. After graduating from high school he began serving as a clerk at one of the local construction sights. During this time he made friends with a dozer operator who taught him how to run that piece of machinery. It was at that point that Babin, Jr., knew he wanted to become an operating engineer. In 1941, Babin, Jr., went to work as a crane operator in a ship yard and joined Local 406 of the Operating Engineers.

Prior to becoming an operating engineer, Babin, Jr., was working as a driver for a newspaper. He says of the work, "worst job I ever had; we worked seven days a week, three hundred and sixty five days a year for $15 a week."[33] Babin, Jr., felt he could improve the plight of the drivers by getting them organized and finding a union to represent them. For this effort he got fired. However, Babin, Jr.'s initial failure in organizing did not deter him from being a union leader.

In 1956, while Babin, Jr., was working as a business agent for Local 406, he was elected the secretary of the New Orleans Central Trades and Labor Council, the number two position in the organization. In May of that year he took an active and influential role in ensuring that the general contractors agreed to set up a health and welfare plan for all of the building trades unions in Louisiana. Having secured medical care for union members, Babin, Jr., went to work on their retirement. Ten years later, the Operating Engineers of Local 406 obtained old age security when they joined the CPF. Babin, Jr., describes his motivation to continue to push the membership to adopt a pension plan during this time period:

The only pension we had at this time was a hat we would pass around when retirees would come to the union hall to get something to do because they had no money. I hated to see a good and respectable aged man who did not have any income after he retired. In those days the equipment was different and the operator had to be strong to handle it. You had to have strong shoulders and knees, and after thirty years of work the machinery would wear you down.[34]

It took ten years after installing the health and welfare plan for Local 406 to join the CPF, due to the slow growth of real wages for Local 406 members. In the four-year period preceding the implementation of the health and welfare plan, real wages for Local 406 Operating Engineers had increased 20 percent. Rapidly rising real wages made it politically feasible to implement benefit programs because the membership did not mind giving up a portion of their paycheck. When real wage growth slowed, Babin, Jr., found it more difficult to convince business agents and local members to add additional benefits to their total compensation package. In the year the health and welfare plan was implemented, real wages for Local 406 members fell 1 percent. In the subsequent four-year period, real wages rose only 6 percent. It was not until 1965 that real wages rose 20 percent beyond the 20 percent boost experienced between 1952 and 1955. From 1956 onward Babin, Jr., was working diligently to get a pension plan instated, but the economy was holding him back from reaching his goal. He says of that time period: "The membership had a kind of bitterness about a pension plan because it was going to take money out of their wage increase and they wanted the money in their pockets. I had to convince them that they had to think about the time when they were old, twenty years from now."[35]

Babin, Jr., did not want Local 406 to have a pension at the Local level. He was adamant in insisting that Local 406 join the CPF because he was well aware of the benefits of a nationwide fund. Babin, Jr., believed that if the local economy took a downturn, his memberships pension would not be in jeopardy because the fund would not collapse: "We set up the health and welfare locally and had an office here for it. I ran the damn thing and it really ran well but I was always concerned about having bad times. I knew if it was a bad time everything would go under. If you have a nationwide fund there is not that threat unless the whole economy collapses."[36] The membership trusted Peter Babin, Jr., and therefore trusted his idea that Local 406 could not house its own pension fund.

While serving as a representative from the Central Trades and Labor Council to the AFL-CIO Building Trades meetings in Washington, D.C., Babin, Jr., met Reese Hammond. Babin, Jr., told Hammond of the problems he was encountering in establishing a pension fund, and Hammond decided to pay a visit to New Orleans. Hammond describes the typical situation he faced when trying to get locals to join the CPF:

Well, I had found out that a major problem is if a lot of young people show up at a meeting while they are quite supportive of health and welfare benefits, pension is something that is deferred and is something that they really don't think much about. They think, why should I put money in there for those old bastards when I could use the money in my paycheck right now. And so you had to face that attitude and in this particular instance, if you have done enough organizing you know when you have got a crowd coming with you. You know just from the nature of reactions and maybe a question or a groan or something like that you know where your problems are. And I made the pitch, and I thought it was pretty well received except there was a number of younger fellows who weren't very happy about it. I went right after him and said, "Listen my friend, what are you making per hour?" And let's say he said "$5.75 an hour." I said, "Do you know what the nonunion guys are making around here?" and before he could reply I said, "Don't bother telling me because I know they are making $3.75 an hour," and I continued on with, "Every hour that you work you are getting two bucks because of the old guys in this building." And then I really started to lay on the chauvinistic business, that if it wasn't for the older guys they wouldn't have this local union and this nice meeting hall. You could see him begin to cross over.[37]

In addition, Hammond told the membership that for every nickel per hour the participating employers contributed to the CPF, the eligible retirees would get $25 per month, regardless of how soon they retired or how little they had put into the CPF. This was a very popular idea, especially among those about to retire.

The combination of Reese Hammond, Peter Babin, Jr., and rising real wages proved to be enough to convince the members they needed a pension plan, and consequently they voted in favor of it in 1966.

COMMUNICATING WITH LOCALS

A central problem facing a new union-management trusteed pension fund is membership distrust. Until a pension fund is well-established and paying tangible benefits, participants will be leery about whether or not promised benefits will be delivered. Therefore, it was imperative that the CPF develop a strategy to communicate with participating locals to ensure the participants that the present and future actions of the CPF would be prudent.

In the 1950s and early 1960s, many union-management trusteed pension funds were in their infancy, and union members did not believe that boards of trustees would invest their pension contributions wisely if left to their own judgment. Thus, pension promises would never be delivered. Due to this suspicion on the part of the rank and file, many local union-management trusteed pension funds began their retirement programs as annuities provided by insurance companies.

Northern California IUOE Locals 3 and 39 both followed this route, as did Southern California Local 501 and New York Local 94. John Sweeny, chairman of Associated Third Party Administrators, which serves as a third-party administrator to over 100 union-management trusteed funds, describes the general climate of union-management trusteed pension funds in the Bay Area in the 1950s: "Nobody really thought the unions were going to try to run away with the money, except for the members. The members really felt they would not get anything out of these pensions. Initially, many unions had an insurance company come in to provide annuities, and that gave the members confidence that they would have money for their retirement."[38]

With IUOE locals having difficulty convincing their membership that pension fund money would be administered in a prudent manner, one can imagine the difficulty that would confront a nationwide fund such as the CPF. In 1962, the Board of Trustees of the CPF appointed Reese Hammond and Richard Dennis to address this problem of communicating with the membership. The initial plan developed by Hammond and Dennis was a three-legged program. They decided the CPF should (1) hold national and regional workshops and make presentations at conferences, (2) support the local unions by keeping the leadership informed of the CPF's actions, and (3) communicate directly with the participants. By following this strategy, the CPF trustees believed the leadership of local unions would be informed and the participants would not be leery of malfeasance.

By 1965, the CPF had developed a filmstrip, a statement of a participant's fund record that was to be sent four times a year, and a brochure. The brochure was thorough in summarizing the benefit structure of the CPF. It detailed how to apply to go on pension, gave several examples of how to calculate a benefit amount, and included all amendments to the plan.

The brochure was probably received differently by the participants based on their age and employment. Younger members most likely never bothered to read about the CPF. Members who were near retirement had to be enthusiastic about the breadth of material in the pamphlet and the careful attention to explaining everything in laymans terms. Stationary engineers probably scrutinized the brochure more thoroughly than hoisting and portable engineers. Art Viat, business manager of IUOE Stationary Local 39, claims his members are very aware of their pensions. Viat says his members are "readers," and one thing they love to read about is the management of their pension money:

Stationary workers are different when it comes to trust funds. They have a lot of time to read and they do a lot of reading. You cannot read girlie magazines and stuff like that because you will get fired, but they have no qualms about you reading about things which improve yourself and your knowledge. This makes stationary engineers readers and they all got opinions. They are always jumping up at the meetings and saying, "we are only getting 3.5 percent out of this pension I don't want any more of my money going into a pension, I can do better on my own." You have got to be careful what investments you are making or these guys will complain.[39]

In the years following its initial issue, the brochure was constantly updated as the CPF benefit structure was changed. Worksheets and examples of how to calculate a benefit were always included to make sure participants would not have any doubts or fears about how much money they would be receiving on retirement. The CPF trustees, administrators, and staff often boast that the CPF already had in place many of what would become ERISA's mandates. Education of the participants is one area in which those involved with the CPF are to be commended. ERISA required that participants have their pension plan explained to them in layman's terms, but the CPF was already doing this for seven years prior to the legislation. Bill Riehl, the CPF's actuary for thirty years, summarizes the importance of the CPF's commitment to serving the participants when he says: "I think the CPF provides a very high level of service. They put out brochures and benefit statements and participants always get their questions answered when they call the fund. This makes the participants very comfortable with the CPF."[40]

The board of trustees, however, decided that simply sending out materials to the participants was not enough. The CPF needed to hold a national seminar to provide face-to-face education. In 1973, the CPF hosted such a conference in Vail, Colorado, which was attended by 145 delegates from various IUOE locals.[41] The delegates were required to do homework and were quizzed on the subjects of proper wording of pension coverage in collective bargaining agreements, accurately reporting basic data to the CPF, delinquency procedures, and the CPF's benefit formulas. A follow-up seminar to the 1973 meeting was conducted in 1978 with the central topic being ERISA compliance.[42] It is the attention to "nuts and bolts" items such as the ones listed above that have made the CPF the sound institution it is today.

SELF-ADMINISTRATION

The CPF was in its tenth year in 1970, and that year was the occasion for the boldest move the CPF trustees would make. They decided the time was right to break from MICA and administer the fund themselves. Jack Johnson explains: "In 1970 the CPF had reached what I call its "critical mass," where it could support its own staff and go out and do what it wanted to. The trustees felt that by going to self-administration they could exercise more care and concern for the participants."[43] The hiring of Johnson, at Frank Gould's recommendation, was one of the first moves made by the board of trustees after going self-administered and Johnson has become a key individual in the CPF's leadership core. Bernie Baum, a Chicago lawyer who represents IUOE Local 150's pension fund and a large number of union-management trusteed pension funds, was impressed with the team of Gould and Johnson. In comparison to other union-management trusteed pension funds, Baum says: "They were more sophisticated early on. I realized that the first time I ran into Frank Gould and saw an internal investment person like Jack Johnson. I had never seen it before. Now that might have been true for other international unions, I don't know. But I had never seen it before. Their operation was just very sophisticated.''[44]

In the late 1960s the fund was being run out of the MICA building in Chicago. When the decision to go to self-administration was made, the fund was moved to Washington, D.C. Johnson says, ''The trustees had previously moved the operation of the Fund to a different floor in the same building where the third party administrator was. So it was just a matter of turning the switch off and turning another on.''[45] When asked why the board voted to go to self-administration, Reese Hammond responds:

I can't give you a specific; we made the determination to go self administered for a number of reasons . . . we didn't do this by pulling it out of our pocket. . . . We commissioned a study by Lybrand, Ross Brothers and Montgomery. It had all the details of what we needed to do including who we should take with us as the core of leadership from the Central Pension Fund unit of MICA. We ultimately got Frank Gould, Doris Hoffman, as head of the Employer Records, and Dick Olson . . . it was a relatively seamless transfer. The only thing that the participants and the participating employers knew was that the address changed where they mailed the reporting forms from Chicago to Washington.[46]

Hammond also wants to clarify that the move had nothing to do with the performance of MICA:

We did not go self-administered because we thought MICA was incompetent. MICA had a lot of other accounts. We were a fairly good sized one near the end of the '60s, and certainly the potential was there to be much bigger. But MICA was not as responsive to what our board of trustees felt we needed and friction built up over a period of a year or eighteen months or so. . . . We were one of 35 funds they had, and in their professional judgment they developed a system which was satisfactory for 34 funds and were not in any hurry to tailor or modify that system simply for the Central Pension Fund, their theory being we are the professional administrators, and we know what it takes, and this is what we will do.[47]

In addition to MICA's inability to tailor an administrative package for the CPF, the investment performance by Chase Manhattan Bank was cited as an additional reason for the move to self-administration. At one point, Chase Manhattan's representatives were recommending that the Fund go to a portfolio structure of 100 percent equities. That was the "final straw." The trustees did not claim to be financial geniuses, but they knew that their involvement with Chase had to be cut off. Hammond explains:

The kindest thing I can say about Chase Manhattan was that they simply were not geared up in the decade of the '60s to handle jointly trusteed pension funds. They are not a collective bunch of idiots. They are a very successful bank, but boy, when you see the track record for the investments they made on our behalf you could easily believe they were a bunch of idiots. . . . You look back and I think you will find that our compounded return was like 1 percent for the nine years that Chase Manhattan ran this Fund. It was really awful. The returns were horrible. They were sensitive to the fact that we were really pissed off and they came into one meeting and said "look, we have the answer to the problem and will get everything right back on track. We are going to put 100 percent of the investment in equities." That was the last straw as far as I was concerned, and I think the other trustees also. While equities over the long run are a healthy part of the American economy, they are also the riskiest of the investment opportunities.[48]

With the firing of Chase Manhattan, the CPF's trustees had no visions of conquering the financial markets alone. The trustees surrounded themselves with reputable financial consultants, in conjunction with Jack Johnson, to educate and advise them on matters of investment. The trustees remain the final authority on how the CPF invests money on behalf of the participants and participating employers, but the influence of the consultants and Johnson in their decisions cannot be understated. This reality is reflected in a statement by Jack Cullerton, chairman of the Board of Trustees since 1981, who said, "the key to the success of this fund is the caliber of the professionals, outside counsel as well as the staff, and we think we have the best in the business."[49]

In an expression of the CPF's continuing desire to be autonomous from the international, a building to house the CPF in Washington was chosen far away from IUOE headquarters. Hammond states, "It was never a viable consideration that we move into the International Union."[50] Hunter Wharton was general president of the IUOE in 1970, and when he learned the CPF was going to move to Washington he made no efforts to bring the Fund into the International: "Hunter was very sensitive to the problems that the Teamsters had and I guess one or two others (the Laundry workers perhaps) with their pension funds. So he had established a philosophy of keeping an arms length between the pension fund and the International Union to the extent that if you were on the pension board you could not be on the executive board of the International."[51]

Thus, the move to self-administration represented a change in outlook and philosophy in regard to serving the participants. The CPF had reached its critical mass, which made self-administration efficient. The trustees had confidence in their ability to manage a large fund, as well as in Frank Gould's administrative capabilities. Therefore, in 1970 it seemed the time was right to take control of their own destiny.

RECIPROCITY

A problem equally as challenging as communicating with locals was to see that participating construction workers received the entire benefit they were entitled to, or in other words earned, through a reciprocity agreement.

The nature of construction work often leads individual IUOE hoisting and portable members to work in the jurisdiction of several locals. The need for reciprocity agreements among local pension plans and the CPF was paramount if hoisting and portable members were to receive the highest level of benefit possible or, in fact, any retirement benefit at all. The itinerant status of those working within several different locals jurisdictions created the problem of never earning enough pension vesting credits to qualify for a benefit in a local's plan. One of the enduring complaints about the Teamster and Laborer's pension plans was that they offered high benefits but denied pensions to workers who moved between locals and for other small breaks in service. In 1973, a reciprocity agreement to end this problem for members of the IUOE was reached between locals participating in the CPF and those locals with their own pension fund.

In the northeastern section of the country, representatives from the locals with pension plans would get together and exchange work records of members from out of their locals and transfer funds contributed for the work. There was no written reciprocity agreement among these locals, and the exchange of records was done on a purely informal basis. On the West Coast the situation was very different. The West is composed of very few locals, each with large jurisdictional territories. This geographical arrangement made it difficult for representatives from different locals to meet in the same informal manner as the northeastern locals did. Thus, hoisting and portable workers would often lose credit for pension contributions. In addition, they might never qualify for a benefit in their home local because they did not meet the years of service vesting requirement.

The initial attempt to begin nationwide reciprocity was made at the Annual Educational Conference of the National Foundation of Health, Welfare and Pension Plans in 1967. Hammond served as vice chairman of the conference and twenty-one IUOE locals sent representatives.[52] Ideally, when an IUOE member retired he would have all his pension contributions transferred to the local fund in which he was eligible for a pension and could receive the highest benefit. In 1973 this goal was almost achieved, as the majority of local unions entered into a reciprocity agreement that made the transfer of money possible. However, many local pension funds decided only to sign on to a pro rata agreement (Table 3.3).[53] The pro rata agreement meant that the total hours worked as an operating engineer for any employer contributing to any local's fund or the CPF would qualify an individual for a pension benefit. For instance, if John Smith worked as an operating engineer within the jurisdiction of three different locals with three different pension funds, each with a ten-year vesting rule, but had only nine years of service in each local, he would still qualify for a benefit in each fund. John Smith would be considered as having twenty-seven years of vesting service under the pro rata agreement. Suppose the three pension plans from which he was qualified to receive a benefit did not determine benefits in the same manner as the CPF. For instance, suppose, they were defined-benefit programs, based on years of service rather than contributions. In that case, John Smith would earn a pro rata pension from each reciprocal pension fund—a

Table 3.3
IUOE local unions with their own pension programs that signed the reciprocity agreement in 1973

Local Union	Type	Signed to A or AB	Local Union	Type	Signed to A or AB
3	HP	A	137	HP	A
4	HP	AB	138	HP	AB
12	HP	A	150	HP	AB
14	HP	AB	302	HP	A
15	HP	AB	324	HP	AB
17	HP	AB	370	HP	A
18	HP	AB	400	HP	A
25	HP	AB	410	HP	AB
30	S	A	428	HP	A
37	HP	A	463	HP	AB
39	S	A	478	HP	AB
57	HP	A	513	HP	A
66	HP	AB	542	HP	AB
68	S	A	545	HP	AB
77	HP	AB	571	HP	A
98	HP	AB	612	HP	A
101	HP	A	675	HP	A
106	HP	AB	701	HP	A
115	HP	A	825	HP	A
132	HP	AB	832	HP	AB

A = Signed prorata agreement, B = Signed transfer of funds agreement.

percentage of determined by dividing each locals required service by the actual time the member worked in each local. In other words, he would receive one third of each local's defined benefit ($9/27 = 1/3$).

CONCLUSION

The CPF has grown from a $10,000 loan from the International to the sixth largest union-management trusteed pension fund.[54] The key individuals on the CPF Board of Trustees and in its administration have had unusually long years of service. They joined CPF operations in the early and middle 1960s and early 1970s and defined the course the Fund would take to the present. These individuals established a culture of decision making with regard to the CPF's involvement with the International, the relationship among the union and management trustees, the trustees' relationship to the administrators, and the influence of outside professionals.

The 1990s will mark the exit of the initial leadership core of the CPF. Reese Hammond and Robert Fox have recently stepped down as union trustees (Hammond in 1991 and Fox in 1993), with Hammond becoming a consultant to the CPF. Hailey Roberts' influence is still strong despite the fact he never assumed the chairmans mantle. Frank Gould has announced his retirement date as December 1994, and Jack Johnson is within five to ten years of retiring. As this leadership core transfers power to the next generation, it remains to be seen what direction the CPF will take. The challenges of a mature fund in a declining union environment will not be the same as the problems faced by the individuals who built the CPF.

In June 1994 it was announced that IUOE General President Frank Hanley would become a member of the CPF board of trustees, replacing Richard Griffin. Griffin has become General Counsel for the IUOE, replacing Michael Fanning, who has become the chief executive officer of the CPF. It is assumed that the culture the pioneers established of honesty, reliance on in-house and outside professional advice, conservatism, and an autonomous arm's-length relationship with the International will be the mindset used by future CPF leaders to tackle the new problems of maturity.

NOTES

1. *The International Operating Engineer* (Washington, D.C.: Operating Engineer Press, June 1959), 13.

2. Letter from Ralph Crammer to Hunter Wharton, 2 April 1958, CPF, Washington, D.C.

3. Letter from Ralph Crammer to Lane Kirkland, 21 April 1959, CPF, Washington, D.C.

4. Ray Tucker, interview by Jeff Petersen, tape recording, Redlands, Calif., 2 August 1993.

5. Lane Kirkland to George Kall, 21 July 1960. Kirkland to Richard Dennis, 21 July 1960. Kirkland to James Egan, 5 July 1960. All letters at CPF, Washington, D.C.

6. "Report of Proceedings of the Twenty-Sixth Convention of the International Union of Operating Engineers," *The International Operating Engineer* (April 1960).

7. *The International Operating Engineer* (October 1960): 27.

8. Robert Fox, interview by Jeff Petersen, tape recording, Los Angeles, 2 August 1993.

9. Ray Tucker, 2 August 1993.

10. *The International Operating Engineer* (November 1960): 29.

11. Richard Ennis, interview by authors, tape recording, Chicago, 27 August 1992.

12. Ibid.

13. Robert Fox, interview by Peter Philips, tape recording, Los Angeles, 30 December 1992.

14. Garth Mangum and Jack Walsh, *Union Resilience in Troubled Times: The Story of the Operating Engineers, AFL-CIO 1960–1993* (New York: M.E. Sharpe, 1994), 21.

15. Reese Hammond, interview by Peter Philips, tape recording, Washington, D.C., 28 April 1993.

16. Frank Gould, interview by authors, tape recording, Washington, D.C., 19 September 1992.

17. Ibid.

18. Richard Ennis, interview on 27 August 1992.

19. Bob McCormick, interview by authors, tape recording, New Orleans, 29 November 1992.

20. Bill Riehl, interview by Peter Philips, tape recording, New Orleans, 29 November 1992.

21. Frank Gould, interview by Jeff Petersen, tape recording, Washington, D.C., 12 August 1993.

22. Jack Johnson, interview by Jeff Petersen, tape recording, Washington, D.C., 27 August 1993.

23. Membership numbers are from 1975 for Tables 3.1 and 3.2. That year was used because that was the earliest year the IUOE had this figure. Source of membership numbers is IUOE Headquarters, Washington, D.C. Source of pension fund commencement is the CPF, Washington, D.C.

24. Art Viat, interview by Jeff Petersen, tape recording, San Francisco, 22 November 1993.

25. Tom Stapleton, interview by Jeff Petersen, tape recording, Alameda, Calif., 17 November 1993.

26. Membership numbers are from the IUOE. Pension fund commencement is from the CPF.

27. Hammond, 28 April 1993.

28. Gould, 12 August 1993.

29. Hammond, 28 April 1993.

30. Ibid.

31. Ibid.

32. Peter Babin, Jr., interview by authors, tape recording, New Orleans, 30 October 1992.

33. Ibid.

34. Ibid.

35. Ibid.

36. Ibid.

37. Hammond, 28 April 1993.

38. John Sweeny, interview by Jeff Petersen, tape recording, San Francisco, 17 November 1993.

39. Viat, 22 November 1993.

40. Riehl, 29 November 1992.

41. "145 Attend Central Pension Fund Seminar," *The International Operating Engineer* (January 1974): 24–25.

42. "Training Seminar Participants Bone-Up on Central Pension Fund," *The International Operating Engineer* (January 1978).

43. Johnson, 27 August 1992.

44. Bernie Baum, interview by Peter Philips, tape recording, Chicago, 28 August 1992.

45. Johnson, 27 August 1992.

46. Hammond, 28 April 1993.

47. Ibid.

48. Ibid.

49. Jack Cullerton, interview by authors, tape recording, New Orleans, 29 October 1992.

50. Hammond, 28 April 1993.

51. Ibid.

52. The IUOE locals with representatives present were 18, 450, 302, 3, 324, 137, 132, 77, 37, 825, 66, 94, 891, 14, 15, 98, 12, 571, 965, 318, 542, and 673. Reported in "Reciprocal Pension Pacts Receive Strong Boost," *The International Operating Engineer*, 16, (December 1967).

53. "Signatories to the International Reciprocity Agreement," *The International Operating Engineer*, 22 (March 1973).

54. The 25 January 1993 edition of *Pensions and Investments* reported the five largest union pension funds as (1) Central States Teamsters ($11,822,000 in assets), (2) Western Teamsters ($11,745,000), (3) United Mine Workers ($5,722,000), (4) National Electrical Contractors ($4,830,000), and (5) Boilermakers-Blacksmiths ($3,020,000).

Chapter 4

Collective Bargaining for Pension Contributions

In the long run, the CPF is only as strong as its participating union locals and contractors and the industries that they organize and serve. In recent years, the IUOE, and thus the CPF, has faced the problem of declining participant work hours associated with declining union coverage in the construction industry. The smaller pool of CPF participants has been partially offset by rising hourly contributions and favorable investment returns. However, rising real hourly contribution rates are at least in part a reflection of an aging union membership in construction, and therefore are more a reflection of, rather than a solution to, a decline in union work.

Building a union-management trusteed pension fund begins at the bargaining table, where a union's bargaining power and goals confront management's ability to pay and compensation strategies. This is done in a context where government policies can also affect the outcome by taxing wages and benefits differently and by encouraging or discouraging collective bargaining.

The CPF was started in a legal and economic bargaining environment that favored the growth of union-management trusteed pension funds. Economic growth was strong. Unemployment was low. Real wages and benefits were rising across the economy, and union membership was healthy. However, during the 1970s and 1980s, the economic and legal environments turned increasingly hostile to collective bargaining, while in the construction industry, economic and legal forces encouraged the spread of the open shop. Union membership declined, unemployment rose, real wages and benefits fell, nine states repealed their construction prevailing wage laws, and the proportion of nonunion contractors rose. Thus, the CPF emerged in an environment favorable to unions and to pension funds, but it grew during a period of rising difficulties for unions and, therefore, their members' pensions.

Ironically, the CPF continued to grow financially stronger in the 1970s and 1980s while the collective bargaining on which it was based fell into crisis. This strength in the face of adversity was partly due to successful investment strategies pursued by the CPF in a favorable investment climate. This will be discussed in the chapter on pension investments. The CPF has also maintained rising total contributions from participants, despite declining total hours worked by participants after the late 1970s. These rising contributions in the face of a shrinking work base were due in part to the aging of participants from hoisting and portable locals. The aging of the construction-union workforce has led locals to increase their hourly contribution rate, even though their real wages have been falling and the cost of their medical benefits have been rising. In addition, as the Fund has grown and steadily increased the level of benefits it pays out, the participant's faith in the trustees' capabilities to manage their money has increased, making the participants more willing to put money that might otherwise have been allocated to current wage income into the CPF.

The rising CPF contribution rate is also due to the stationary locals within the IUOE benefitting from the broad switch within the U.S. economy from manufacturing to service employment. Real wages for stationary engineers have not been falling, nor has the membership of stationary locals been aging on average. Instead, they are increasing their pension contributions because they continue to be successful at the bargaining table. Future events will tell us whether there will be a rebound in unionized bargaining in construction to provide renewed support for the CPF. This chapter outlines the changing economic and legal structures that once fostered, but are currently making problematic, efforts to bargain successfully for greater pension contributions.

COLLECTIVE BARGAINING IN A CHANGING ECONOMIC CLIMATE

The fundamental economic context into which the Central Pension Fund emerged can first be viewed by placing the early 1960s in historical perspective. Figure 4.1[1] shows the U.S. gross national product (GNP) from 1869 to 1991 evaluated in 1991 dollars. Over this long-term period, the U.S. economy grew at a compounded rate of over 3 percent per year. This long run growth trend can be approximated by fitting a smooth exponential growth curve over the actual uneven rise in GNP. By superimposing this trend line on Figure 4.1, one can see various periods within U.S. economic history when the economy grew faster or slower than the long-term trend. For instance, actual GNP during the Great Depression of the 1930s fell well below the long-term growth trend, whereas GNP levels during World War II were above long-term growth projections. After fluctuations in the 1950s, the CPF came into being just as the overall economy was beginning to exceed long-term GNP growth patterns. However,

Figure 4.1
GNP growth, the long-term trend, and the deviation from that trend

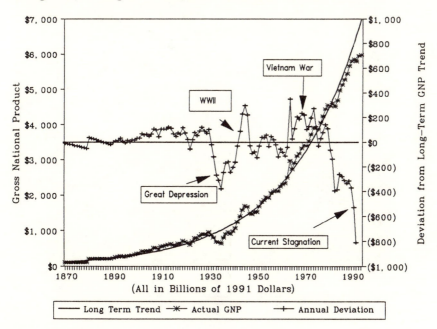

(All in Billions of 1991 Dollars)

this auspicious beginning was offset after the early 1970s by a period of protracted economic stagnation in the United States. This ongoing period of stagnation presents the Fund with serious problems and challenges. Although the relatively slow growth from the 1970s to the early 1990s is not as notorious as the economic crisis of the 1930s, Figure 4.1 shows that the U.S. economy fell more precipitously away from long-term growth trends in the recent period than it did during the Great Depression. Furthermore, the recent stagnation has lasted longer than any previous period of economic slowdown. Not surprisingly, good times enhance both union bargaining power and the employer's ability to pay additional wages and benefits. Bad economic times both weaken unions and strengthen the employer's resolve to resist wage and benefit demands.

Figure 4.2[2] shows the weakening of the union movement. Union membership has been. declining as a proportion of the labor force since the mid-1950s, although it increased in absolute numbers until early 1980s. The civilian labor force increased 22 percent from 1970 to 1980, whereas union membership increased only 8 percent in that decade. Declining in absolute numbers thereafter, the percentage organized became half what it had been three decades earlier.

After 1970, union negotiators were caught in the pincers of declining membership and rising unemployment. Unemployment, which had risen somewhat toward the end of the 1950s, was nonetheless low by historical standards and

Figure 4.2
Union membership in the United States from 1930 to 1992

had been falling throughout the 1960s when the CPF was getting started.[3] As the CPF matured, however, the trend in unemployment steadily worsened. After the early 1970s, declining union membership and rising overall unemployment in the context of a stagnating economy brought an end to a long-term trend of rising real wages and benefits for American workers.

Figure 4.3[4] shows that average real wages have fallen persistently since the early 1970s, whereas benefits have stagnated, sustained from decline by rising health care costs. These economy-wide trends in sluggish growth, declining unionization, rising unemployment, and falling real wages and benefits make bargaining for pension contributions into the CPF increasingly difficult. Trends in the construction industry reinforce this overall negative pressure on union negotiators, whereas trends in the service sector relieve some of the pressure on representatives of stationary engineers.

CONSTRUCTION UNIONISM

As Figure 4.4[5] shows, the construction industry has historically been one of the most unionized sectors of the U.S. economy. However, construction union membership after starting higher, has fallen faster, farther, and sooner, and to a percent almost as low as union membership in the overall economy. In 1947

Figure 4.3
Real wages and real total compensation for American workers

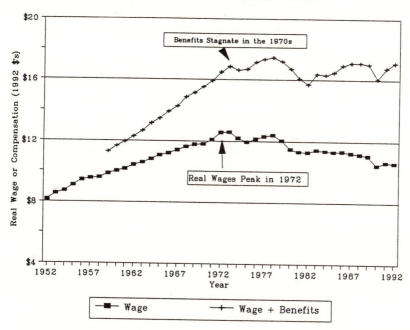

construction workers were 87 percent organized, whereas at the inception of the CPF in 1960, half of all construction workers were unionized. In 1991, construction worker unionization stood at 22 percent. This precipitous decline occurred despite the fact that construction employment was maintaining a constant 5 percent share of the overall U.S. labor force.

Real wages fell 26 percent between 1970 and 1991 in unionized construction, and nonunion wages declined a similar 27 percent (Figure 4.5[6]). Thus, despite the decline in union coverage in construction in the last two decades and the fall in real union wages, the union wage premium has persisted. Along with construction unionism in general, the IUOE endured a heavy decline in membership in the early 1980s. From 1980 to 1985 the IUOE lost 22 percent of its membership. This is somewhat less than the loss suffered by the building trades in general[7] and may be due to the better performance of the nonconstruction stationary division within the operating engineers. Stationary engineer membership in the IUOE has increased 14 percent since 1975 (Figure 4.6[8]). Hoisting and portable membership declined 20 percent during this same time period. The stationary gain may be due mainly to the shift in the American economy toward service producing industries that now employ nearly 80 percent of American workers,[9] a 20 percent rise from 1945. Construction employment as a percentage of all employment has held steady at 5 percent from 1945 to the present. The

Figure 4.4
Union organization in construction and the wage premium for construction union labor

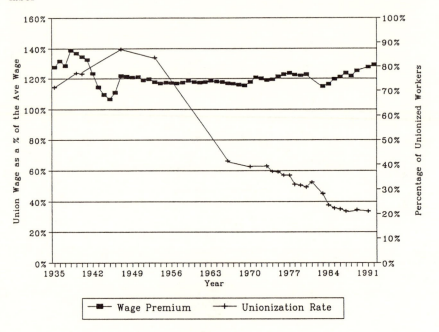

sector that has seen the most dramatic change is manufacturing. Manufacturing employment accounted for 36 percent of all employment in the 1940s, but currently stands at less than 20 percent. The switch to service employment has increased demand for building maintenance and custodial services. Energy price increases during the 1970s also put a premium on having skilled stationary engineers in charge of heating and cooling equipment. Union negotiators for stationary engineers have been able to translate this rising demand for stationary engineers into rising real wages, despite the overall trend within the economy toward lower real wages.

Figure 4.7[10] shows that medical costs have risen faster than inflation since the 1950s, and that the pace of medical cost inflation accelerated in the 1980s. Real wages and real total compensation are adjusted for the overall average rise in the cost of living. This is measured through the U.S. consumer price index. However, union negotiators have had to deal with the fact that medical costs have historically risen faster than other costs faced by consumers. This puts additional pressure on union negotiators seeking to divide falling real total compensation between wages, health insurance, and pensions.

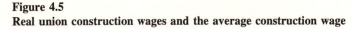

Figure 4.5
Real union construction wages and the average construction wage

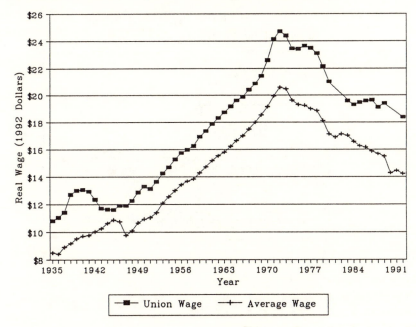

COLLECTIVE BARGAINING FOR PENSION CONTRIBUTIONS: A VIEW FROM THE LOCAL LEVEL

The first section of this chapter explored the broader economic and legal forces that, in the last two decades, have created an environment antagonistic to unionism, resulting in declining real wages and benefits for union members. IUOE locals within and outside of the CPF have had distinct experiences adapting to the rapidly changing environment of the U.S. economy. Three construction locals, Louisiana Local 406, Indiana Local 103, and Northern California Local 3, and two stationary locals, Southern California Local 501 and Northern California Local 39, are selected to view the effects of the economic environment of the 1970s and 1980s (see Figure 4.8[11] for membership numbers).

The stationary locals were selected based on their ability to provide comprehensive wage and benefit data, which are difficult undertakings due to the diverse nature of stationary employment. Locals 39 and 501 have done very well in the 1970s and 1980s, and their stories may overstate the case that the stationary side of the union has seen relatively better times than the construction side. In the case of both locals, the data show that real wages have held steady while total compensation (wages + health + pension) has increased. Stationary

Figure 4.6
Change in membership in the IUOE: hoisting and portable versus stationary

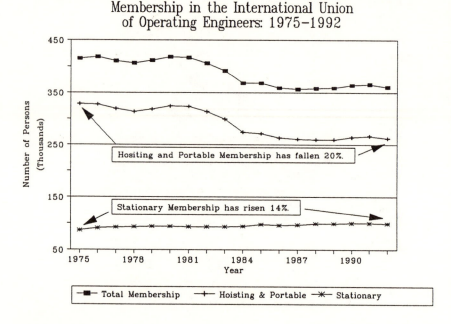

engineers have seen their total wealth increase because of their ability to adapt to the rapid technological changes in their field, beginning at the time of the energy crisis of the middle 1970s. However, this increasing wealth has been primarily diverted into rising health care costs.

The construction locals were selected because their experiences over the past two decades appear representative of the construction side of the IUOE. Figure 4.9[12] shows that the three construction locals have followed the national average in terms of real wage performance. Real wages peaked in 1974 and have subsequently declined. The total compensation package (the sum of wages, health, and pension) has been relatively steady for Local 3, but Locals 406 and 103 have seen substantial decreases. Figure 4.10 highlights the fact that health care costs have eaten away at pension contributions. Historically, in all three locals, pension contributions have accounted for 60 percent of the benefit package. However, that equilibrium level has changed dramatically from the middle 1980s to the present. Pension contributions are now less than 50 percent of the benefit package. Figures 4.9 and 4.10 will be referred to often in the case studies that follow.

Figure 4.7
Medical costs as a percentage of the U.S. Consumer Price Index

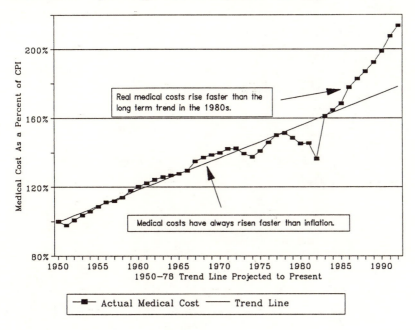

Actual Medical Cost —— Trend Line

Louisiana Construction Local 406

On August 19, 1976, Peter Babin III was elected business manager of Local 406 at the age of thirty-eight. The new business manager was to be tested early, as he came into office during a politically heated time. Louisiana had repealed its right-to-work law in 1956, and in 1976 the push was on to re-instate it. During the vehement battles over this law, violence broke out at a nonunion construction site and shots were fired. One of the bullets went astray and hit a man living in a trailer. While going through the trailer, the bullet was mangled, and the gun from which it was fired could not be determined. There was a strong anti-union feeling among the public at this time, and many people concluded that the union members were responsible. This event ensured the passage of a new Louisiana open shop law.

The passage of the right-to-work law in 1976 and the anti-union climate of the early 1980s spelled doom for wages and benefits for the membership of Local 406. From 1977 to 1980, real wages for Local 406 members fell 17 percent and real total compensation fell 11 percent. While the rest of the economy was experiencing the recession of 1982–1983, real wages for operating engineers in Local 406 rebounded, increasing 10 percent from 1981 to 1983. However, the rebound was short-lived. From 1984 to 1991 real wages in Local

Figure 4.8
**Membership in IUOE Construction Locals 406, 103, and 3 and Stationary Locals
39 and 501**

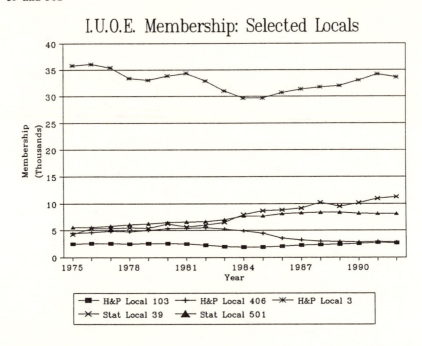

I.U.O.E. Membership: Selected Locals

406 plummeted. Babin (III) attributes the decline in union power in construction
to the open shop movement sponsored by the Business Round Table:

> I say this, they conspired to destroy the unionized sector in the construction industry,
> and they did it in two areas as far as I'm concerned. The first area they did it in is
> through sending the word from the national Associated General Contractors to all the
> local Associated General Contractor chapters, both state and locally, to cease bargaining
> on a multiemployer basis. We used to sit down and bargain with committees that rep-
> resented all the contractors and they pushed for the contractors all to be a member of
> the association, the same way we had our association. That was when we sat down and
> we negotiated a contract, that contract then was for all the construction companies. That
> way the terms and conditions were for all the labor organizations. Well, the first thing
> they did was send a message to disband that. So, if one guy knocks you down a little
> bit and another guy knocks you down a little bit more, then the third guy demands the
> same deal. It just screwed up bargaining something awful. The second thing that they
> did is they encouraged national contractors to form non-union double-breasted[13] com-
> panies.[14]

The decline of construction union power in Louisiana has directly affected
the CPF. With membership falling off in Local 406, the number of hours re-

Figure 4.9
Wages for IUOE construction locals

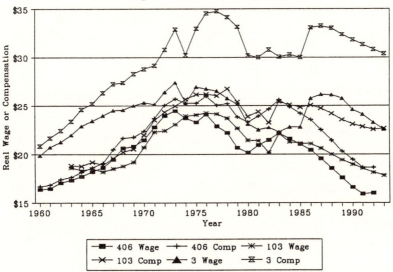

IUOE Construction Locals 406, 103, & 3:
Real Wages and Total Compensation

ported to the CPF has decreased, and pension contributions have been squeezed by falling real wages and health care costs. The hourly contribution from Local 406 to the CPF reached a high point of a $1.42 in 1983. It then declined to $1.25 the next year and stayed at that level. Pension contributions as a percentage of total benefits fell from 60 percent in 1981 to 48 percent in 1991. The health care cost squeeze of pension benefits has not been as great in Local 406's case as in other locals' cases within the CPF. Babin III attributes this to his encouraging members to a go to a network of hospitals where they get good care for reasonable prices. Thus the falling pension contribution is more attributable to a falling real wage, which is a direct result of declining union power.

Indiana Construction Local 103

A relatively recent addition to the CPF board of trustees is Dan Smart, current business manager of Local 103. Smart says the members of Local 103 were not initially in favor of putting part of their pay check toward a pension, but that attitude has changed dramatically over time. He says that unlike earlier decades, the younger members are solidly in favor of the hourly contribution to the CPF. Smart attributes this support to the Local's education on Social Security and personal finances. This education has the effect of awakening younger workers to the necessity of early planning for retirement.[15]

Figure 4.10
Benefits as a percentage of the compensation package

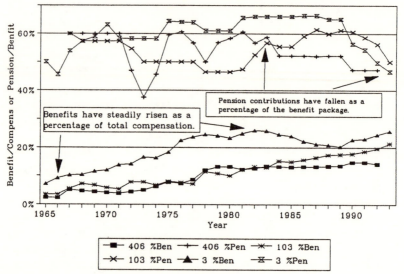

IUOE Construction Locals 406, 103, & 3:
Where Does the Benefit Package Go?

Membership in Local 103 has been stable since 1975. The local had 2,520 members in 1975 and currently there are 2,690 members. Relative to other IUOE construction locals the membership increase is impressive, especially considering that 80 percent of the members are employed in highway construction. The end of the national highway program has meant layoffs for a large proportion of the operating engineers who worked in that field.

The membership of Local 103 has shared with the construction industry as a whole a decline in their real wage. Real wages began to stagnate in the early 1970s and then began to fall later in that same decade. The decline halted from 1979 to 1986, but real wages have steadily fallen since that time. In 1993, real wages were at 84 percent of their 1986 level.

Benefits have not suffered as much as wages. The total compensation package to Local 103 members is at the same level as it was 1981. Pension benefits have only recently been squeezed by health care costs. The current benefit package received by Local 103 members is evenly divided between pensions and health and welfare. Pension contributions remain equivalent to health care contributions for two reasons. First, is the membership's attitude towards the CPF. Smart comments, ''Our members are very well educated about the CPF and its benefits; they are willing to put money into the fund because they know they will earn a good return.''[16] Second, Local 103 pools its resources with other locals to purchase health care services. This helps keep costs down.

Northern California Construction Local 3

Local 3 is the largest local in the IUOE with membership in excess of 33,000 persons. From 1975 to 1993 membership dropped off 2 percent. Membership stability has been maintained by bringing in public employees outside of the construction industry. However, real wages and real total compensation have stagnated. Even with the stagnation of wages and benefits, however, members of Local 3 remain some of the highest paid persons in the union community.

The benefit formula for Local 3 is the same as for the CPF. Thus, hourly pension contributions determine the benefit level in conjuncture with the percentage payout determined by the board of trustees. Currently, employers who enter into a collective bargaining agreement with Local 3 must pay an astounding $3.75 per hour to the pension plan of Local 3 on behalf of each construction worker they employ. This per-hour pension rate is $2.25 higher than the average contribution rate to the CPF. However, the current hourly pension contribution rate was established seven years ago. After becoming business manager in 1982, Tom Stapleton instituted a philosophy among the board of trustees to always look five years ahead in the decisions they make. Stapleton instructs the actuarial firm Martin Segal to do the same when advising them. Thus, the $3.75 rate was collectively bargained for in 1986 with the idea that it would hold until 1991. However, the local has not tried to impose higher pension costs on its employers since that date for one reason—Local 3 is not in jeopardy of incurring unfunded liability.

More persuasively, the pension contribution rate has not been increased due to rising health care costs. "Health costs are killing us,"[17] rages Stapleton, and the numbers confirm his statement. From 1989 to 1993, real health and welfare contributions have risen from $2.29 an hour to $4.17 an hour, an increase of 82 percent. Pension contributions historically accounted for 60 percent of the benefit package. That equilibrium level has been significantly offset in the past four years. Pension contributions have been squeezed by health and welfare costs and currently account for 47 percent of the benefit package.

Southern California Stationary Local 501

The members of Southern California Stationary Local 501 working in the service sector of the local economy have benefitted from the economic shift from a goods-producing American economy to service production. Figure 4.11[18] shows that unlike the construction side of the IUOE, these engineers' wages and benefits have held steady at their early 1980s level. Wages and benefits for stationary engineers working in the manufacturing sector of the local economy have not performed as well as those in service employment and are currently at their 1970 level.

In the early 1950s, wages of stationary engineers within the local had been steadily increasing, and market conditions would have permitted wages to rise

Figure 4.11
Wages and total compensation for Local 501 members

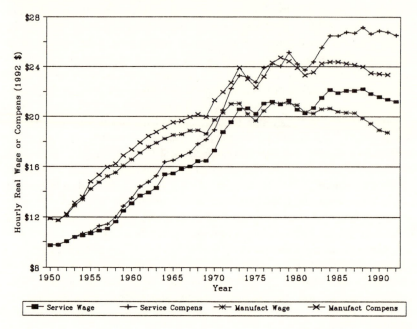

above the Korean War wage controls instituted at the time. Bob Fox, long-time business manager of Local 501, recalls, "the reason we put the health and welfare plan into place was because we were running into the wage control limit."[19] Wage controls did not prohibit rising compensation being put into a health insurance program, so the local negotiated compensation increases by establishing a health and welfare plan.

Real wages for members of Local 501 continued to rise throughout the 1950s and 1960s but have risen only slightly since then (Figure 4.11). This corresponds roughly to national trends in real wages over this period and real wage trends for operating engineers in general. However, the pattern of real wage growth has not been uniform within the local. The wages of stationary engineers working in industries such as breweries, dairies, and ice and cold storage had higher real wages throughout the 1950s and 1960s compared to stationary engineers working in service sector jobs such as hotels and office buildings. From the late 1950s onward, the wages of stationary engineers in the service sector grew faster than wages in manufacturing. Wage growth slowed for both groups around 1970 and declined for stationary engineers in manufacturing after 1980. This relatively better real wage growth for service sector engineers in the 1980s has led to higher real wages for this group compared to industrial sector engineers, reversing the ranking of the 1950s and 1960s. Neither group has experienced the wage fall-off that occurred for hoisting and portable engineers in this study. The relative success of these stationary engineers in Local 501 is due in part to the superior growth of the southern California economy over this period, and in part to the shift of the American economy from goods production to service production.

In addition to favorable economic conditions, technological change has made the stationary engineer a more highly skilled person. During the energy crisis of the 1970s, businesses noticed that a well-trained core of stationary engineers could save them a substantial amount of money on their utility bills. Dan Goodpaster, a Local 501 member, has taken every course the local has offered and worked his way up to the chief engineer at TRW in southern California. He credits Bob Fox with "the foresight to institute a new training program in the 1970s to elevate the stationary engineer to its current role."[20] Fox says of Local 501's training program and the evolution of the stationary engineers role:

In the 1970s we rebuilt our apprenticeship and training programs to get the membership back into classes to update their skills to the new technology. The technology was moving faster than any one individual could handle. Energy conservation became a big item when employers figured out that a competent crew of stationary engineers could reduce a million dollar a year utility bill by $300,000. Up until the guys who pulled the purse strings figured that out, the stationary engineer was looked upon as a necessary evil that you never saw any income from. For example, in a bank building they put in new guys out of our local. They increased the crew, paid them almost twice as much money, and bought a lot of new equipment. It turned out the bank saved $84,000 in the engine room in the first year.[21]

This ability to save company's money in several different arenas has made stationary engineers more valued employees, thus increasing the demand for their services. This leads to wage and benefit increases.

Following national patterns, benefits have performed better than real wages for Local 501 (Figure 4.12). In the 1950s, benefits for the manufacturing sector within the local were higher than service sector benefits. However, from 1960 to the late 1970s, benefits for both sectors were basically the same. This pattern broke in the late 1970s, and in the 1980s service sector benefits were systematically higher than manufacturing sector benefits among the members of Local 501. This break in benefit patterns is another reflection of the relative strength of service sector work compared with manufacturing work for stationary engineers.

For both the manufacturing and service segments within Local 501, benefit contributions have been a rising portion of total compensation over the entire postwar period. However, rising health costs in the 1980s have reduced the pension share of total benefit contributions. Bob Fox relates: "We are willing to pay if we have to take some money out of the wages to put over to health and welfare. Health and welfare is probably number one in the working man's

Figure 4.12
Benefits as a percentage of the total compensation package

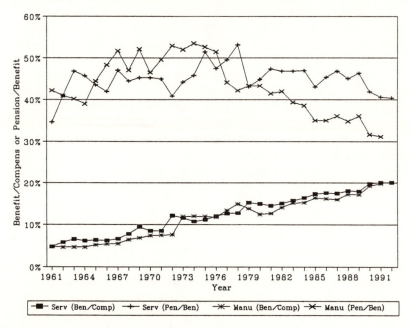

mind today, forget wages, forget pensions, forget other things. Health and welfare is really the number one issue.''[22] The decline in pension contributions as
a share of total contributions has been much greater for the manufacturing segment within Local 501. This is because real wages and total compensation have
been falling faster among these workers than among those in the service segment. Faced with the same rising medical costs, the better performance of wages
in the service segment has allowed this group to preserve its pension contributions more effectively than the manufacturing segment of this local.

Northern California Stationary Local 39

Art Viat, business manager of Local 39, has lived with the union movement
and collective bargaining process his whole life. His father was a union member
and a labor leader in Indiana. Viat says of his father and growing up in a union
family:

My dad was a sheet metal worker by trade. He was always in the labor movement. He
was running Fort Wayne Federation of Labor in Indiana. It was like a central labor
council and was primarily responsible for Magnavox Corporation, International Har-
vester, corporations like that. I grew up on picket lines, because that is what my dad did.

You did not have good legislation then, so it was not unusual for my dad to call everyone out at lunch time and say we were not going back to work until we got what we wanted.[23]

Local 39 had been formed in 1947 as an affiliation of nine different local unions in northern California and Nevada. The various groups had never coalesced, and the local had been rife with factionalism. Viat took over as the business manager of Local 39 in 1965 when his predecessor received a vote of no confidence from the membership and decided to step down.

Early in his tenure Viat adopted two strategies: first, "every member of this local union is an organizer," and second, "every member of this local union will have a high level of education."[24] Viat claims that the emphasis on organizing and training in Local 39 has fueled the increase in its membership and, as was the case with Local 501, the growing importance of the stationary engineers to their employers:

We have been growing ever since because we had a vision to get outside of our true blue engineers; there just is not enough of them. I felt that if this union was ever going to go anywhere we needed to train and diversify. I have spent my whole life training and diversifying, and the International has adopted much of what we developed many years ago. Our current General President is the first one who really believes that the future of this union is in diversity and education. Because of the way we did things we continued to grow during the times that the rest of the union was decreasing. We went from 2400 members, to today, with 15,000 members.[25]

Local 39 currently has a contract with nearly every high-rise building, hospital, hotel, airport, and waste water treatment plant in the San Francisco Bay Area. Viat was also one of the first people in the IUOE to cross traditional bloodlines in organizing efforts. "You can't spit in this town without hitting one of our members,"[26] claims Viat.

The divergence in wages and total compensation between stationary engineers working in the service sectors of the local economy and those in the manufacturing sector is more dramatic in Local 39 than in Local 501. From 1986 to the present, stationary engineers in the service sector have earned more in wages than stationary engineers in manufacturing are earning in total compensation (Figure 4.13[27]). Employment in the service sector has also provided stationary engineers with increasing real total compensation and a real wage equivalent to what they earned in 1985. Real pension contributions for service sector employment have risen 37 percent in the last ten years. Employers currently contribute $2.60 per hour worked on behalf of service sector engineers to Local 39's pension fund. On the other hand, manufacturing stationary engineers' real wages are at the same level as 1974. Their real hourly pension contribution rate is $2.54, which represents a 28 percent increase in the last ten years.

Stationary engineers participating in the pension plan of Local 39 have not had their pension contribution rate "squeezed" to the extent as members of

Figure 4.13
Wages and total compensation for the membership of Local 39

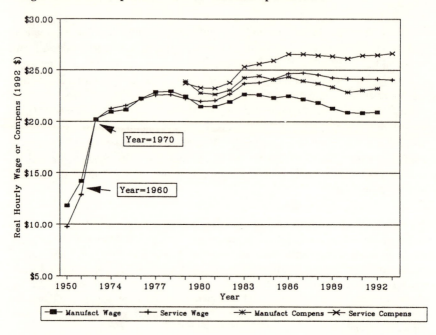

Local 501 participating in the CPF (Figure 4.14). In Local 501, service sector engineers have 40 percent of their benefit package going to their pension, whereas manufacturing engineers have only 30 percent. In Local 39, both service and manufacturing engineers have 50 percent of their benefit package going to their pension. The difference is attributable to the relative costs of health care, not the relative strength of the two pension funds. Viat claims that Local 39 has been able to keep down their health care costs by making each employer pay a set monthly amount for each stationary engineer they employ. By running the health and welfare program in this manner, the local minimizes administrative costs. Reducing this monthly amount to an hourly contribution rate shows that the participating employers are paying only $2.60 per hour for health care. This contribution rate is 57 cents lower than the rate of Local 501's and $1.57 per hour lower than that of Local 3, which is located in the same geographical area as Local 39. All three locals provide full medical and dental coverage to their membership. By keeping health care costs down, the leadership of Local 39 is able to divert money into the pension plan through their collective bargaining agreements.

Figure 4.14
Benefits as a percentage of the total compensation package

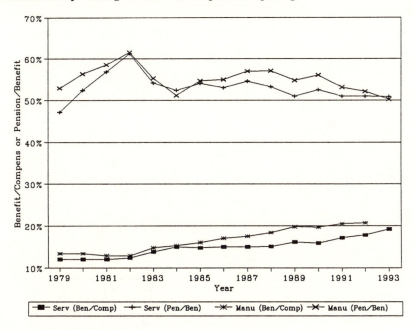

THE EFFECT OF ECONOMIC STAGNATION AND UNION DECLINE ON THE CPF

The CPF has navigated through the troubled waters of rising unemployment, declining union coverage, increasing real health costs, and falling real wages.[28] These underlying economic forces have altered the age composition of CPF participants, shifted the balance between construction and stationary local participation, induced a dropoff in work-hours reported into the Fund, and yet increased, at least in the short run, the real hourly pension contributions.

The CPF was originally established to serve the needs of smaller locals within the IUOE that could not establish their own pension funds. Figure 4.15 shows that stationary members initially accounted for almost half of all CPF participants. By the late 1960s, however, construction workers came to account for 80 percent of the CPF participants. The first locals within the Fund were disproportionately stationary locals, but they had lower average membership than the construction locals. As the number of locals within the CPF climbed through the 1960s, the percentage of construction locals within the Fund rose. By the late 1960s, the mix of stationary and construction locals stabilized, and the additional locals entering in the late 1960s and early 1970s were evenly divided between stationary and construction. The percentage of construction participants

Figure 4.15
Stationary engineers and hoisting and portable engineers as a percentage of CPF participants

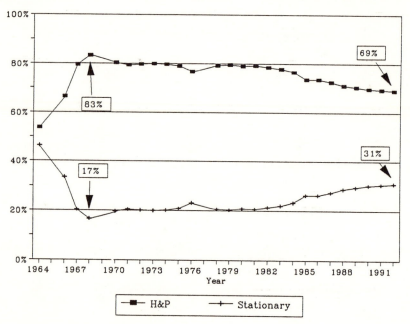

within the Fund began to decline in the early 1970s, and this decline accelerated in the 1980s. Even though the number of construction locals within the Fund held constant, their average membership fell. Although stationary locals on average had a steady membership of 500 engineers per local, the construction locals obtained a peak average membership of 2,000 in the late 1960s, and this average declined to 1,100 by the early 1990s.

During its formative years in the 1960s, the CPF recruited a rapidly growing percentage of overall IUOE membership. Figure 4.16[29] shows that by 1972, CPF participants accounted for 20 percent of all IUOE members. This increase was due primarily to the movement of locals into the CPF, rather than growth in the size of the initial locals. From 1961 to 1972, sixty-eight locals joined the CPF, of which thirty-three were stationary locals and thirty-five were construction locals. From 1972 to the mid-1980s, the CPF gained an additional 7 percent of the total IUOE membership. During 1976–77 the concept of "dual participation" was initiated when six local unions in upstate New York voted to join the CPF in addition to maintaining participation in their independent Engineers Joint Pension Fund (EJPF). Retirees who participated in both the CPF and EJPF receive benefit checks from both funds each month. Some CPF Trustees saw this move as a wave of the future, with the potential of all members in the IUOE

Figure 4.16
The percentage of IUOE members participating in the CPF

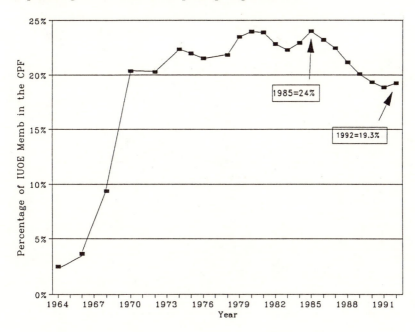

eventually covered under the CPF. Despite negotiations with other Northeast local union only one, Local 98 in western Massachusetts, signed up with the CPF.

The wave of universal dual participation ebbed with only 5,500 members covered under both an independent local union fund and the CPF. Reese Hammond, while secretary of the Fund, was a strong supporter of dual participation, and remains an advocate of universal participation in the CPF by all IUOE members.

From 1985 to 1993, only two additional locals joined the CPF, while the Fund's share of IUOE members fell to 21 percent. This dropoff is partly inherent in the initial purpose of the Fund, which was to provide pension services to the smaller locals. Although not all locals within the CPF are small, the smaller locals coming from weaker union areas have been disproportionately affected by the overall decline in union coverage, especially within construction. Thus, the growth of the CPF after its formative period in the 1960s was primarily due to IUOE locals within the CPF growing faster than the average for locals within the overall union. The relative shrinkage of the CPF's share of union membership in the late 1980s was due to CPF locals losing members faster than the average for the union as a whole. There is an irony here. The CPF was founded to provide greater stability for the pension contributions of smaller locals by

Figure 4.17
Wages and total compensation for IUOE members participating in the CPF

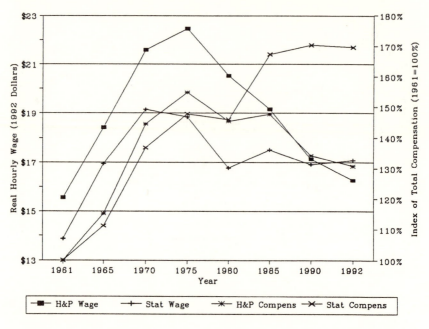

allowing them to pool their resources into one larger pension fund. However, by aggregating disproportionately smaller locals within the union, the CPF may have inadvertently acquired greater instability of membership compared to the union as a whole, growing faster in good times and shrinking faster in difficult times. The exceptions to this rule are the small stationary locals, whose members work primarily in the service sector.

Figure 4.17[30] shows that the real wages of hoisting and portable engineers have declined steadily over the last two decades. This follows the national pattern for average real wages. Although construction wages have been falling, total benefits have continued to rise as construction workers shift their total compensation from the paycheck to health and pension benefits. The real wages of stationary workers within the CPF continued to rise after construction wages began falling, and the subsequent decline in stationary wages has been moderate. Consequently, stationary engineers within the CPF are now better paid than their construction counterparts, and they receive higher benefits. A rebound in organization and union power within construction could reverse these trends, but there is nothing on the horizon to support such a prediction.

Figure 4.18 shows that both stationary and construction locals have increasingly shifted total compensation toward benefits and away from wages over the entire history of the CPF. This allowed both groups to raise their real benefit

Figure 4.18
Benefits as a percentage of total compensation and pension contributions as a percentage of benefits

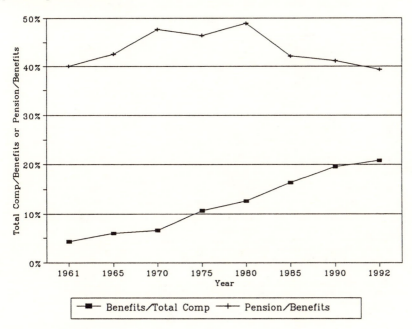

contributions despite drastically falling real wages in the case of construction workers and moderately falling real wages in the case of stationary engineers. Interestingly, stationary workers with rising total compensation were choosing to shift a greater percentage of their benefit contributions into health insurance, whereas construction workers, whose total compensation was falling, were choosing to maintain a more steady division of their benefit contributions between health and pensions. In other words, both groups chose to raise their real pension contributions by roughly the same absolute amount, and both chose to split their total compensation between wages and benefits along the same percentage. Because stationary engineers' total compensation was not falling drastically, however, this left more money for them to put into their health insurance programs.

Figure 4.19 depicts the results of both groups raising their real pension contribution rates. Total hours reported by CPF participants fell sharply after 1978. For a while, total real contributions to the CPF fell correspondingly. However, as the dropoff in hours reported slowed, total contributions into the Fund began to rise. Half the loss in total contributions between 1978 and 1985 was recouped in the next six years due to rising hourly contribution rates with no renewed increase in hours reported.

Figure 4.19
Hours worked and dollars contributed by CPF participants

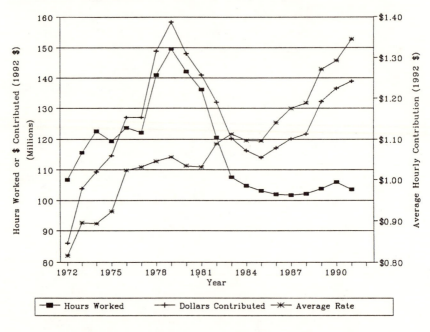

Figure 4.20 indicates that the rise in the real contribution rate is associated with an increase in the average age of CPF participants. This is not surprising, because workers typically become more inclined to contribute to their own retirement as they get closer to retirement age. Only the hoisting and portable division within the CPF, however, shows a rise in average age. This may be associated with declining union coverage within construction, leading younger new entrants into open shop employment. It may also indicate declining attractiveness of construction as a career, with workers spending a few years in the industry before incurring family responsibilities and moving on to more stable types of employment. The stationary section is not aging. This, of course, raises the question why real pension contributions of stationary engineers are increasing at a pace equal to construction pensions contributions.

Figure 4.21 resolves this puzzle by comparing portable and stationary locals within the CPF along three dimensions: (1) age, (2) total compensation, and (3) pension contributions. Age is read off the left-hand vertical axis and is represented by the bars in the graph. As the gray bars indicate, the average age of stationary engineers has not changed much between 1975 and 1992, whereas the lighter bars show that construction operating engineers have become significantly older. Total compensation is indexed on the right-hand vertical axis, with

Figure 4.20
Average age and hourly contribution rate for CPF participants

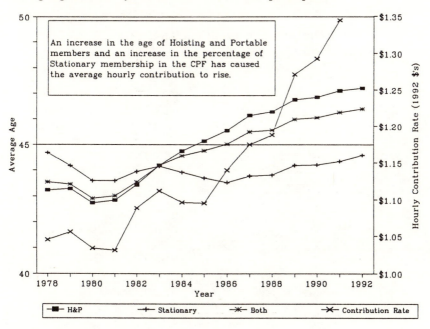

An increase in the age of Hoisting and Portable members and an increase in the percentage of Stationary membership in the CPF has caused the average hourly contribution to rise.

the real value of total compensation equaling one for stationary engineers in 1975. Thus, hoisting and portable total compensation in 1975 is indexed at 1.22, indicating that it was 122 percent of stationary compensation in that year. By 1992, hoisting and portable compensation had fallen to below one, equalling only 88 percent of the total compensation of stationary engineers in 1975. In contrast, stationary total compensation had risen to 1.18 by 1992, 118 percent of its level seventeen years before. In short, construction locals were aging and getting poorer, whereas stationary locals were not aging and were getting richer.

Pension contributions are also indexed on the right-hand vertical axis, with the average value of stationary pension contributions in 1975 equalling one. Hoisting and portable pension contributions in 1975 were slightly less than stationary contributions. In the subsequent seventeen years, real pension contributions into the CPF from both groups rose, but the portable contributions rose faster and farther. They also rose for different reasons. The construction contributions rose because the construction locals were getting older, whereas the stationary contributions rose because the stationary locals were getting richer. Evidently, given pocketbook and medical cost pressures, getting older was a greater incentive to contribute to a pension fund than getting richer.

Figure 4.21
Total compensation, average pension contributions, and average age of CPF participants

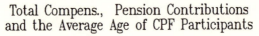

Total Compens., Pension Contributions
and the Average Age of CPF Participants

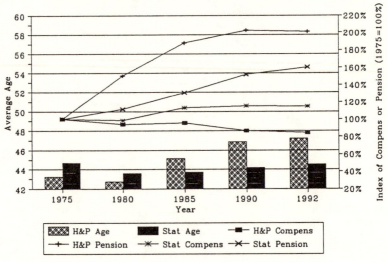

CONCLUSION

The CPF has limited means to alter the shrinking pool of participant hours, which has proved problematic for the last decade. To the extent that declining hours are a result of the CPF's declining share of the IUOE membership, it is conceivable that the CPF could merge with the pension funds of various IUOE locals. The locals that have recently shown an interest in merging with the CPF, however, have not come from union strongholds and are not the larger and better financed local pension funds within the IUOE. These smaller local funds are not likely to provide a long-run increase in participant hours, nor are they likely to reverse the current aging of the construction membership within the CPF. To the extent that declining participant hours are a result of declining union employment, particularly in construction, the CPF could gear its investments to serve the several purposes of solid returns and job creation, and to enhance the bargaining hand of local unions.

In the short run, the shrinking pool of participant hours can be and has been offset by rising per capita contributions. However, to the extent that rising hourly contribution rates are the result of an aging pool of participants, this cannot be a long-term solution, simply because these participants will soon retire. To the extent that rising contribution rates are the result of rising real wages, as appears to be the case among stationary locals, this can significantly offset falling participant hours in the short run. In the long run, it may be that the stationary locals will account for a rising proportion of CPF participants, sufficient to reverse the current stagnation in participant hours. A boom in construction employment or a revival of union coverage in construction would have the same effect.

Ultimately, CPF participant hours and contribution rates will be decided by people and developments beyond the direct control of the trustees, managers, and workers within the Fund. Future economic and legal processes will determine the relative health of collective bargaining in the construction and building service industries. Pension fund money cannot substitute for a healthy economy, favorable laws, effective organizing, and hard bargaining. The CPF's main job is to ensure the financial health of its investments and the generosity and reliability of its benefits. In the final analysis, the CPF can probably help union bargainers the most by simply developing a long track record of consistently delivering on its pension promises.

NOTES

1. GNP data for the years 1870–1970 is from the U.S. Bureau of the Census, *Historical Statistics of the United States: Colonial Times to the Present* (New York: Basic Book Publishers, 1975), 224. GNP data for 1971–1992 is from the Council of Economics Advisors, *Economic Report of the President* (Washington, D.C.: Government Printing Office, January 1993), 171.

2. Labor union membership and union membership as a percentage of the labor force for 1930–1970 is from the U.S. Bureau of the Census, *Historical Statistics of the United States*, 178. For 1970–1990 the numbers are from the U.S. Bureau of the Census, *Statistical Abstract of the United States* (Washington, D.C.: Government Printing Office), pages vary by year.

3. Council of Economic Advisors, *Economic Report of the President*, 390.

4. Ibid., 396.

5. Union construction wages for 1935–1970 are from the U.S. Bureau of the Census, *Historical Statistics of the United States*, 171. Union construction wages for 1971–1992 are from the U.S. Bureau of the Census, *Statistical Abstract of the United States*. Average construction wages are from the U.S. Department of Labor, *Employment, Hours, and Earnings, United States, 1909–1990, Volume I* (Washington, D.C.: Government Printing Office, 1991), 38–39. Unionization rates in construction are from Steven Allen, "Declining Unionization in Construction: The Facts and the Reasons," *Industrial and Labor Relations Review* 41, No. 3 (April 1988): 343–59.

6. Ibid.

7. U.S. Bureau of the Census, *Statistical Abstract of the United States*.

8. Membership numbers are from IUOE headquarters, Washington, D.C.

9. Council of Economic Advisors, *Economic Report of the President*, 394–95.

10. Ibid., 411.

11. IUOE.

12. Wages and benefits were provided by each IUOE local.

13. Double-breasting companies consists of forming a holding company with two wholly owned subsidiaries, one generally operating union or government projects and the other nonunion or private projects.

14. Peter Babin III, interview by authors, tape recording, New Orleans, 17 December 1992.

15. Dan Smart, interview by Teresa Ghilarducci, tape recording, Indianapolis, 13 January 1994.

16. Ibid.

17. Tom Stapleton, interview by Jeff Petersen, tape recording, Alameda, Calif., 17 November 1993.

18. Wages and benefits are from Local 501 of the IUOE, Los Angeles, Calif.

19. Robert Fox, interview by Peter Philips, tape recording, Los Angeles, 30 December 1992.

20. Dan Goodpastor, interview by Jeff Petersen and Andrew McDiarmid, tape recording, Compton, Calif., 2 August 1993.

21. Robert Fox, interview by Jeff Petersen, tape recording, Los Angeles, 3 August 1993.

22. Ibid.

23. Art Viat, interview by Jeff Petersen, tape recording, San Francisco, 22 November 1993.

24. Ibid.

25. Ibid.

26. Ibid.

27. Local 39 of the IUOE, San Francisco.

28. The source of all data, unless otherwise noted, in this section is the CPF, Washington, D.C.

29. IUOE membership numbers for 1964–1974 are from U.S. Bureau of the Census. *Statistical Abstract of the United States*, pages vary by year. IUOE membership numbers for 1975–1992 are from the IUOE. CPF participation is from the CPF.

30. Hoisting and portable wage and total compensation data are from Locals 16, 17, 103, 139, 147, 181, 320, 382, 406, 463, 673, 819, 832, 841, and 917. Stationary wage data are from IUOE Locals 20, 94, 501, and 835. Stationary total compensation data are from Locals 94 and 501. Locals 501 and 94 are situated in Southern California and New York City, two predominately union strongholds. This may make the total compensation figure not representative of the stationary engineers as a whole in the IUOE. However, the favorable economic conditions for stationary engineers would indicate that total compensation index is representative of the stationary members of the IUOE.

Chapter 5

Planning for the Golden Years: What Does the CPF Deliver?

People plan their retirement income so they can maintain their current lifestyle after stopping work. Because taxes and work-related expenses are lower and other spending falls with age, the amount of working income needed to be replaced in retirement is lower than 100 percent of pre-retirement income. For lower income workers, such as those making $15,000 per year, the required replacement rate is approximately 82 percent. The replacement rate is lower for high-income individuals—those earning over $80,000 per year—at 66 percent because work-related expenses and savings for retirement represent a large share of this group's working income.[1]

The prevailing view of retirement income security, one that reigns today as a rule of thumb in public policy circles, is that a worker should retire with income from three sources: (1) personal savings, (2) Social Security, and (3) a pension. These three sources are commonly referred to as a "three-legged stool," the one used presumably to sit out retirement. The stool is an abstract concept; reality supports the image of a wobbly four-legged table. Currently, a middle-class retiree receives more than 32 percent of his or her income from Social Security, 25.7 percent from working, about 10.5 percent from private sector employer pensions, and the rest from welfare and savings.[2]

One of the reasons employer pensions provide as little as they do is because in 1992 only 45 percent of the workforce was covered by an employer-provided plan. Many times a leg of the mythical retirement platform is missing. Being a union member, however, helps substantially toward securing an employer pension. Ninety percent of unionized workers are covered by a pension plan from their employer.[3]

At the time the operating engineers established the CPF, retired workers in their income brackets (as opposed to all retirees) were receiving about 47 percent of their pre-retirement incomes from Social Security and were relying on the rest from their savings, odd jobs, family members (especially their children), local pension fund and other sources. Widows had Social Security survivor's benefits, but this was obviously not enough, and the lack of an employer-based plan really hurt women, who on average live about eight years longer than their husbands.

In 1992, the average unionized operating engineer earned about $17.00 per hour (not including fringe benefits) and worked approximately 2,021 hours per year; the average annual income is thus $34,357.[4] Unionized stationary engineers work more hours at an average wage of $17.08 per hour; their average annual income is $35,357. Current retirees from the trades receive over half of their income from Social Security, with less, about 40 percent, coming from other sources—mostly their union-management trusteed. For operating engineers over age 60 (including people who may have retired 15 years ago), the average annual income is $12,500. This puts them squarely in the middle class.

An operating engineer retiring in 1993 who had worked in the trade under the CPF pension for twenty-five years would receive about $1,000 a month in Social Security and $1,420 in a CPF benefit. This yields an upper-middle-class retiree income of $29,040. With good health and a reduction in work-related expenses, the operating engineer and his or her spouse can easily maintain their current living standards without working. This is not only good for the retirees' families, but also for the younger members who need jobs.

The CPF avoids many of the problems that plague employer-based pension funds. One is that the CPF has a benefit structure that is simple to understand and administer, as well as being fair and portable. This benefit structure works for a workforce that is peripatetic. In an economy where workers are becoming more mobile, the CPF and union-management trusteed plans offer an interesting model. This chapter examines the benefit structure of the CPF and the history of its improvements, compares the CPF with the pensions of other IUOE locals, makes some predictions about what the plan will look like in the next ten years, and reviews what policymakers can learn from the benefit structure of the CPF.

THE BASIC BENEFITS OF THE CPF

The CPF and many other union-management trusteed plans have a structure that ensures most everyone contributing to the CPF will get a pension. Most of those who will not are workers who will not achieve vesting, which takes five years of credited vesting service. The CPF is unique among union-management trusteed plans because it has a five year vesting rule. ERISA requires only a ten year vesting rule for union-management trusteed plans.

The plan is portable. If workers move from contractor to contractor, they are still provided the credits that the collective bargaining agreement requires be contributed by the employer to the CPF (see Chapter 3). This multicontractor coverage minimizes "breakage," which in many plans results in the few benefiting at the expense of the many. Breakage is the amount of money contributed on behalf of people who are covered in the plan but never become eligible for a benefit. The implication is that those who get the pension are subsidized by those who do not. Operating engineers have become virtually immune from the problem of breakage, due to the internationals' reciprocity agreement of 1973 and the lower vesting rule.

Benefit Formula

The monthly benefit paid under the plan is a percentage of the total contributions made on behalf of the worker throughout his career. These contribution accounts increase over time as the worker accumulates more service and receives higher negotiated contributions. For example, if a worker has $50,000 contributed by 100 employers over a lifetime, that worker would receive $1,650 (3.3 percent of $50,000) a month for the rest of his or her life under the current formula. This amount does not run out as the retiree ages; there is no individual account that is being depleted.

In some ways this formula may seem like a defined-contribution plan, in that the ultimate benefit is related to the total amount of contributions and years of service. Nevertheless, it remains a defined-benefit plan because a percentage of the contributed amount is payed out in a defined manner. Another shared characteristic of a defined-contribution plan and the CPF is simplicity. Workers covered by the CPF can easily calculate their monthly benefit. In fact, it is easier for a worker to estimate his or her pension in this type of defined-benefit plan than if they were in a defined-contribution plan because in a defined-contribution plan a worker knows only the account balance, not the pension amount.

The CPF is a defined-benefit plan. That means the total amount of benefits received is determinable and depends on contributions, the expected mortality of the pensioner, and the number and expected mortality of his or her survivors. In addition to the redistributive aspects, another distinction that will be covered extensively later in the chapter is that in defined benefit plans the Trustees can increase retiree benefits. Annuity contracts with life insurance companies or individual accounts never increase the retiree's benefit.

The Lure of Past Service

In the beginning of the CPF, a worker (anyone in the plan, a current or future retiree or beneficiary) could earn past service credits prior to their initial participation date in three ways. Operating engineers earned a year of past service credits for each year they worked as an IUOE member after age thirty-five up to their initial participation date. Second, when an employer begins contributing to the CPF, an employee's total years of service with that employer (after age thirty-five up to their initial participation date) counts as years of past service credit. Again, the contributions were presumed to be whatever the prevailing contribution rate was when the worker actually entered the plan. Third, an employee's years of work experience within an industry in the IUOE's jurisdiction was counted as credited past service (after age thirty-five up to their initial participation date) that served the needs of the pipeline workers.

This generous way of crediting past service had one major goal: organizing. Past service credits were sign-up enticements and potent incentives to join the CPF. In the early to mid-1970s, local unions with older members took notice and entered the plan in droves as we saw in Chapter 3. The rules were so generous that some members received substantial benefits from credited past service. Because these credits were calculated at the rates in effect at the date of entry, those who entered during the 1970s sometimes received larger pensions than members who had entered the plan during the 1960s, when employer contributions per hour of employment were substantially lower. In response to this explosive situation and because the enticement to enroll in the CPF was no longer necessary, the CPF's trustees limited the eligibility rules for past service. By 1990, however, the staff felt these restrictions were too extreme and recommended their modification. The restrictive rules, which began in 1975, limited the amount of industry credit by linking it to actual participation in the CPF. A participant with five or more years in the industry would immediately get five years of industry credit and one by one for every year they were in the CPF. The definition of industry was also tightened. Further restrictions were established in 1977 that required five years in the CPF before any industry past credits were applied. Between 1978 and 1981, the contribution rate for past credit was also limited.

When the CPF was first established, there was a tremendous incentive to make the benefits attractive to locals not yet in the plan. For that reason, the fund gave past service credits. This was expensive, but a new fund can usually afford such incentives because there are few retirees and many active workers. Now past service is a minimal expense because most members begin their careers with a local already in the plan. Nevertheless, crediting past service represented a significant subsidy of older members by younger members.

Disability

A distinguishing feature of a union is the belief in collective action as well as mutual aid. Examples of collective action are the union's motivation to garner clout for workers as a group and, especially in the construction trades, to provide and certify certain types and levels of skill and education. American unions can also be quasi-fraternal organizations.

Disability provisions in union plans are designed to defend against the inability to do work in one's profession. Because disabled workers are often young, the provision of a pension on disability can be expensive. One way to reduce the costs and still adhere to self-help principles is to require confirmation of disability status. This feature is, of course, not unique to any disability insurance scheme. In the early 1990s, the California workers compensation insurance program sent spies to examine the activities of disabled workers and terminated benefits in celebrated cases. In the union case, the enforcement is different. Each local has an incentive to turn a member in for working while disabled. Of the 750 or so disabled workers in the CPF in 1992, the CPF staff reckons less than 5 percent are not disabled, based on the rate at which locals report disabled members working. The major way the CPF confirms disabled status, however, is to require the beneficiaries to confirm their disability every other year during their first four years of eligibility. In May 1992, for instance, eight participants were dropped because they did not respond to the request for confirmation.

Cost-of-Living Allowances

Cost-of-living allowances (COLAs) are an important feature of any pension plan because inflation can rapidly erode a pensioner's living standards. The rule of seventy-two is a good way to estimate the devastating effects inflation can have on the standard of living for a person dependent on a fixed income. The rule of seventy-two states that buying power will be cut in half in the number of years equal to seventy-two divided by the rate of inflation. For instance, if the rate of inflation is 7.5 percent the number of years it will take for a person on a fixed income to suffer an erosion of one-half of their buying power is 72/7.5 or 9.6 years.

The average benefit for CPF retirees has increased every year since 1965. When adjusted for inflation, however, the real buying power of the benefit increased in thirteen years and decreased in fourteen years (Figure 5.1[5]). The buying power of the average pension decreased in the 1970s when inflation was high and somewhat unpredictable. In the 1980s and early 1990s, the trend has been to increase both the monetary value and the real value, or buying power, of the pension. The real value increased in five out of the past six years, from 1986 to 1992, and the total real benefit increased 30 percent during this same time period.

Social Security payments have increased less than CPF benefits (Figure 5.2[6]). Since 1964, the real CPF benefit has increased 53 percent, whereas Social Security payments have increased 45 percent. In 1964, the average yearly Social Security benefit was $4,260. Currently that number is $7,831. The CPF's average yearly benefit was $1,626 in 1964 and $3,455 in 1992. The overall average is somewhat misleading because of wide differences in local averages, due primarily to the variability of contributions different locals have been able to negotiate from employers. Social Security benefits are higher because the recipients have had many more years of contributions. Most of the current CPF pensioners have substantial amounts of past service determining their benefit.

Figure 5.1
The CPF's average yearly benefit

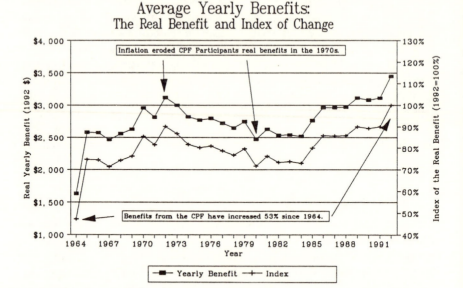

Average Yearly Benefits:
The Real Benefit and Index of Change

Newer retirees will have many more years of contributions, and the CPF benefit amount will increase over the coming years.

Although the CPF trustees stemmed the erosion of the benefit due to inflation in the years between 1972 and 1979, the real yearly benefit fell substantially throughout the 1970s and remained stagnant in the early 1980s (Figure 5.1). Benefit increases in 1984, 1986, 1988, and 1991, along with low inflation, caused the real benefit to escalate rapidly. This reversal may be attributed to the trustees' active and conscious commitment to alleviate the destructive effects of inflation on retirees' income. In fact, that a pension plan would increase benefits for retirees is remarkable when considering that employers usually pay pensions to affect worker effort and loyalty to the company. By providing a benefit that increases with service to the employer or trade, the employer can ensure that the worker's skills he or she acquired with more work experience will be to the benefit of that particular employer. Vacations that accrue over time and other seniority-related benefits serve similar economic functions. That is, however, less of a consideration in the construction portion of the CPF. There, the question is loyalty to the industry as workers move about among contractors through the union-run referral system.

As a political institution, the union wants the pension to garner support for itself. Therefore, it would make sense for locals to give COLAs to retirees when the retirees vote in local officer elections. Indeed, our interviews with operating engineer locals support that political motive. The motive is more indirect for a

Figure 5.2
The average yearly Social Security benefit

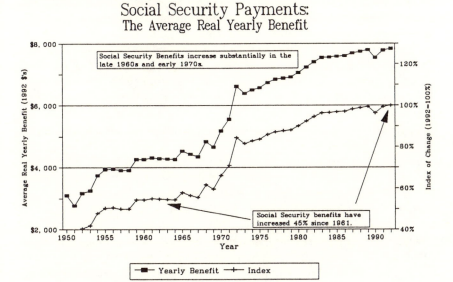

Social Security Payments:
The Average Real Yearly Benefit

nationalized pension fund that is far removed from local politics. IUOE Stationary Local 39, for instance, does not increase its benefits for past service. Benefit increases are not retroactive, as is the case with the CPF. Art Viat, Business Manager of Local 39, states:

Once somebody is retired, they are retired. We do not even give COLAs to our retirees. For so many years the people in the plan were not getting anything out of it. We were buying things for everyone else—past service credits, different improvements and they never put anything into the plan. My theory was that there had to be an end to it sometime. So at a given period in time we just stopped doing it. We said look, the future people are entitled to something, and we're going to stop paying the tab.[7]

When asked if the retirees in Local 39's pension plan complain, Viat replied:

A handful of them. But they never put any money in. In six months they would get out of it what they put in. I took a position that the pension is never going to be worth anything unless we put something into it. My predecessors used to say you can have it on pension or you can have it on wages. Anyone under forty-five wanted to have it on wages, not pension. Then they would come in here to retire and they would not have any benefits. I took a position that we would say where the money would go and tell the employer where the money would go.[8]

By choosing the same policy as Local 39, the CPF could offer increases in future service benefit calculation rates for the benefit of younger workers. But the trustees have always followed a policy that benefit increases should be retroactive. What explains the expensive increases in retiree benefits from the CPF? The answer may lie in the other roles a union plays. It can perceive itself as an institution that raises the living standards of its members throughout their lifetimes, rather than just during their working years. If the union meets this goal, it gains a reputation that can be helpful in its relationship with current members and in organizing. Giving retirees increases that have not been contracted signals a commitment to members that reaches beyond their working life and prevails throughout their life cycle. This concept will be referred to again in the chapter on the CPF's investments.

Like most pension plans in the corporate and public sector, the CPF provides survivors benefits. Many are concerned that the existence of a survivor's benefit means that married men receive more than single men. That is not true. The married worker's benefit is reduced according to a set formula that is based on the expected life spans of the worker and his or her spouse. Benefits are redistributed, and just as in any insurance plan, the people who gain are the people who beat the average. If a retiree and his or her spouse are extraordinarily healthy, they may live much longer than the expected average retiree. Therefore, they benefit at the expense of the couple who live for a shorter time than expected. Because the retiree must accept a decrease in pension in order to guarantee a survivor's benefit, many retirees opt for more money and forgo the survivor option. The Retirement Equity Act of 1984 (REA), sponsored by former Congresswoman and vice presidential candidate Geraldine Ferraro, changed ERISA and required that the retiree can only receive the full benefit without the survivor option on the notarized permission from his or her spouse. By the time REA was passed in 1984, a majority of new retirees in the CPF were choosing the spousal benefit.

Range of Current Benefits by Local

The average benefit for Local 612, which is not a contributing local but participates in the reciprocity agreement, had nine pensioners collecting an average of $57.93 per month in 1993. Local 501, which uses the CPF as a primary plan had its 1,711 pensioners in 1993 averaging $458 per month (Table 5.1[9]). Why does the average pension benefit amount vary so widely by local? There are several reasons. For the locals that use the CPF as the sole pension plan, the benefit generosity reflects each local's relative bargaining power to secure high rates of employer contributions. That will depend on both the extent of organization and the state of the local or regional economy. A second factor explaining average pension differences is the percentage of retirees who have been retired for a long time to the total retiree population. Long-time retirees have less pension because their contribution rate was low when they retired.

Table 5.1
The twelve largest IUOE locals participating in the CPF by size, type, contribution rate, and pension benefit

Local	Type	Number of Employees	Entry Date	Average Hourly Contrib.	Average Monthly Pension	Ranking of Contrib. Rate	Rank of Pension
49	HP	8200	1967	$1.85	$258.81	4	11
139	HP	5759	1967	2.58	448.32	1	2
94	S	5293	1968	1.10	338.50	6	6
501	S	5163	1965	1.97	452.57	3	1
399	S	3099	1960	.74	277.93	12	10
9	HP	2987	1968	.94	400.49	10	3
181	HP	2859	1965	1.35	312.69	7	7
406	HP	2722	1966	.96	296.96	9	8
103	HP	2599	1962	2.18	400.47	2	4
18	HP	2116	1971	.75	223.15	11	12
841	HP	2096	1962	1.48	356.97	5	5
400	HP	2089	1966	1.07	280.48	8	9

Recent retirees have worked substantial hours at significantly higher rates of contributions. The third factor explaining local pension differences is that locals that can provide their members with large numbers of hours will have more contributions, and thus larger pensions. For the same reason, pay rate differences among locals will make the pensions different. The important issue for a pension fund is not so much the size of the variance across locals, but rather that the variance is perceived as fair by the participants.

As noted in Chapter 3, Fred Dereschuk, CPF trustee and business manager for Local 49, the largest local in the CPF, has speculated out loud whether his group would get a higher benefit rate if it had its own pension. It is evident from Table 5.1 that his local does not have either the largest contribution rate or the largest pension. However, his union local is growing relative to the other construction locals in the CPF. His members know this and pressure Dereschuk to explain why Local 49 is subsidizing shrinking locals. Of course, only an actuarial analysis could determine if Local 49 would be better off with its own pension plan. Bill Riehl, the CPF's actuary from 1961 to 1991, addresses the issue: "Dereschuk has been very aggressive about benefit increases since he has been on the board. He has good reason because his local is very big and puts in a lot of money. It is possible that if his local had a fund of its own it could provide a higher benefit than the CPF. That would depend upon the demographics of Local 49."[10] Thus, Dereschuk would be correct, in general, if Local 49 had a larger rate of new entrants and if the new entrants lowered the fund's average participant age.

Despite the strong suspicion that Local 49 could pay a larger benefit if it had its own plan, Dereschuk insists he will stay in the CPF because he declares, "that is what a union is for.''[11] The next section explicitly discusses the key issues of solidarity, redistribution and mutual aid in a pension plan.

TRADE-OFFS AND REDISTRIBUTIONS IN THE PENSION FUND

As Fred Dereschuk's concerns illustrate, it is normal and expected that one of the key issues in any collective action process, whether it be a strike, paying taxes, cooperating on a project, or being in a pension, is the perception that some groups are taking out more relative to their contributions. In other words, one group is pulling the weight of a weaker group. Defined benefit plans are social insurance plans, and thus everyone in a population enters the plan to defend against the risk of retiring without enough money. People buying fire insurance insure against the financial loss of having a house burn down. Therefore, those people whose house does not burn are paying for houses that do. Likewise, the retiree who dies before he or she is expected to is helping out those who live longer than expected. The problem with the analogy is that with fire insurance everyone in the pool is confident that the risks of fire are being reduced by the efforts of the insurance companies.

But in a retirement plan the incentives for the participants is to live as long as possible—to beat the odds, not to reduce them, as is the case in disaster insurance. In a pension plan, there are rules that ultimately determine which group gets more than another. In trade union-management trusteed pensions, such as the CPF, there is a tendency both to distribute benefits on the basis of need and to maximize contentment among the membership. The pension plan also helps the union, and to some extent the contributing employers, to regulate labor supply. These regulators are addressed in the next section, which discusses how the plan treats working pensioners, and later in the discussion of breakage.

Working Versus Nonworking Pensioners

One of the most discouraging consequences in the union decline in the construction industry is the growth of the free rider. One free rider problem the CPF tries to prevent is subsidizing the nonunion employer with a trained union worker willing to work for less because he is receiving a union-management trusteed pension. One of the key features of multiemployer pension plans is their restrictions on working while receiving a pension. Most union-management trusteed plans suspend benefit payments to retirees if the retiree works while collecting a pension. However, Ian Lanoff, the ERISA enforcer for President Carter, took on the building trades in 1981, despite the fact that before coming to the Department of Labor, Lanoff served in the general counsel's office of the Teamsters and the United Mine Workers. Lanoff constructed the "suspension of benefit rules" that limit the ability of union-management trusteed funds to restrict those working in any capacity from collecting pensions. During hearings on ERISA, there were stories of Teamsters locals that had cut off pensioners for minor infractions, including doing odd jobs.

The current law allows union-management trusteed plans to suspend benefits for pensioners who work more than thirty-nine hours, or seven days or shifts in a month in the same trade, industry, and geographical area. The pension plan would be at cross-purposes with the union if the plan allowed pensioners to undercut wages by working for a nonunion employer and subcontract wages or to take jobs from younger members. The pension is for retirement income security, not a wage subsidy.

The CPF deals with suspending pensions of working pensioners on a routine basis. How are they caught by a fund administration that is far away in Washington, D.C.? The local must report them. For instance, the plumbers, sheetmetal workers, and bricklayers do not consider this to be a big issue; the political and actual costs of monitoring and spying were not worth the reimbursement to the fund. In addition, one non-IUOE staff member close to the pension fund expressed the opinion that if workers tried to work a little to supplement the pension, who was the union to tell them they earned too much, especially if working helped them retain some semblance of worth and dignity.

Young Versus Old Workers

One of the enduring beliefs about retirement programs is that the young do not care as much about pensions as the older workers. This condition led us to expect that as a local's members age, the local would push for more and more of its compensation to be put in the pension fund, yet the health care crisis has overwhelmed this propensity. In the building trades, as is true elsewhere, contributions to the pension fund are for the first time less than contributions to health insurance. As described in Chapter 4, pension contributions have been eroded by health care costs. Yet in the stationary locals where the average age is not increasing, workers are bargaining for a greater percentage of their total compensation to go into their retirement plan. Therefore, age is not the only factor explaining a desire for pensions. Although a commonplace nostrum may be that young workers do not place as high a priority on pensions compared with older workers, there seems to be no proof of this in the CPF. There is little evidence of any rift between generations because of the pension plan. Union education about retirement planning and controversies around Social Security in the 1980s may have made younger people more appreciative of pension coverage than they were in the 1950s and 1960s.

RECORD OF BENEFIT IMPROVEMENTS

The first substantial amendment to the CPF took effect in the early 1960s when the credited service provisions for the hoisting and portable locals were increased. In 1965, the death benefit was raised. In early 1967, the first large future service benefit increase occurred: 1.75 percent to 2 percent for hoisting and portable and 1.25 percent to 1.6 percent for stationary employees. Two years later in 1969, the future service crediting was made uniform across stationary, pipeline and hoisting and portable. The retirees received a huge 10 percent increase as well, and the disability age was lowered from fifty to forty. From then on, improvements were a bit more uniform and simple. Increases in the benefit formula and cost-of-living adjustments for retirees were common amendments. A series of benefit improvements, retiree cost-of-living increases, and the maintenance of the other ancillary benefits have generated a plan that pays 3.3 percent of the participant's "account level" for every month of a retiree's life, along with an expectation of periodic cost-of-living allowances and a very generous disability benefit.

In actuarial simulations that project future costs and earnings of pension plans, the increase of retiree and future retiree benefits while employment and pay is not growing show that a mature pension plan could quickly become underfunded. Before we examine the implications of the maturation of this thirty-one year old pension plan, it is important to compare the union-management trusteed plans and the corporate plans in order to put the union-management performance in context. There are significant differences between them that make generalizations and blanket regulation inappropriate. We argue that the full-funding limitations do not make sense for union-management trusteed plans.

CRUCIAL DIFFERENCES BETWEEN CORPORATE PLANS AND UNION PLANS

The strength of the improvements and the level of benefits in the CPF is made even more starkly apparent when compared with corporate plan behavior. Instead of raising benefits in response to the bull financial market, corporations lowered pension contributions in the 1980s. There were many reasons. Lowering pension contributions—in contrast to outright pension plan terminations—can be a milder and less conspicuous way for firms to "borrow" from workers in order to stabilize firm finances or execute a corporate strategy. Why does it matter that a firm lowers contributions and shrinks the gap between assets and liabilities? Because COLAs are usually paid when funded ratios are high.[12] Indeed, the corporate pension funds routinely paid out COLAs in the 1970s, but have done so rarely in the 1980s. Moreover, a fund's financial condition is an important determinant of the generosity of these COLAs.[13]

In a comprehensive and influential 1987 study of the changes in pension fund contributions, Economist and current Deputy Treasury Secretary Alicia Munnell found that the stock market boom from 1979 to 1987 led to lower pension contributions by some $20 billion. She blames the trend not on corporate ill will, but on ERISA's full funding limitation to prevent excessive loss of tax revenue. Under this limitation, firms are prevented from getting tax breaks on

Table 5.2
The authors' and the DOL's estimates of the ratio of vested to non-vested participants

	AUTHORS (All Plans)			DOL (100 or more participants)		
	Only Actives		*All*		*Only Actives*	
	Single	Multi	Single	Multi	Single	Multi
1985	48%	41%	40%	30%	51%	50%
1986	47	40	40	29	50	51
1987	46	40	37	29	49	52

contributions to the pension fund if the value of the assets in the fund exceeds the plan's liability by 150 percent. Thus, as plan assets increased because of the stock and bond market boom of the 1980s, firms would sharply decrease contributions once they hit the full-funding ceiling.[14] Munnell implies that if it were not for the full-funding limitations, firms might have increased contributions to take advantage of the higher returns. The implication is that if corporations had contributed more, there would have been a higher probability that more pensions would be paid.

However, Munnell does not explain why the corporations did not avoid the full-funding liability by raising benefits. She did not distinguish between the unilateral corporate plans and the jointly run union-management plans, which represent about 13.8 percent of all private plans assets. The explanation is that union-management trusteed funds behave differently since their level of contributions is determined by collectively bargained contracts. In the face of a stock and bond market boom, union-management trusteed funds might be expected to raise pension benefits rather than reduce contributions because the joint management-union trustees are inclined by their fiduciary duty to increase benefits when the fund does well, not to maximize the profits of the employer. Therefore, Congress should make the full-funding limitation apply only to corporate plans.

When Lanoff directed the Pension and Welfare Benefits Administration in the DOL, ERISA regulation was in a formative stage. Lanoff's and the public's attention on pension abuse was focused on the union-management trusteed plans, yet when the DOL compares the breakage in corporate plans and union plans by calculating the percentage of all working participants who are vested, there is not much difference. But if union plans have more retirees than corporate plans, simply examining the active population does not reveal the extent to which union plans pay benefits and tolerate breakage. When we compare the non-vested population to the entire number of participants, corporate defined benefit plans do worse in vesting their participants (see Table 5.2).

Our estimates include the ratio of non-vested participants to all participants, whereas the DOL calculates the ratios only for the plans with more than 100 participants. That excludes 84 percent of all single-employer defined benefit plans and 20 percent of their participants, whereas 8 percent of union-management trusteed plans and 0.9 percent of participants are in plans with fewer than 100 participants.[15] The authors use all plans and use the same data as Form 5500.

Technically, the CPF has minimized breakage in two ways. First, the shorter the vesting period, the lesser the breakage. The CPF has a vesting schedule of five years which is shorter than most, whereas the ERISA minimum for union-management trusteed plans is ten years.

Second, CPF participants have been covered by the International Union Reciprocity Agreement since 1973. This arrangement provides that individuals working under IUOE pension agreements anywhere in the United States will have all contributions made on their behalf aggregated to avoid a break in service and the resulting benefit loss. Under reciprocity, a pensioner at retirement time may receive several pro rata pensions as a result of working under several pension funds during his career (the low average pension benefit attributed to Local 612 is attributed to the pro rata effect).

Some inevitable (if minimal) breakage occurs when non-career transients, such as college students, work on a union job for a few months and then move on to other careers. Pension contributions made on their behalf ultimately wind up in the general fund to be used for benefits for career operating engineers.

In trade union terms, Dick Griffin, CPF trustee from 1986 to 1994 and current general counsel for the IUOE, argues that snow birds and temporary workers, like college students working in the summer, enjoy the benefit of the union's vigorous efforts to secure high wages and benefits. Therefore, Griffin argues, some breakage is fair. Hammond provides an illustrative metaphor. Temporary workers contribute to pensions they won't collect to pay for the union's house they benefit from. The house has a floor of bargained wages, walls of negotiated working conditions (including health and safety), and the roof of income security.

HOW DOES A UNION-MANAGEMENT TRUSTEED PLAN DECIDE TO RAISE BENEFITS?

Every year at the October meeting, the CPF trustees are presented with an "asset-to-liability" study prepared by the Fund actuary. An actuary is the single most influential professional among those hired by a pension plan. On the surface, his or her role seems like that of a technician. Much of what an actuary is trained to do is now contained in several software programs. The actuary determines the present value of the current promises and benefit levels and comes up with one number. That may sound simple, but actually the software has to be fed the data to make those calculations. Most of the data is based on

Figure 5.3
The CPF's assets-to-liability ratio

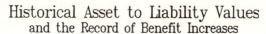

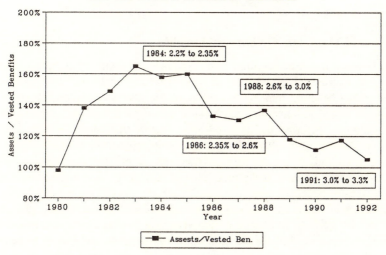

Historical Asset to Liability Values
and the Record of Benefit Increases

predictions about the future. Based on past trends, the character of the industry, and the particular work force the actuary has to decide which mortality table to use and what turnover assumptions to make, and so forth.

The actuary also decides what interest rate is to be used to discount the liability. The lower the interest rate assumption, the higher the value of the liabilities. The CPF actuary chose and the trustees approved what became a lower than actual interest rate in the 1980s. This meant that the fund had what is called actuarial windfalls for a number of years. It is on this basis that the asset-to-liability study is performed, enabling the trustees to make benefit decisions. The study also helps determine if the plan can afford a certain benefit level, based on what the fund is reasonably expected to earn in the future. Let's look at each of these decisions separately.

The CPF trustees used the ratio of the market value of assets to liabilities to gauge whether the fund could raise promised benefits, give current retirees an increase, loosen up eligibility standards, and so forth. Examining the relationship between the plan improvements and the asset-to-liability ratios from 1980 and 1992 (Figure 5.3[16]), one can see that the asset-to-liability ratio was high before an improvement and fell dramatically thereafter. The trustees said they were aiming for a target cushion of 10 percent meaning that the ratio of assets to liabilities was targeted at 110 percent, but, what one observes while looking at the table is a clear downward trend in the asset-to-liability ratio. What is to be made of this downward trend and the fact that the stated target has not been achieved? Not much, we conclude. As was noted in the section comparing the other plans, the choice of a target is idiosyncratic. It is determined by a trade-off between how important it is to give benefit increases and how important is it to protect one's participating employers from exposure to withdrawal liabilities.

What is Too Low: Withdrawal Liability

Withdrawal liabilities require that an employer who withdraws from a union-management trusteed fund not be allowed to simply walk away by paying off the expected benefits from its own workers. As noted in Chapter 2, if there is unfunded vested liability the withdrawing employer has to pay, regardless of what company incurred the debt. Clearly, a union-management trusteed fund that has withdrawal liability will repel new employers from the fund.

Is debt so bad? There are good reasons why a pension fund may want to tolerate debt for a while. If the fund remains in debt for too long, however, the ability to raise benefits in the future decreases and the flexibility of the fund is crimped. In 1980, the funded vested ratio was below 100 percent. By 1983, the fund rapidly built up to a ratio of approximately 160 percent, exceeding what became the tax-free, full-funded ratio limitation imposed in 1987. In March of 1984, the Trustees increased the benefit from 2.2 percent to 2.35 percent of contributions. As expected, that increase caused a big dip in the ratio to just less than 150 percent. Two years later, the stock and bond market boom enabled the trustees to increase the future benefit formula again to 2.6 percent and retirees got a 5 percent raise. This increase caused the asset-to-liability ratio to fall near the target and stay there for several years. In 1989 several improvements were made, the largest being another benefit increase. In 1991, the benefits were increased again to 3.3 percent and retirees got a 10 percent increase, bringing the asset-to-liability ratio to approximately one.

The character of an organization is often revealed by its response to a crisis, or to a situation some see as a crisis. In a few short months after former President Bush and the Federal Reserve Bank pursued a policy to lower interest rates to spur the economy before the 1992 election, the investment rate predictions fell so much that the likelihood actuarial gains fell and the fund was faced with the possibility of having to cut benefits. The combination of the benefit increase in 1991 and the downturn in interest rates and real estate values caused the nearest thing to a crisis this fund has ever seen. It so happened that in 1993 the actual return far exceeded what was predicted—12.9 percent. But the trustees did not know that would happen. How they handled the bad news gives some indication of the delicate judgments to be made in maintaining a pension plan.

The staff and consultants presented the trustees with an analysis that essentially said the fund has about a 50 percent chance over the next five years of earning a rate of return that could pay for the benefits. To most of the trustees that meant there might be a problem. The staff was thought to have implied that something ought to be done, such as reduce benefits. However, the overwhelming feeling among the trustees was that participants would not readily accept a benefit cut in a boom market. Indeed, this sentiment went further. A benefit cut was not wise or legitimate, regardless of the readiness of the participants to accept one. One philosophical position was to err on the side of the larger benefits.

Paul Rizzuto, who has been the CPF actuary for two years, puts it succinctly: "It was premature to talk about remedial action."[17] Previously, the trustees had primarily looked at one ratio, the withdrawal liability—the market value of assets to the vested benefit liability. That focus on withdrawal liability made sense because that is what employers cared about. If the withdrawal liability was greater than zero, new employers would be wary of joining the fund as contributing employers responsible for part of a liability they did not create. Past asset-to-liability studies and benefit increase studies did present minimum funding credit balance data, and unfunded entry age liability. The trustees gave the withdrawal liability surplus by far the greatest weight in deciding benefit increases.

Paul Rizzuto wants the trustees to examine the funded position of the pension plan, or in other words, the actuarial value of the fund over what is called the "entry age" normal liability. Rizzuto sounds almost apologetic when uttering these words but he does so with the patience of a math high school teacher who never abandons hope that understanding a quadratic equation will lead to a better life for his students (Rizzuto is, in fact, a former high school math teacher).

The funded position of the plan is another barometer of the fund's health. It compares the expected value of the fund over a period of time to a broader notion of liability. A fund can be in surplus relative to its vested benefit liability, and deficient relative to its entry age normal liability. For instance, in 1993 the CPF had a $235 million surplus on vested benefits, but was $892 million underfunded on an entry age liability basis.

In the past, the trustees kept the market value of assets-to-vested liability ratio at about 120 percent on an ongoing basis. When the ratio rose above that level they would increase benefits and allow it to fall somewhat below the mark. In 1991, when they raised the benefit formula to 3.3 percent the ratio fell nearly to 101 percent. Did this mean the trustees were overreaching? Rizzuto thinks it could have been a completely reasonable move to a board that wanted to, needed to, or felt compelled to offer the maximum benefit they could for their active members. The point is that neither the actuary nor the investment consultant or the staff can be certain of the best trade-off between a comfortable funding cushion and benefits for their members. It is a judgment call, the type of decision only the trustees are empowered to make.

Pension Actuaries and the CPF Actuaries

The CPF is fortunate in terms of the continuity of the actuarial firm and the actuary. Bill Riehl had been the actuary for more than thirty years when Paul Rizzuto took over as principal in 1992. Sol Weinberger is the peer review actuary. The continuity, however, was challenged during J. C. Turner's term as IUOE president. Martin Segal company was the actuary for the international's staff plan, and Turner wanted the CPF to switch from Mercer to Segal. Segal is known as a union firm and has the highest percentage of union funds in the country. Turner felt it would be politically advisable for the CPF to dump Mercer and retain Segal. The CPF trustees, however, were not going to be told what to do. As was stated in Chapter 3, the CPF has always maintained an autonomous, "arm's-length" relationship with the International, and in this case they were happy with Riehl as the funds' actuary and were not about to change. Riehl tells the story:

One of the General Presidents, Turner, tried to get Segal to be the actuarial firm and the trustees voted for Segal to come in and do three studies, Actuarial, Administration, and Investment. Three very big expensive studies. It took many, many pages and dollars for them to say that they had nothing significant to offer in the way of changes. Even with differing assumptions they came within 99.8 percent of our numbers. The word went back to Turner, no way Jose, but then he still put a bunch of pressure on the Board. He finally realized the Board was not going to change its mind, but he did manage to get a Segal employee to sit in on the Board meetings for a while, about a year and a half, and then that employee died. This goes back to the CPF's commitment to guide its own course.[18]

The role of the actuary at the trustees' meeting also conveys its importance. The CPF has never granted a benefit increase that the actuary did not approve. The actuary is trusted with having a great deal of judgment based on the complications of the calculations. Bill Riehl had a unique relationship with the board. As noted in Chapter 3, the board would look to Riehl for approval if they wanted to raise benefits. Riehl would say "I am comfortable with that" if he felt the action was fiduciarily sound. As the possibility of plan improvements arose, the staff surveyed the local union leadership to determine what improvements were important to the local members. If there were a multitude of issues up for debate, Riehl would offer the CPF trustees several different options and the trustees would select the option they felt contained the most important benefit increases. Riehl says: "I confirmed at what level benefits could be increased. Sometimes there would be a package and we were asked to cost out specifics, possible increases in different areas. Maybe ten different possible combinations. And I would say OK guys, six of these ten you cannot do right now. And they would pick the ones they wanted to do."[19]

The actuary is trained to have several variables in mind at the same time. The trustees ask the actuary to change one of those variables and the actuary's job is to see how it affects everything else. Therefore, when the actuary says "I am comfortable with that," the trustees presume the actuary considered how it would affect the fund's ability to reach their goals such as avoiding withdrawal liability and how it would affect future ratios, given the particular situation of the fund in terms of the industry and the demographic profile of the group.

CONCLUSION

This chapter describing the CPF's benefit structure illuminated a few basic facts about pensions and union-management trusteed pension funds in particular. First, the case study shows that sponsors know explicitly that pension funds redistribute pension benefits from some participants to others, just as in any insurance scheme (the burned-out family receives a "subsidy" from the fire insurance holder who has no losses; in groups health insurance the smoker is subsidized by the nonsmoker). The union trustees are not defensive about the breakage though there were some exceptional cases uncovered in ERISA testimony among Teamsters, Bakery Workers, and others. Union trustees, Richard Griffin in particular, actually defends breakage.

Second, there are key distinctions between corporate plans and union-management trusteed plans. The union-management trusteed plan is a hybrid between the defined-benefit and defined-contribution plans. It allows for mobility and periodic COLAs when they can be afforded. These features are in stark contrast to corporate plans. The second distinction is how the two systems respond to a stock market boom or any other special or unexpected windfalls. The corporation takes the surprise gain and gives it to capital holders, whereas the union-management trusteed plan uses the rapid gains to increase benefits to the workers.

It should be clear from Chapter 3, "Building the CPF," and this benefit chapter that the actuary is a key professional to the fund. Only an actuary can answer the question, "Can we reasonably expect to earn enough on the portfolio to fund a certain level of benefits?" The trustees have to make tradeoff decisions constantly. Should we pay a COLA or raise disability? Do we pay more to the hoisting and portable workers by lowering the retirement age, or improve benefit accrued for future service, a gain to all stationary workers? Only an actuary can assign costs and benefits to those decisions. In the next chapter we will look at the more straightforward task of investing the pension fund to pay the benefits.

Last, it should be clear that the trustees must make the difficult decisions. This chapter and the next describe the technical aspects of the pension payout and fund investment decisions that ensure that the political decisions concerning the priorities on organizing (giving past service credit and keeping withdrawal liabilities low), and maximizing and trading of benefits among workers, retirees, and the disabled can all be controlled by the trustees.

NOTES

1. Robert Clark and Joseph J. Spenger, *The Economics of Individual and Population Aging* (Cambridge: Cambridge University Press, 1980), 51.

2. Employee Benefit Research Institute (EBRI), *Tabulations of the March 1993 Current Population Survey* (Washington, D.C.: EBRI, 1993), 15.

3. John A. Turner and Daniel J. Beller, *Trends in Pensions* (Washington, D.C.: Government Printing Office, 1992).

4. Survey sent to locals participating in the CPF.

5. CPF.

6. Social Security Administration, *Social Security Bulletin* (Washington, D.C.: Government Printing Office, January 1993).

7. Art Viat, interview by Jeff Petersen, tape recording, San Francisco, Calif., 22 November 1993.

8. Ibid.

9. CPF.

10. Bill Riehl, interview by Peter Philips, tape recording, New Orleans, 29 November 1992.

11. Dereschuk, interview by authors, tape recording, New Orleans, 28 November 1992.

12. Mark J. Warshawsky, "Pension Plans: Funding, Assets, and Regulatory Environment," *Federal Reserve Bulletin* (November 1988): 717–30.

13. Steven G. Allen, Robert L. Clark, and Ann A. McDermed, "Post-Retirement Benefit Increases in the 1980s," in Turner and Beller, *Trends in Pensions*.

14. Alicia Munnell, "Pension Contributions and the Stock Market," *New England Economic Review* (November/December 1987): 3–14.

15. Turner and Beller, *Trends in Pensions*, 590–95.

16. CPF.

17. Paul Rizzuto, interview by Teresa Ghilarducci, tape recording, date unknown.

18. Riehl, 1992.

19. Ibid.

Chapter 6

How to Deliver the Promised Benefits: The CPF's Investment Policy

The wealthy understand the enormous benefits of investing money and living off the interest. With enough money wisely invested, one can live off the earnings without ever touching one penny of capital. Because higher-income families can meet their financial needs more easily, they are more likely to have retirement savings than the average worker. The exception is unionized workers. Union members are more than twice as likely to be covered by a pension than nonunion workers, 90 percent coverage compared to 40 percent.[1] In 1992, the decline in unionization explained almost one third of the decline in pension coverage among men. Being in a union means being connected to pension programs. Such programs are institutions that help workers easily defer spending now to build a capital base for spending in retirement. Prefunded pension funds are trust funds for the working class.

This chapter is divided into two parts. The first part is a primer on investment practices and a history of the CPF's investments. The second part describes the criticisms of union pension funds and the struggles trustees face when striving to maximize profits when profits are increasingly obtained by lower labor standards and destroyed unions.

PART ONE: THE PRINCIPLES OF INVESTMENT AND THE CPF

Prefunding and Investment Earnings

Pension funds build up reserves and aim to have sufficient investment returns to eventually pay for a significant portion of current benefits. When a pension plan is first established, the number of workers paying into the fund greatly outnumbers the few retirees drawing pensions. Under these circumstances, each worker only has to contribute a few cents per hour to pay generous benefits to current retirees. But as the number of retirees begins to increase, contributions begin to play a secondary role to investments in paying pensions. For example, in 1962, investment returns constituted less than 1 percent of income to the CPF, but in 1992, 54 percent of the fund's income came from investment earnings.

Another way to finance a pension scheme is to have current workers pay for current retirees benefits. This is called pay-as-you-go or pay-go. The Social Security system is a pay-go example. A trust fund is maintained as a cushion, but that fund is far from sufficient to earn the revenues to pay the present let alone the future obligations of the system. There was consideration in 1935 of a prefunded system first collecting taxes to amass a fund and then paying benefits. However, politics is rarely that patient. The Depression devastated incomes, and the political pressure from intrepid elderly groups precluded any such possibility. The first Social Security benefits were originally scheduled to be paid in 1942, but five years earlier the Social Security Administration began paying benefits based on "credit" for past service, that is, service during which taxes (or contributions) had not been collected.[2]

The U.S. economy flourished after World War II. National production grew an average of 4.8 percent between 1947 and 1973 compared to 2.7 percent between 1973 and 1988.[3] During the period immediately following World War II, prosperous workers had many children who also found good jobs and paid healthy Social Security contributions. These postwar baby boomers helped finance Social Security benefits for their parents' generation. This group of fully employed workers, assisted by their baby-boomer children, could also afford to improve Social Security benefits considerably for two decades. The first big improvement was in 1952, the last in 1977.

In the early 1990s, the politics of the young versus the old have taken center stage. Politicians and analysts have begun to argue that young adults and children are not getting a fair share of social resources in comparison to the elderly. This indicates that the social consensus for a pay-as-you-go social insurance system is eroding.[4] The fact that vigorous opposition is brewing to the mildly redistributive aspects of Social Security, a program with a great deal of history and political legitimacy, reveals why smaller plans avoid many of these objections by being prefunded.

With the pay-go method causing even the broad-based Social Security system to come under pressure, a fund with a much smaller base, such as that of one industry or one employer, has less certainty that the industry or company will last as long or be as economically powerful as the U.S. government. Therefore, there are economic and political sides to the argument that a fund with a smaller base has more difficulty running on a pay-go basis and must have reserves. The economic argument is that it is much cheaper to have investment earnings paying

Figure 6.1
Beginning in 1984, investments account for a higher percentage of earnings

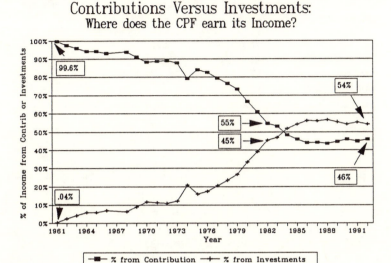

Contributions Versus Investments:
Where does the CPF earn its Income?

for benefits. The political argument is that no generation knows what a later generation's commitment or ability to pay will be. The task of pre-funding the CPF is the subject of this chapter.

The Importance of Investment Earnings in the CPF

In 1961, 99.6 percent of the CPF's income came from employer contributions ($371,092) and 0.4 percent from investments ($1,304) (Figure 6.1[5]). As the years passed, contributions continued to represent a higher percentage of CPF's income, but investment income was steadily gaining ground. In 1984, investment income was greater than contributions for the first time. In 1992, investments accounted for 54 percent of income, whereas contributions accounted for 46 percent. The trend toward investments representing a higher percent of income will continue in the future.

HOW MUCH RISK ENSURES A GOOD RETURN: THE SCIENCE OF MODERN PORTFOLIO THEORY

Contrary to the perceived wisdom in the 1950s that union pension funds recklessly invested in "brother-in-law" construction companies or in opulent resorts for union bosses, the vast majority of union trustees take their fiduciary duty seriously. To avoid the worst possible scenario—that retirees would have

Table 6.1
Fluctuations of returns, 1983–1992

	Best Year	Worst Year	Average Return
Intl. Stocks	70%	-12%	17%
U.S. Stocks	32	-3	16
Intl. Bonds	37	-5	14
U.S. Bonds	30	0	13
Real Estate	13	-7	7
Money Market	12	-6	7
Diversified Portfolio	29	1	13

no pensions—many trustees simply put the funds in long-term, low-yielding government bonds.[6] Many stock analysts argued that this strategy was unduly conservative, but before ERISA, it was not suspect. After ERISA, a fund would have to justify such an extreme avoidance of risk. A fund may want to avoid all financial risk if it has negative cash flow, that is, if ongoing expenses are greater than income, or if liabilities are perfectly known and fixed. However, the fiduciary responsibility affixed by ERISA makes undue conservatism as violative as undue risk.

An improper and superficial way to judge whether a pension fund, or for that matter any investment, has done well is to measure its return over a certain length of time. The temptation is to conclude that the fund that earned the highest return is the best investment, yet high returns often come with higher risk. For instance, over the ten-year period from 1983 to 1992 international stocks earned 17 percent; U.S. stocks, 16 percent; international bonds, 14 percent; and money market and real estate, 7 percent (Table 6.1[7]). One might conclude that any smart portfolio would have only held international stocks because they have the highest return. There are two reasons that holding a single class is not a good idea. One reason is high risk, and the other is the common sense of diversification. The common sense of diversification was modeled and formalized in the 1970s under the name "modern portfolio theory."

One way to understand risk and the common sense of modern portfolio theory is to see what happened to each investment category over a ten-year period (Table 6.1). The best performers, international stocks, earned 70 percent in their best year and lost 23 percent during their worst. On the other hand, the money market fund earned 12 percent in its best year and earned 6 percent in its worst. The lesson is that conservative investments, those without much volatility, do not on the average earn spectacular relative rates of return. What is curious and needs explaining is how a mixed or diversified portfolio seems to get a higher return for less risk. Compare the diversified portfolio with U.S. bonds. The average return was the same, but a portfolio with only U.S. bonds would have had a year with no return and a year with a 30 percent return, whereas the diversified portfolio has a smaller spread 1 percent to 29 percent.

The diversified portfolio takes advantage of the fact that elements in the economy that make international stocks go up or down are different from those that make bond rates change. The investment consultant illustrated the benefits of diversification by showing the trustees a table in the 1994 Investment Alternatives that showed some categories of stocks move almost perfectly with the broad index of stocks, the Wilshire 5000. The risk of the stock market is the risk born by holders of equity in large capitalized U.S. firms or small companies. That risk is shown by their "coefficients of correlations," or the index that measures how closely together each asset moves, which are 97 percent and 98 percent, respectively. However, the stocks of companies in the Pacific Basin move with the U.S. stock market only about half of the time. The coefficient is 0.51, or 51 percent. This coefficient, which is far different from 100 percent, means there are potential benefits from diversifying.

If one owns a mixture—so that half of one's portfolio is going up when the other is going down—one has less overall fluctuations or volatility. The portfolio investor tries to find an investment within each level of volatility, or risk, that has the maximum return.

One of the board of trustees' first steps in constructing an investment philosophy is to decide how much risk to accept. This helps determine the percentage of assets the fund holds from each asset class. The second element of an investment philosophy is to choose vehicles within each asset class.

After deciding how much risk to bear, which in turn implies what percentage of "risky" assets to hold, the board of trustees can hire the best real estate picker, the best small firm picker, and the best large firm pickers to buy and sell in each asset class. In addition to this strategy, or as a replacement of it, the fund can take a more passive approach and buy a bit of each asset class. The third role of the investment strategy is to evaluate the performance of the money managers.

THE EVOLUTION OF THE CPF'S INVESTMENT STRATEGIES

Union-management pension funds often suffer the false images generated by abuses that occurred forty years ago. The personal and petty greed of trustees motivated some improper uses. The most celebrated cases, however, involved unions using their pension funds to enhance their bargaining power. They could reward union employers with below-market rate loans.

Although many expecting scandal may regard it as dull, the CPF's financial management was precocious in its sophistication. CPF's noteworthy financial finesse evolved from typical multiemployer plan practices. Unions sponsoring multiemployer pension funds—the Teamsters, the International Garment Workers, the Bakery Workers—did make their own investment and managerial de-

Table 6.2
Historical schedule of investment earnings, 1961–1970

	CPF	10 year U.S. Treasury Bonds	Other Plans
1962	-7.40%		
1963	6.97	4.00%	
1964	7.29	4.15	
1965	4.28	4.21	
1966	-10.11	4.66	
1967	23.90	4.85	
1968	3.10	5.25	8.4%
1969	-13.16	6.10	-5.2
Average 1963-69	3.11%	4.15%	
Average 1968-69	-5.06	1.6%	

cisions but they also contracted for actuarial services and used bank trust departments for investment management. Smaller locals with their own funds— for example, the carpenters, some operating engineer locals, and other building trades—used banks exclusively.

1961–1970: The CPF's Birth and "Let the Bank Do It"

When the CPF was established in 1961, contributions from employers represented most of the fund's value. Income earned from investments was fairly insignificant. As noted earlier, employer contributions in 1962 were 99.6 percent of total additions to the fund, and in 1969 they were 94 percent. Therefore, the first CPF trustees reasonably focused on benefit rules, portability, past service, and employer contributions rather than investment management.

In this context, Lane Kirkland and the original trustees of the CPF decided to do what many pension funds and individual investors did at the time: hire a well-known bank, Chase Manhattan, to create and manage a portfolio of investments. The fund also hired an overseer, the investment firm of Smith Barney and Co., to monitor Chase Manhattan's performance. In the 1960s this was typical practice for institutional investors. The original investment philosophy, for the nine years between 1961 and 1970 could be summed up in Reese Hammond's quip, "We let the bank do it."

The investment returns were quite disappointing. Chase earned, on average, just 1.44 percent between 1962 and 1969 (Table 6.2[8]). However, what most concerned the trustees were inconsistencies in the bank's investment recommendations. Wild swings in the proportion of assets allocated to equities varied between 70 percent and 25 percent from year to year. The trustees fired Chase in November of 1969, as noted in Chapter 3.

The financial performance of the CPF reveals some of the sources of concern leading up to Chase being fired. The CPF took a big hit in 1969. The CPF's performance did not necessarily reflect broader trends in the market. The Standard & Poor's (S&P) 500 averaged a 3.24 percent return, with an even performance ranging from 3.0 percent to 3.83 percent. Table 6.2 compares the yearly yields of the CPF with the much less volatile yields on ten-year Treasury Bonds, which were 4.15 percent. The two years (the earliest data available) we have for other pension plans also shows the CPF did worse.

1970–1975: ERISA and Transition

In 1970, the CPF took the first steps to take their "investment destiny" into their own hands. This maturity combined the trustees' developing sense of accountability and activism with their intellectual appreciation of the need to diversify advisors, managers, and assets. This was an evolving condition contingent on several related and unrelated events happening at once. The trustees' disappointment with Chase required a self-examination of their focus on investments. The trustees also knew that investments would be increasingly important for the fund's income and sustenance of benefits.

The experience with Chase Manhattan Bank disabused the trustees of two notions: (1) that there was a straightforward science to investing, and (2) that the stalwarts of finance, the banks, were the best agents to do the work. The trustees realized that investing is more than an art or simple science, but rather a sophisticated process that accounts for the particular needs, desires, comfort, and even philosophy level of each individual fund. Investing for a pension fund, the CPF trustees were learning, requires constant monitoring, evaluation, debate, resolution, self-confidence, and informed decision making.

In 1970, Max Cooper helped the CPF find two investment consultants, J. Parker Hall, former University of Chicago treasurer, and Corliss D. Anderson, an ex-trustee of the United Methodist Fund, to evaluate the performance of the money managers and advise on the management of the portfolio. They advised the fund from 1970 to 1976 before being caught up in the financial revolution explained in the following.

The CPF trustees realized that investing fund assets needed more involvement from them and the expert advisors close at hand. One of the increasingly sophisticated developments in the CPF's investment policy was the use of modern portfolio theory principles ten years before they became widespread in the financial community. That was also more than a decade before it became a standard part of ERISA enforcement. This section explains how that forward-looking investment management practice came about.

The first development was the trustees' realization that prudence was not defined by the trustees picking the best expert. Prudence required a process by which the trustees picked the best expert and made the expert accountable. Over time, the trustees would realize prudence required competent staff and consultants, longevity on the board, and individuals identifying with the status of "trustee" rather than "representative" of union or management. Prudence also required trustees to be responsible, they would have to undertake tremendous self-education in areas in which most union leaders and management representatives do not have substantial background: finance, accounting, and law.

A 1973 quote from Reese Hammond gives a good indication of these early sensibilities that prudent management required of the stewards (the trustees) in order to account for and understand the fund's performance. In an interview for the Department of Labor's journal *Monthly Labor Review* Reese Hammond described the investment goals of the CPF: "because we have an obligation to maximize return within the restriction of prudence, we couldn't leave our money with some mutual fund management whose track record looks like the Teton mountains."[9]

Another development that indicates the value of accountability is the fact that in 1973 the CPF also adopted an "investment policy statement" three years before ERISA required one. An "investment policy statement" is a benchmark and set of goals that the trustees can use to monitor their progress. Jack Johnson's metaphor helps describe its function: "I guess it's my years in the Navy that made me think of it. When you go on ship there are standard orders we, as a crew, constantly referred to. The investment policy statement is like those standing orders."[10]

In sum, one of the CPF trustees' first significant departures from what was then standard practice was their early recognition of the importance of *trustee accountability*.

The second notable development in the CPF's evolving investment practices was that between 1970 and 1979 the fund practiced what would become a logical extension of the modern portfolio theory. Ten years before it became a recommended practical application of the prudent expert standard, the CPF began to construct a well-diversified portfolio, not just by determining an asset allocation but also by diversifying managers.

The strategy was to select a broad asset mix between cash, money market funds, bonds (both fixed-interest and index-linked), corporate equities (both actively managed and indexed), and real estate (both direct placements and pooled trusts). A fixed asset allocation does not attempt to "time" the market. In fact, it prevents the trustees having to time the market and replace bonds with equities when they think the stock market will rise relative to bonds. A fixed allocation embodies the principle of modern portfolio theory that no one investor will know better than any other when this time will be. The mix reflects the belief that each sector will have rates of return that are comparable after the risk, or variability of returns, is taken into account. The second step in the asset allocation strategy is to select managers to make detailed selections within these categories. The CPF had Hall and Anderson to retain and monitor several managers and to help develop an investment strategy. This development, notable for CPF's early use, is called *manager diversification.*

In 1970, four years before ERISA, the CPF was ahead of its time by being concerned with avoiding both conflicts of interests and incompetent investment managers. The CPF showed this concern by paying attention to the investment *process.* This became the ERISA standard for judging prudent and legal investment practices—considering the investment process as well as the results. In October 1969, the board of trustees heard from their Smith Barney consultant, who "cautioned against a dual relationship between a Bank serving as Corporate Trustee and a Financial Advisor. His advice was that fund assets could be split up, but not in too many pieces, and that the investment managers chosen by the board should be given discretion."[11] The dilemma facing the trustees was clear. They had to give leeway to their professionals, but they could not be as distant as they were in their relationship with Chase.

In order to deal with this in the 1970s the CPF began a practice of *active engagement.* As Jack Johnson tells it, "When I first came on board (in early 1970) I had to pick up a lot of routine tasks. I had to trace decisions, follow up on policies. Really I was a comptroller. One thing I found crazy was that we had four separate custodian banks who reported in four different formats. I brought them all together and said "Hey, guys, can't you consolidate these accounts.""[12]

State Street Bank of Boston was the only bank that responded to Johnson's sensible request. They set up their first master trust for the CPF. The bank's wisdom in entering this new field at the CPF's request is a remarkable story, considering that State Street Bank is now the largest master trust manager in the world. The CPF's active engagement made a significant impact on the money management field. The CPF was able to consolidate its control, drop the other custodians, and rationalize its pension fund management.

Another example of active engagement is the CPF's adoption of a policy in the late 1970s to systematically communicate to money managers the importance of voting the CPF shareholder proxies. The trustees and staff recognized that ownership of financial assets entailed a variety of benefits. The chief benefits were of course the direct monetary returns from fund dividends and capital gains. The ability to monitor and exert voting power on underperforming corporations is also a benefit attached to owning shares. Not using those rights was equivalent to squandering fund resources. In 1988, over a decade later, the Department of Labor also realized this, and in the Avon decision, the DOL fine-tuned its regulations to acknowledge that prudent management required trustees to have explicit proxy-voting guidelines, a conclusion the CPF had reached years before. Prudent management required active attention to the potential benefit of owners acting responsibly and scrutinizing management behavior. Considered use of proxies can make the company more valuable to the shareholders.

1976–1992: "Fine-Tuning"

In June of 1978, Jack Johnson organized a seminar on modern portfolio theory for the trustees that was conducted by the A.G. Becker consulting firm for $20,000. This trustee seminar was a watershed event. The trustees learned how complicated asset allocation, diversification of risk, and accountability could be and hired A.G. Becker to serve as consultant, with Richard Ennis as the key Becker staff member involved. When Ennis left Becker in 1980, the CPF hired Ennis, Knupp, and Gold, which later became Ennis, Knupp, and Associates to proceed with the third phase of the CPF's management.

Richard Ennis, along with the staff of A.G. Becker, did the first of a series of studies of the plan in 1979. These studies examined the efficient frontier, the technical name for the combination of assets with the same risk-adjusted rate of return determine how the fund could get maximum return for least risk. Here again, the CPF was ahead of its time by accounting, in a less formal way, for the structure of liabilities as well as assets in the late 1970s and early 1980s, although the first formal asset-to-liability study was done in 1986. Much of the CPF's precocity can be explained by the incentives that come with bad luck. The poor investment performance in the 1960s and 1970s encouraged the CPF to pursue the best thinking and cutting-edge innovations in asset management.

The CPF first commissioned their investment policy study in 1979 by simulating with a computer various kinds of risk and return possibilities. Most importantly, the study examined how various possibilities would effect the "funding standard account" (FSA) and the ratio of plan assets to vested benefits. The effects were shown under three hypothetical situations: a boom, a bust, and a normal situation.

Evaluating the investment philosophy in terms of the effect on these accounts, the funding standard account and the ratio of assets to liabilities reflect the heart and soul of an investment creed. In the end, these are the two measures for which the trustees are held accountable. Therefore, it is worthwhile to describe what they are.

The FSA demonstrates that the plan has satisfied ERISA's minimum funding standard. Projections of the FSA indicate the projected well-being of the plan, or whether the plan is affordable. The ratio of market value of assets to vested benefits is more straightforward. It is the figure that would be relevant if the plan stopped operating today. This ratio measures withdrawal liability.

In 1979, the study recommended that the trustees periodically specify the desired target level of equities. To understand this recommendation, one needs only to recall the rule-of-thumb advice given to individuals: hold a percentage of your portfolio in stocks equal to 100 minus your age. This tactic rejects the philosophy that one can "time" the stock market, moving in and out when one expects the market to change and no one else thinks so. This philosophy is also derived from modern portfolio theory, which says diversifying to get maximum return for minimum risk should be every investor's goal.

In 1982, real estate was added. In 1984, small company stocks and assets with different maturities were also added. In 1993, the consultant suggested increasing the asset allocation in equities from 37 percent to 40 percent, exploring alternative fixed-income and value-added equity strategies (this refers to different kinds of active equity investing, which amounts to only 9 percent of the CPF's equity holdings), reducing the real estate target to 5 percent from its actual 6 percent allocation, reducing its allocation in short-term government bonds, and reviewing international equity mangers. The board accepted all recommendations but the last.

"Indexer"

The CPF's unusual investment policy harkens back to its origins—a commitment to professionalism and independence, and a suspicion of professional portfolio managers. CPF leadership decries pension funds paying large fees to active stock and bond managers, who do not beat the market but merely "window dress" to show high returns at reporting time, or who the leadership suspect of "churning" to generate fees.[13] Therefore, in 1993 the CPF's equities were 82 percent passively indexed, whereas its bonds were 81 percent passively managed.

Indexing means that the stocks owned are weighted according to their value in the Wilshire 5000 index, a portfolio that attempts to exactly match the capital market return. The management fees are a fraction the fees active managers charge, and performance is about the same or better. When the trustees hired Jack Johnson in 1970, they hired someone with a high degree of concern for workers' old-age security that led to a passion for the financial literature and personal dedication to the fund. He essentially rewrote his job description and steered the fund toward modern and efficient practices. Twenty-five years later these concerns are summarized by his personalized license plate, "INDEXER."

Why not all passive? In the words of the former long-time trustee and "CPF-grandfather," Reese Hammond, "We do not want to turn our backs on the capitalist system." Hammond echoes the more technical critics of indexing, who argue that markets will not work if every one stops seeking information they hope will yield a self-opportune profit.

The commonplace criticism to indexers is that if everyone was indexed there would be no one left to "make the market." How would the market deliver information if everyone stopped trading on information? This is the classic fallacy of composition. What is good for the one is not always good for the whole. Johnson replies that there needs to be far less financial trading than there is, but he also acknowledges that some active trading is necessary.

The argument embodied in Hammond's quote is that pension funds have a "social service" duty, or that pension funds should do some active trading so that meaningful, new information causes share and bond prices to change accordingly. This argument for active trading illustrates how pension investment

Table 6.3
The CPF's portfolio: 1976–1991

Year	Equities	Fixed Income	Cash	Real Estate	GIC's
1976	49%	23%	18%	1%	9%
1977	44	26	16	1	13
1978	39	25	18	1	17
1979	31	30	14	1	23
1980	32	32	10	2	22
1981	31	22	20	2	23
1982	30	31	16	1	20
1983	30	31	16	3	18
1984	29	36	13	5	15
1985	29	35	17	6	11
1986	30	38	15	7	7
1987	31	40	12	10	5
1988	32	38	14	11	3
1989	30	39	16	11	2
1990	30	40	15	12	2
1991	35	42	10	9	2

advisors see themselves and their behavior affecting a wider world. This "social responsibility" of capitalism may also explain why another part of the CPF's investment strategy flies directly in the face of passive indexing, making the CPF out as an aggressive, self-actualizing group of investors. These self-conscious and socially conscious investment strategies are discussed in Part Two.

CPF Performance in the 1982–1990 Benchmarks

The CPF is a bit more conservative than most other union-management trusteed pension funds. Table 6.3 shows that the CPF actually reduced its equity holdings and increased its bond holdings from 1978 to 1992 the opposite of the average tendency of union-management trusteed plans to increase stock holdings relative to bonds.[14]

The trustees have to continually evaluate whether the outcomes of their decisions make sense. The relevant criterion is whether, given a certain tolerance for risk, the fund received a satisfactory rate of return when compared with other investors and funds. The benchmark has to compare returns of other funds that have similar risk levels. The CPF depends on the investment consultant, the same consultant who advises on the level of risk and the way to achieve it, to devise the benchmark.

The consultant creates a standard and unique benchmark that serves the large universe of union-management trusteed plans. The standard benchmark compares the CPF's fund to a hypothetical fund made up of the assets that receive actual average yields for that asset category. The consultant calculates this standard performance benchmark by assuming the hypothetical portfolio holds the same share of each asset class the CPF does. Clearly, the fund could passively invest in a representative sample of assets from each asset class and get the average return for a given level of risk. Thus, anything over this passive or minimum requirement means superior performance. The CPF earned 11.6 percent between December 30, 1977, and June 30, 1993. The performance benchmark earned 10.8 percent and long-term bonds yielded about 10.7 percent with almost twice as much volatility.

CONCLUSION: TOWARD SOPHISTICATED MANAGEMENT

For most of the CPF's history, what the fund could afford determined the benefits promised. This sentiment is shared by Reese Hammond and Jack Johnson as well as other trustees and staff and made sense when assets were growing much faster than liabilities. The argument that fund size wagged the benefit-promise tail is confirmed by the CPF's record of benefit improvements in relationship to its funded status. When assets exceeded liabilities by about 50 percent, the trustees would raise benefits, increasing liabilities and lowering funded status. In 1991 the Trustees, for reasons discussed in Chapter 5, raised benefits so that the funded status fell below the traditional funding cushion. This has added new focus on asset-liability studies, which concentrate on predicted liabilities and the fund's ability to meet them.

There has been a fundamental shift in the focus of the CPF, and many other mature pension plans from fund size to benefits promised. This shift can be explained by three structural changes moving through time. At first, the fund was so small that the laissez-faire attitude "Let the bank do it" was justified. Later, as investment income soared, managing assets to get the most return for the smallest risk became a key focus. Investing to maximize risk-adjusted returns seeks the largest fund possible. In contrast, asset-liability adjusts the focus away from the sole target of maximizing the fund size and toward fund liabilities, integrated examinations of the fund in relationship to the benefits promised. When liabilities grow faster than income in mature plans, managing and paying for promises (made but not entirely paid for in the past) becomes a crucial concern of pension fund management.

This integrated approach, which makes investment decisions partly based on when benefits are due, can be viewed as a general trend toward a broader and more holistic approach to pension fund management. For decades, some union-management trusteed funds more than others have always taken a broad approach in its investment responsibilities. These have sought to invest in vehicles that bring jobs to the union sector, and to engage in shareholder activism that brings value to the company.

The change from letting the income drive the benefits to the benefits driving the fund illustrates the many roles a pension fund has, such as when it is sponsored by a union and a unionized industry. A pension plan has nuances and dimensions not found in an insurance company. The pension fund exists within the framework of industry and union health. There is a creative tension between the needs of the pension fund as a fund that pays annuities and as an institution that affects employers and workers' loyalty to a trade and to institutions that maintain the trade's status and skilled labor force.

The second part of the chapter is a distinct break from the descriptive analyses of CPF's practices and performance. The next section explores the unique political economy aspects of investing a union pension fund when the fund is succeeding and the unionized industry is faltering.

The developing science of investing brought about significant changes in the institutions doing, advising, and monitoring pension investing. Part Two shows how this science was enthusiastically embraced because it offered an approved code of behavior that, if followed, would blunt criticism that union management was corrupt at worst and inefficient at best.

The CPF and Wall Street's Financial Revolution

It is not easy to appreciate the CPF's investment innovation without understanding a bit about the history of financial management. The 1970s were not kind to Wall Street or the holders of bonds and stocks. The oil embargo, soaring interest rates, and the threat of inflation led to Nixon's wage and price controls. This meant uncertainty about the direction of corporate profits and Wall Street was volatile and depressed. Trustees, who had to make financial decisions that determined many people's livelihood, were nervous. The "Teton Mountain" performance of the stock market in the 1970s caused a financial revolution that led to modern portfolio theory. Table 6.4[15] suggests why there was a "financial revolution" in investing in the 1970s. The CPF's diligent board of trustees and esteemed, hand-picked investment advisors did worse than medium-term, perfectly safe government bonds. The CPF was not alone. Other pension plans did worse than ten-year treasuries, but none as badly as the CPF.

Not only was the CPF ready for new ideas, but the unsteady, lackluster performance of the stock market made Wall Street ready for new ideas as well.[16] The S&P 500 earned an average of 6.6 percent from 1970 to 1978, but it ranged from a high of 37.2 percent in 1975 to a low of minus 26.5 percent in 1974.

Modern portfolio theory had been around in universities and think tanks since the 1960s. It turned conventional theory on its head. What investment and portfolio managers "stock picked" before the 1970s? Investment firms had scads of researchers and analysts who surveyed the "fundamentals" and attempted to

Table 6.4
Historical schedule of investment earnings, 1970–1978

	CPF	10 year US Treasury Bonds	Private Pension Plans
1970	11.14%	6.59%	1.3%
1971	NA	5.74	17.5
1972	16.73	5.63	15.3
1973	5.8	6.30	-15.1
1974	-16.62	6.99	-20.3
1975	-10.05	6.98	23.1
1976	21.07	6.78	17.2
1977	1.95	7.06	-2.2
1978	-1.08	7.89	5.8
Average			
1970-78	3.61	6.66	4.7
1972-78	2.54	6.80	3.4

pick the most profitable companies. This strategy required investors to think they could predict the winners before anyone else. Modern portfolio theory contradicted this conventional strategy.

Modern portfolio theory says basically that no one bank, analyst, or individual could know which stock is better than any other because, as soon as one person knows it, everyone knows it. The only thing an investor can do, the theory continues is to diversify as much as possible, but in a very special way. The diversification should be designed so that risks are minimized by canceling each other out. The savvy investor, modern portfolio theory concludes, knows that all asset values will go up and down. The skill and trick is to own assets that go up when the others you own go down. The performance of Wall Street in the 1970s shook confidence in the old investment regime.

This new idea gradually trickled down to pension trustees. Cheaper computer capacity made constructing a diversified portfolio easier, while deregulation caused trading fees to fall threefold. These developments made modern portfolio theory practical and operational by the late 1970s, whereas the CPF had already adopted elements of modern portfolio theory early in the same decade.

By 1976, the CPF trustees, especially Hammond, felt the advisors were too traditional in their "stock pick" and "buy and hold" strategies and had less than success to show for it. The CPF trustees felt their return and approach was faded and weak. Jack Johnson, although hired as an administrative executive, was on top of the cutting edge of financial market intellectual ideas. The trustees agreed that the consultants from the "Old World" would not meet the challenge and promise of modern portfolio theory head on. Modern portfolio theory's key tenet is to decide on the relative shares of assets in a fund in order to balance risk and return, not to stock pick. The CPF knew that *portfolio diversification* was the wave of the future and began to ride it.

In sum, in the second phase of the CPFs investment policy development we see the CPF engaging in innovative behavior described here as: *trustee accountability, active engagement, management diversification,* and *portfolio diversification.*

PART TWO: CONTRADICTIONS AND CONFLICT IN PENSION INVESTMENT

The CPF was born into the culture of scrutiny, the legacy of suspicion, and the scientific revolution in finance. The CPF's professionalism, clean record, and timely benefit payments, made the CPF a model for the 1974 ERISA legislation that would lead many union plans to professionalize. To professionalize meant to secure an enrolled actuary, report all conflict of interest transactions, to not invest in one's own sponsor, and to diversify within reason. This reasonable standard, also referred to as prudence, put a large premium on a process that privileged conformity, for what was reasonable had been simplistically defined as what the majority practices.

As Chapter 2 documented, the nation's interest in organized labor was partly aroused by the emergence of multi-million-dollar pension funds controlled by unions after World War II. It did not escape notice that these monies represented significant potential power. Indeed a Jesuit priest, Paul Harbrecht, published the well-regarded book about unions and pension funds, *Pension Funds and Economic Power,* in 1959. The high-profile battle between Robert Kennedy and Jimmy Hoffa occurred in the context of the 1958–1959 McClellan Committee hearings that accused unions of many things, including stealing from and misusing pension funds. These hearings prompted Congress to pass the Labor-Management Reporting and Disclosure Act, or Landrum Griffin Act, in 1959, just one year before the IUOE established the CPF. The Landrum Griffin Act has been called the union membership's "Bill of Rights." Although it did not deal specifically with union pension fund activity, its overall effect was to increase the amount of "sunshine" on union activities in general. Sunshine is a metaphor that refers to the benefits of exposure. Exposure of information leads to accountability and hopefully responsible behavior. This requirement of accountability helped fuel the trend in financial management toward science-based criteria.[17] The science, which was the subject of this chapter's first section, reduces financial asset ownership into two characteristics, risk and return. The concepts of investor relationships, owner responsibilities, and creation of jobs are too difficult to measure, and thus are not given as much attention as the solid measures of return and risk.

These science-based metaphors can hinder common sense investment activity. Nonetheless, the trend has to be seen in a context where accountability about investment strategies was slim and performance was terrible. In addition, there were vigorous attacks on union pension fund management. Below, we examine two areas. First, inefficiencies, and second, malfeasance and fraud.

Inefficient Management

Chapter 7 examines the CPFs administrative practices in depth and addresses the issue whether large funds are cheaper to run than small funds. It is presumed in 1994 as it was in the 1970s, that practicing modern portfolio theory takes computer capacity and financial expertise, placing obvious advantages on having large amounts of money handled by one office. For instance, the Department of Labor's report on construction bargaining cited many problems in construction, including the administrative costs incurred by the proliferation of local health and pension plans: "Contractors have charged for years that the large number of units in this industry has been a major cause of jurisdictional disputes, whip-sawing tactics which escalate wage settlements, and a proliferation of pension and welfare funds which inflates costs and reduces labor mobility."[18]

Olivia Mitchell and Emily Andrews found in 1980 that multiemployer funds experienced scale economies in administrative expenses. By being a national centralized plan, the CPF eliminated many of these diseconomies of scale and has achieved impressive decreases in relative fees as its assets have grown. The economies of scale come mainly from consolidating operating costs of collection, auditing, and distribution of checks, and paying smaller fees to twenty-six separate investment managers. Yet blaming the construction trades for inefficient proliferation seems misplaced since 84 percent of all single-employer defined benefit plans have fewer than 100 participants compared to under 9 percent of multiemployer defined benefit plans.[19]

Conflict of Interest: SEC Recommendations for Union-Management Trusteed Plans

"The specter of Teamster pension abuses hangs over the entire pension field,"[20] said the Securities and Exchange Commission (SEC) in 1977. The SEC was complaining of conflicts of interest due to union-dominance and limited employer scrutiny that could cause malfeasance—noncriminal mistakes or poor judgment—or fraud in attempts to meet union political goals or obtain valuable kickbacks from vendors and investment projects. The SEC recommended three changes in union-management trusteed funds to curb malfeasance and fraud that never were implemented: (1) reorganize the boards to have three-year terms for trustees, neutral third parties, and mandatory high quorums to encourage management-trustee participation; (2) federal supervision of employer contributions to decrease the role of the union in collecting delinquencies; and (3) reconsider the ERISA "prudent expert" rule, interpreted to limit the ability of pension funds to target investments for their ancillary benefits.[21] For example, union funds are inhibited (but not curbed) from targeting funds to create union jobs. Single-employer plans also may not invest more than 10 percent of their own stock.[22]

The SEC used the experience of the United Mine Workers fund to argue for a third-party trustee on union-management trusteed pension fund boards of trustees. The courts appointed Paul Dean as the third-party trustee of that fund. Dean served in that role from 1974 to 1994, although no one replaced him. Ian D. Lanoff, a prominent fiduciary lawyer specializing in pension plans and the former administrator for the Pension Benefits Welfare Administration under the Ford and Carter administrations who started his career working with Dean, assesses the SEC recommendation by noting that

human nature makes it almost impossible for employer and union trustees to always take off their hats as labor or business representatives and act like trustees whose only interests are the interests of the participants. The third party trustee can strengthen the aims of ERISA to take collective bargaining away from the pension management table. The third party trustee can sometimes solve the two hat problem.[23]

But Lanoff is careful not to endorse a blanket requirement that third-party trustees be imposed on all pension trusts. Any potential benefits depend on the situation and the character of the trustees. He confirms that third-party trustees are unnecessary when trustees identify themselves with the overwhelming goal to manage the fund for the sole benefit of the participants. Yet Lanoff acknowledges that new trustees have difficulty appreciating the differences between the interests of those who appointed them and the interests of the plan participants. As the trustees stay on the job longer, this confusion diminishes.

Lanoff's general comments describe the CPF's character well. The longevity of the trustees had made them confident enough in their trustee role to act as good independent counsel. A good example is the 1993 CPF debate over foreign equities. Ironically, in this case, the trustees boldly asserted the legitimacy of questioning whether their interpretation of their fiduciary responsibility required them to invest in anything that may have a marginally higher rate of return.

The fact that the trustees have so much tenure makes them independent from the staff and from other parties-in-interest, such as the union. They did not rebuff staffer Ennis' suggestion to invest in global equities, but they did ask detailed questions about the way the equities would be selected and gauged.

The CPF is unusual among pension plans in trying to minimize conflicted interests. It has an explicitly written ethical statement and it requires that all trustees report contact they have with vendors. The CPF rarely allows vendors to make sales pitches to the board (the few exceptions are the AFL-CIO affiliated trusts, ULLICO and the HIT/BIT). Many large union-management trusteed plans have a constant stream of vendors and are managed by a large investment management and benefits firm that has few funds among its clients that are not union dominated. CPF trustees wonder how difficult it might be under those circumstances to separate the interests of the union from those of its potential retirees.

The CPF prides itself on its integrity and professionalism. The tenure of the trustees is quite long, which, in contrast to Blodgett's conclusions, seems to have created a sense of loyalty to the role of trustee and independence from union politics. The CPF is also atypical of union-management trusteed funds by having in-house professionals. When the job is to be accountable and responsible in obtaining the best risk-adjusted return, the funds staff believes that following modern portfolio theory is the professional course of action. But administering the CPF requires more than a staff of professionals. It also requires the decisions and vision of the trustees. The next section focuses on the union pension fund trustee.

Social Investing and the Two-Hat Problem

The conflictual roles trustees have stem from ERISA, its intellectual roots in modern portfolio theory, and the way the professionals have interpreted ERISA during the last twenty years. It also stems from the two-hat problem. When union trustees wear their trustee hat they want high rates of return, even if it might possibly mean investing in companies that slash workforces and cut wages. When they wear their union hat they want high standards of living for workers and long-term growth.

The discussion of investment management above has described the science in portfolio management. Ennis, Knupp and Associates, with the competent help of Jack Johnson, have purged investment decisions from political pressure and sleazy pitches by vendors. The CPF is in the vanguard for using indexed funds and state of the art, finely tuned benchmarks to judge performance.

But the fund is not run by the professionals and their scientific and necessarily narrow perspective. The trustees are forceful, independent, and responsible, partly because, as was argued in Chapter 3, they have long tenure. The trustees are committed to run the fund, but they also bring the concerns of the industries, companies, and unions they represent to the trustee table, the finance committee table, and indeed, to the dinner table. One cannot separate conflicting roles within one body and one mind.

Coping with Conflict of Roles

Human psychology does not like conflict and the human mind finds many ways to overcome it. Some people actively seek ways to resolve the conflict, such as searching for investments that simultaneously earn a high rate of return and have good social value. The dilemma inherent in being a good representative and a good neutral can be solved by tactics and institutions that create statements that both maximize profit and social welfare. They want to do well by doing good. These institutions and tactics are called, for the purposes of this section, the growing field of economically targeted investments (ETIs), investments that have attractive ancillary returns in addition to having high monetary rates of return. These ancillary benefits are long-term growth, stability, and job creation.

The other strategy used to cope when people or institutions try to meet two conflicting goals is to decide which goal is more important. If two conflicting goals are good, such as earning the highest rate of return on an investment and building housing with union labor, solve the conflict by picking the most important goal. ERISA and its intellectual foundation, modern portfolio theory, along with the capital asset pricing model, solve the conflict through the latter method by choosing sides. Risk-adjusted rates of return are more important than any other collateral benefit. The retort to this focus is the concern that maximizing income to the fund could threaten the survival of the fund itself.

Modern Portfolio Theory and What Is "Prudent"

The current interpretations of ERISA answers this question and solves the human conflict by establishing that rates of return adjusted for risk are the most important goal for a pension trustee. Most union trustees then presume they need not be haunted by the critical questions about how to solve their two-hat problem. These challenges have been solved by ERISA and modern portfolio theory.

If union trustees were true believers in modern portfolio theory, they would believe that maximizing return for the least risk is the best way capital gets allocated in the financial markets. Poorly managed firms in undesirable markets will be punished by investors seeking the risk-adjusted highest rate and the best firms will have the highest risk-adjusted rates of return and will be rewarded by pension funds buying their shares and bonds.

The return-maximizing trustee would not be anguished. He or she would be confident that even if Kodak loses jobs and hurts the New York economy, a firm that can best use the resources will hire the workers, borrow capital, and do better than Kodak did. All this time they would reward the pension fund with good returns and profits. All the more, if the best use means paying less than workers have been earning, then it is the workers' fault for not being more productive and valuable. This scenario may or may not happen, but the conviction that it will makes the investment decision easier.

Sacrificing even one percentage point can make a big difference. Compound interest makes it necessary to get the highest rate because small increments can make a big difference. The way the market is supposed to work is summed up by President Bush's Assistant Labor Secretary for pensions, David George Ball, who warned that we should guard against artificial incentives to investments that would not otherwise be made in a free market. In his view, unfettered capital markets have been and will continue to be the lifeblood of economic growth.[24]

Regulated Markets and the Financial Revolution

This view that markets are not to be interfered with is rather new and unorthodox given recent American history. The Great Depression was very much seen as a failure of the financial sector and a result of the dangers of speculation. A complex system of rules and regulations was designed to get capital to needed areas and to minimize panics. The attitude described in Ball's quote came along with the financial revolution of the early 1970s. This financial revolution had five characteristics and greatly influenced how the CPF operates today.

First, ERISA passed in 1974 mainly because of the tragedies that occurred when companies reneged on their pension promises because of corporate restructuring, bankruptcy, and underfunded pension plans. After ERISA was passed and minimum funding standards were established, money flowed into pension funds and began to transform institutional investors into major market players. Second, the October 1974 stock market crash (the worst since 1929) shook confidence in the old regime of investment practices. This made the premier issue of the *Journal of Portfolio Management* (the first issue happened to be published in 1974)—an outlet for academics promoting modern portfolio theory—particularly welcome on Wall Street.[25] As described earlier, modern portfolio theory advises a diverse portfolio to minimize risk by reducing each equity to just two components, risk and return, thus supplanting the buy-and-hold strategy of equity purchasers. Liquidity became a favorable portfolio characteristic. Third, in the early 1970s, cheaper computer capacity became available to implement a large number of trades and stock analysis, making modern portfolio theory practical. Fourth, the Securities Act amendments in 1975 fully deregulated broker fees and commissions and average fees fell from $0.34 to $0.26 per trade to $0.075 so that investor behavior was no longer dominated by the social rules and customs of a few traders. Last, but of paramount importance, the profitability of American corporations declined considerably in the 1970s and 1980s.[26] Furthermore, rapid trading and a market for corporate control was propelled by a growing group of institutional investors. In sum, ERISA biased investor behavior toward maximizing short-term rates of return to separate managers from owners.[27]

But what if seeking the highest rates in the short term has collateral effects that reduce the rate of return for the fund in latter periods? What if there are feedback effects, such as closing down a plant, which has a multiplier effect downward, making a geographical location an unattractive environment for investment, and no firm comes in? What if poor management can be corrected by means other than threatening to leave? What if market rate of return is not a good signal for estimating performance? If these questions are legitimate, there is no longer a simple choice between choosing goals and creating ETI. The trustee life becomes more complicated, yet modern portfolio theory tends to make it simple. In some respects modern portfolio theory did make regulation and trustees' decisions easier by simplifying the criteria investment decisions had to meet. Pension funds are for pensions, but pensions rely on investment returns and jobs.

ERISA and modern portfolio theory modernized the investment activities of the pre-ERISA fund managers and of all portfolio managers. With its sophisticated formulas, the theory demonstrates that if one invests in vehicles that have covariance risk, the firm reduces its overall risk. That means that almost no investment is too risky if it has a high enough return. The prudence of the choice to buy a particular vehicle has to be seen in the context of the entire portfolio. This meant that high-risk real estate venture capital and safe yet boring bonds all needed to be in each portfolio.

The Case of Foreign Investing

In 1993, Richard Ennis, with the assistance of Jack Johnson, recommended to the trustees that they could get higher return, based on the past performance of the different accounts, if they moved some of the fund into global equities. The International Foundation for Employee Benefit Plans' National Opinion Survey in 1991 reported that 72 percent of multiemployer plans said they would increase their international investments. The AFL-CIO pension committee has also examined the conditions in which foreign investing may be a good alternative for union pension funds.

Vocal trustees arguing against investing in foreign funds objected and in 1994 rejected the professional's and staff's advice to buy globals. They had two objections. First, Johnson and Ennis proposed to choose nations and then choose the best companies within those nations. Richard Griffin reports that the experts could not give enough persuasive examples. The trustees pressed for details and learned that although such examples made sense theoretically, no fund had successfully operationalized these principles. Second, the trustees wondered how pension funds would perform their role as engaged shareholder activists if they owned foreign shares. If the pension fund's goals, they argue, are to take on responsibility along with ownership, vote proxies, and introduce shareholder resolutions, there is no plan to participate in the corporate governance of foreign firms. In fact, U.S. corporate pension funds are demanding that non-U.S. firms allow for more shareholder participation in corporate governance. They want English-language meetings and reports, access to proxy votes, and shareholder resolutions.[28]

The foreign investing conflict between the CPF trustees and its professionals illustrates the acceptance of modern portfolio theory in the pension management industry and its use in interpreting what is meant by prudence under ERISA. Modern portfolio theory merely requires maximizing return adjusted for risk. This eliminates any musings and quandaries about shareholder responsibility. Modern portfolio theory does not quantify the benefits of shareholder resolutions. The risk and return rule directs the professionals to recommend that the CPF invest in global funds, even if the advantage to the fund is equal. In some ways, ERISA embracing modern portfolio theory was refreshing. It changed investment norms of behavior and sanctioned funds investing in many more risky assets, such as venture capital and stock. However, it did not challenge socially conscious investing.

The pension fund trustees, CPF included, have had to lead contradictory lives. On one hand, they are there to promote participants' well-being, both while they are working and after they retire. On the other hand, they seek to earn the highest yield in order to enlarge fund assets. It is in this context that they resist investing in international stocks, feeling that many U.S. projects still need funds. However, modern portfolio theory and ERISA do not help trustees who try to maximize the fund size and the size of the participant base. The only way trustees can avoid lending to firms that threaten union construction, for instance, is by boycotting egregious firms on an ad hoc basis. The CPF boycotts Marriott, Haliburton and Boise-Cascade, three aggressively anti-union companies.

The Pension Fund as Shareholder Activist

The crack in ERISA's adherence to modern portfolio theory came in the form of the Avon letter. In 1988, the letter suggested that proxy votes were a valuable part of the ownership and that managers had a fiduciary responsibility not to passively vote for management initiatives as a matter of policy. The CPF had decided in the mid-1980s that the fund would always record each manager's vote. The fund has its own proxy voting system, which requires investment managers either to vote proxies in accordance with their shareholder voting proxy guide or explain any variance with the CPF's directives. This policy has had some effect. In 1989, the CPF managers voted with management 98.2 percent of the time and by 1993 they voted 93 percent of the time.

Another way that unions have increased their clout vis-à-vis management is by being a part of the Council of Institutional Investors (CII). Jesse Unruh, the fiery and innovative California state treasurer, realized early in 1975 that the pension funds cannot do the "Wall Street walk." That was the rule that if a stock does poorly, sell it and just walk away. Unruh formed the Council of Institutional Investors to represent pension funds collectively in their dealings with corporations as owners.

There is some controversy because the CII has invited corporate pension funds to be represented. The most important controversy, however, is indicated by trustee Griffin's lament: Who does the CPF represent? Pension funds as shareholders, or pension funds that maximize participant interests?

Creating Jobs

The CPF has supported the AFL-CIO's forays into social investment, but mostly for political reasons rather than any ideological commitment to using the money to create new jobs or to bypassing capital markets that do not value what is meaningful to labor. The CPF was always aware of the union's ability to use pension funds as leverage and in creating jobs. Part of the fund's policy with signatory locals and their employers was that the direct investment portion of the fund—almost all real estate—would be spread proportionately to the different conferences.

An independent consulting service, the Marco Group, reported that union-oriented investment funds had similar and sometimes superior performance compared to standard mortgage and real estate funds. In the three, five, and ten years previous to 1992, the ASB Capital Management's Employee Benefit Real Estate and the Multi-Employer Property Trust outperformed the industry standard benchmark, the Open End Equity Funds. But consistent with the ETI, one must know that the Housing Investment Trust (HIT) and Building Investment Trust (BIT) funds that have a union-only investment policy have risk and return characteristics competitive with traditional investment vehicles. The jobs created with the union-directed accounts may have been created without the HIT/BIT capital, but perhaps the areas invested may have been invested anyway. What is certain is that because the funds were available only for union labor and that labor did not lose contributions or bargaining strength because of the new construction.

Therefore, union pension funds are known for creating vehicles to use pension fund money to create their own demand by investing in union-only construction projects. Yet the operating engineers are not likely to be in the forefront of such investing to meet individual and narrow goals because union-built, real-estate-related construction involves few workers from their jurisdiction. Highways, however, are a different matter. In 1993, General President Frank Hanley was an active member of the Senate's Commission on Infrastructure. The commission investigated ways to provide taxable bonds used to finance public works. This device would surmount a huge, unintentional problem. Pension funds are not attracted to tax-free municipal bonds because they are already tax exempt. Here tax policy sabotaged itself by attempting to encourage the formation of pension funds and public works by deferring pension fund earnings, contributions, and municipal bonds from tax. But perversely this meant that a large share of the capital markets was excluded from municipal bonds because their rates of return were discounted to attract only investors who needed the tax shelter.

What Can Go Wrong: An ETI Tragedy

In the late 1970s, Dennis Walton, president of an ambitious and aggressive IUOE local in Florida, wanted to leverage his local's pension fund to help his local gain strength. He directed most of his funds into four properties, including his own union headquarters. The investments looked promising and they were made in the heat of the hot Florida real estate market. But in the late 1980s the Florida real estate market crashed and now the fund owes money.

The controversy over unorthodox investment practices by union-management trusteed pension funds is put into perspective by examining the behavior and incentives of corporate plans. The CPF's investment policy explicitly addresses the purpose of the pension funds and the overall objective of the fund. The last sentence reads: "Should the assets of the Trust appreciate on a significant long term basis so that the additional funds do become available, the Board, with the concurrence and assistance of its consultants and actuaries, will utilize such gain to liberalize plan provisions." The next section illustrates an entirely different set of incentives for corporate plans.

Comparing Corporate and Union-Management Trusteed Pension Fund Investment Strategies and Incentives

Before suspicion arises in the minds of the reader that unions will run away with the pension fund money if regulations allow consideration of anything other than rate of return in the investment decisions, one should note what happens when corporations manage their plans without such scrutiny. Corporate sponsors have practiced another kind of social investing.

Single-employer plans are less well-funded than union-management trusteed plans. The union-management trusteed fund at the PBGC ran a small deficit in 1980 and has been increasing its surplus every year since, whereas the single-employer fund has increased its deficit every year since 1981.[29] Much of the credit can be attributed to withdrawal liability and the inherent risk adverseness of union-management trusteed plans. Employers who withdraw from an underfunded union-management trusteed plan are liable for part of the unfunded liabilities, even if they did not create it. Therefore, it is very difficult to organize employers into underfunded plans. This is why management and the union trustees of the CPF want to keep assets greater than liabilities. Another reason union-management trusteed plans are better funded is because they have no corporate treasuries to fall back on if assets come short of liabilities.[30]

As a result, union-management trusteed plans are generally more conservatively invested than corporate plans. For instance, they hold about ten percentage points less equities than corporate plans.

Simultaneously, single-employer plans have incentives to erode funding standards. The corporate profit squeeze of the late 1970s and 1980s encouraged such funds to reduce pension contributions, and to terminate and revert excess assets to supplement corporate treasuries.[31] The single-employer pension fund sponsor incorporates pension funding decisions into their corporate finance decisions so that as firm profits are squeezed, so are the pension fund assets and benefits.

In contrast, employer trustees in union-management trusteed funds are far removed from the financial decisions of their firms. No one employer dominates the management trustees. At worst, the goal of a corrupt trustee would be to maximize the amount of money in the fund and consequently the pension benefits. That would be true even if they want to give consulting work to their friends or invest to meet political needs, although this is illegal.

One piece of evidence that corporate plans are managed differently than union plans is found in the higher actuarial interest rate assumptions in company plans. A higher rate means that companies predict their funds will earn higher returns and they are therefore required to contribute less each year. For 1987, the mean actuarial interest rate for single-employer plans was 7.9 percent compared with 6.9 percent for multiemployer plans and in 1981, the average was again a full percentage point higher, 7.3 percent compared to the multiemployer rate of 6.2 percent. The union plans were much more conservative (authors' calculations for the Form 5500).

CONCLUSION: EVOLVING STRATEGIES AND CHALLENGES

Perhaps the beauty of ERISA is that it attempts to enforce practices that separate the actual participants temptations from their decisions. ERISA and the science of modern portfolio theory represents the philosophy that investors should be unconcerned to an extreme about any aspect of an investment other than risk and return. There is, however, a creative tension between modern portfolio theory and union activism.

The CPF, with little modification, proceeds with its investment policy in a professional manner. There are three reasons for this professionalism: the long staff tenure, the long tenure of the trustees, and the lack of pressure and incentives to curry the favor of vendors or to steer investments into particular areas for peripheral reasons. This chapter emphasized two points: first, that the fund follows standard investment practices inspired by modern portfolio theory, and second, how important earnings are to a fund such as the CPF, which has seen its various funding accounts and cushion disappear. The fund would seem to be in some potential trouble, the same trouble facing all funds that have decreasing participants and lower returns, although the lower returns have not yet occurred. The actual rate of return in 1993 was over 12, which far exceeded the assumed rate of 7.75 percent.

What will the CPF and other pension funds do if and when, after a decade of soaring stock and bond markets, the markets turn down? Underfunded plans will face problems first, of course. One choice will be to increase contributions, as health and welfare funds first did when faced with rising health care costs. The second choice will be to reduce promised benefits, because a trust cannot reduce current explicit benefits (remember the cost-of-living increases are not contractually promised to their retirees). The third response, albeit marginally useful, will be to cut fund expenses, the most important of which are the investing expenses.

The CPF is in relatively good shape. It has already adopted a policy of passive investing so that doing more indexing to lower administrative costs would be difficult. The fund is as diversified as possible, capturing all that modern port-folio theory has to offer. The only exception is a slightly lower exposure to foreign equities. This investment position is rather uncontroversial. The lively challenge to investment policy will be the fund's ongoing struggle with the irony that what has made the fund so rich in the 1980s is impoverishing the labor movement and CPF employers. That paradox remains to be resolved.

NOTES

1. Sophie Korczyk, "Gender Issues in Employer Pension Policy," *Pensions in a Changing Economy*, edited by Richard Burkhaueser and Dallas L. Salisbury (Washington, D.C.: EBRI and NAC Aging, 1993).

2. John Williamson and Frederick Pampel, *Old Age Income Security in Comparative Perspective* (Oxford University Press: Oxford, 1993).

3. Council of Economic Advisors, *Economic Report of the President*.

4. Laurence Kotlikoff, *Generation Accounting* (New York: Macmillan, 1992).

5. CPF.

6. Stuart Dorsey and John A. Turner, "Union and Nonunion Differences in Pension Fund Investments and Earnings," *Industrial and Labor Relations Review* (July 1990): 543–55.

7. T. R. Price reports from Solomon Brothers; Standard and Poor's; Frank Russell International, Russell-NCREIF Property Index; *Insights*, Vol. 1, No. 210, ca. 1993.

8. U.S. Department of Commerce, *Business and Statistics: 1963–1992* (Government Printing Office: Washington, D.C.).

9. J. Quirt, "Labor Leader Profile: Reese Hammond," *Monthly Labor Review* (July 1993), 51.

10. Jack Johnson, telephone interview by Teresa Ghilarducci, tape recording, 20 June 1994.

11. CPF, *Board of Trustees Minutes* (October 1969), 34.

12. Johnson, 20 June 1994.

13. Josef Lakonishok, Andrei Shleifer, and Robert Vishney, "The Structure and Per-formance of the Money Management Industry," Preliminary Draft, University of Chicago, November 1991.

14. John A. Turner and Daniel J. Beller, *Trends in Pensions* (Washington, D.C.: Government Printing Office, 1992).

15. U.S. Department of Commerce, *Business and Statistics, 1963–1992* (Washington, D.C.: Government Printing Office, 1993), and Turner and Beller, *Trends in Pensions*, 253.

16. Peter Bernstein, *Capital Ideas: The Improbable Origins of Modern Wall Street* (New York: Free Press, 1992).

17. Bernstein, *Capital Ideas*.

18. Donald Cullen and Louis Feinberg, *The Bargaining Structure in Construction: Problems and Prospects Labor-Management Services Administration* (Washington, D.C.: Government Printing Office, 1980).

19. Turner and Beller, *Trends in Pensions*, 590.

20. Richard Blodgett, *Conflict of Interest: Union Pension Funds Asset Management* (New York: Twentieth Century Fund, 1977), 31.

21. Ibid.

22. Congressional Research Service, "Joint Pension Trusteeship: An Analysis of the Visclosky Proposal," Hearings before the Subcommittee of Labor-Management on H.R. 2664, Feb. 21–28, 1990, Washington, D.C.

23. Jan Lanoff, interview by Teresa Ghilarducci, tape recording, Washington, D.C., 22 March 1994.

24. "Ball Predicts New Pressure to Increase Targeted Investments," *Labor and Investments*, 5 (Fourth Quarter) 1.

25. Bernstein, *Capital Ideas*.

26. Martin Wolfson, *Financial Crises* (Armonk, N.Y.: M.E. Sharpe, 1994).

27. Randy Barber and Teresa Ghilarducci, "Pension Funds and the Economy," *Transforming the Financial System*, edited by Gary Dymski, and Gerry Epstein, and Robert Pollin (Armonk, N.Y.: M.E. Sharpe, 1993).

28. Institutional Shareholder Services Monthly Newsletter, Washington, D.C., 1994.

29. Pension Benefit Guarantee Corporation, *Annual Report* (Washington, D.C.: PBGC, 1994), 52.

30. "Stuart Dorsey and John A. Turner, "Union and Nonunion Differences in Pension Fund Investments and Earnings," *Industrial and Labor Relations Review* (July 1990): 543–55.

31. Teresa Ghilarducci, *Labor's Capital: The Economics and Politics of Private Pensions* (Cambridge, Mass.: M.I.T. Press, 1992); Fred H. Mittelstaedt, "An Empirical Analysis of the Factors Underlying the Decision to Remove Excess Assets From Overfunded Pension Plans," *Journal of Accounting and Economics* (November 1989): 399–418; Mitchell Petersen, "Pension Reversions and Worker-Shareholder Wealth Transfers," *Quarterly Journal of Economics* 107 (3) (August 1992): 1033–56.

Chapter 7

Administering the Central Pension Fund

The CPF spends its money in three ways: (1) it provides benefits to its retired participants, (2) it incurs costs associated with the collection and auditing of contributions and dispersal of benefits, and (3) it incurs costs associated with financially managing its investments on behalf of the participants. The costs of operating the Fund and managing its investments must be covered before pension benefits can be paid out. Thus, all things being equal, the lower the administrative costs of the Fund, the higher the benefits it pays can be. All things, however, are not always equal. In particular, the CPF must set goals for the desired risk and return from their investments, the desired degree of rigor with which it audits contribution collections, and the level of advice and service it provides its participants.

By spending more money on investment management, the CPF might earn a greater return, and by spending more money on contribution collections and participant services the CPF might gather more money and/or better serve its participants. Furthermore, the operating costs associated with serving participants will vary depending on whether these participants are working or retired.

The CPF has three types of participants: (1) *active* participants, who are currently having contributions made on their behalf by the CPF's participating employers; (2) *retired* participants, who are drawing a pension from the CPF; and (3) *newly retiring* participants, who are in the process of moving from active to retired status. Retired participants, and especially newly retiring participants, are much more administratively expensive because they require more services. Thus, the mix of active and retired participants will greatly influence the level of operating costs. Similarly, the mix of assets will greatly influence the cost of money management. Active real estate assets are more expensive to manage compared to stocks and bonds. Actively traded stocks and bonds are more expensive to manage compared to stocks and bonds, which are passively held for relatively long periods of time.

Being a large pension fund both helps and hurts in the effort to keep administrative costs low. When becoming large cuts average costs, this is called an economy of scale, and when getting larger raises average costs, this is called a diseconomy of scale. We have found that in the collection of pension contributions, small is beautiful. Local pension funds appear to have advantages over a centralized pension fund in collecting and auditing contributions because local pension funds have fewer contracts to consider and fewer employers to monitor. They may have better or cheaper sources of information about employers and more opportunities to piggyback the collection and auditing of pension contributions onto other local activities that would have occurred anyway. Because of these local advantages, 60 percent of the IUOE locals within the CPF collect and audit their pension contributions locally, in conjunction with their health and welfare fund audits.

We will also see that the process of auditing employers is a political as well as an economic process. Just like individual taxpayers who get audited by the Internal Revenue Service may feel picked on and put upon, employers audited by pension funds may feel inconvenienced or worse. Routine audits that select every participating employer for examination within a specified period of time reduce the political aspects of auditing but necessarily raise the economic costs. Targeted auditing lowers economic costs and raises the potential payoff from audits but is open to political manipulation. Because audits have both economic and political costs and benefits, we will examine the relative merits of centralized versus local audits both in economic and political terms.

There are two clear economies of scale that have come with the growth of the CPF. With $3 billion in assets and 8,000 participating employers, the CPF has become a very large union-management trusteed pension fund. Size in assets has helped reduce money management fees per dollar of asset invested. The large number of participants has allowed the Fund to spread computer, personnel, and other operating costs over a large participant base, cutting operating costs per participant. Historically, these net scale economies have been a major justification for smaller locals to join the CPF rather than start their own fund. Three IUOE stationary locals—Southern California Local 501, New York Local 94, and Denver Local 1—had contributions in escrow that they transferred into the CPF.

The CPF's administrative costs are low not only because of net economies of scale, but also because of the Fund's passive investment strategy. Because (as explained in Chapter 6) the CPF has increasingly followed a strategy of holding bundles of assets that are tied to market indexes and infrequently traded, the CPF pays relatively lower investment management fees. Net economies of scale and passively managed asset holdings have helped the CPF attain relatively lower administrative costs per participant served and per asset dollar managed. The CPF, however, will continue to enjoy additional economies of scale only if it keeps growing. In recent years the Fund's assets have continued to grow, bringing more money management savings, but Fund participation has peaked and is gradually decreasing. By itself, falling participation brings on diseconomies associated with smaller size. Furthermore, with a dropoff in participation, the mix of Fund participants has been shifting away from actively working participants who are relatively cheap to service to retired Fund participants who are relatively expensive to service. This participation pattern is also true of many local IUOE pension funds. The future will tell whether the CPF's progressively growing use of computers to automate aspects of Fund operations will offset these upward cost pressures or whether a union-wide search for new economies of scale will instigate a new era of pension fund mergers with the CPF.

ECONOMIES OF SCALE

Money management and pension fund operations typically enjoy economies of scale. In the case of money management, this means that as the value of invested assets grow, the cost of investing these assets also grows, although at an ever-slowing rate. Thus, the per-dollar cost of investing assets falls as the size of those assets grows. In the case of fund operations, as the number of participants in the CPF has grown, the cost of administering their records has grown but at an ever slower rate. Consequently, the per-participant cost of administering accounts has fallen. Economies of scale lower the average cost of doing the Fund's business and this means there is more money to go into benefits. Economies of scale are central to the question of pension fund mergers. Scale economies are also central to evaluating the benefits associated with pension fund growth and the problems caused by declines in union membership. Therefore, we will go more indepth into the dynamics of scale economies within the CPF.

How economies of scale work within the CPF is illustrated by Table 7.1. The data in Table 7.1 are derived from two linear regression models, one predicting money management costs within the CPF and the other predicting operating costs. Both models are based on the CPF's actual administrative costs from 1964 to 1992.

The three hypothetical scenarios in Table 7.1 show what happens to the CPF's costs as (1) the Fund's assets increase, (2) the Fund's participants increase, and (3) the mix of participants within the CPF shifts from active to retired participants. Because economies of scale diminish as the scale of the CPF increases, the results of these three scenarios are partially dependent on the starting point we have chosen of (1) 30,000 participants, (2) 30 percent ratio of retired to total participants, and (3) $3 billion in assets. Starting points two and three accurately reflect the CPF's current status, whereas starting point one significantly underestimates the 1994 participation level. Thus, Table 7.1 overestimates both the

Table 7.1

Hypothetical economies of scale within the CPF

(1)	(2)	(3)	(4)	(5)	(6)
Participants	Retired to Active Ratio	Assets	Total Costs	Avg. Cost per Participant	Avg. Cost per $100,000 Invested
SCENARIO ONE					
30,000	30%	$3,000,000,000	$7,229,172		$157
30,000	30%	$4,000,000,000	$8,733,141		$155
30,000	30%	$5,000,000,000	$10,222,932		$154
30,000	30%	$6,000,000,000	$11,701,521		$153
SCENARIO TWO					
30,000	30%	$3,000,000,000	$7,229,172	$84	
40,000	30%	$3,000,000,000	$7,873,627	$79	
50,000	30%	$3,000,000,000	$8,485,201	$75	
60,000	30%	$3,000,000,000	$9,071,788	$73	
SCENARIO THREE					
30,000	30%	$3,000,000,000	$7,229,172	$84	
30,000	40%	$3,000,000,000	$7,473,419	$92	
30,000	50%	$3,000,000,000	$7,679,092	$99	
30,000	60%	$3,000,000,000	$7,858,469	$105	

current average operating cost per participant and the savings from a doubling in participant size from current levels.

In the first scenario, the number of fund participants shown in column one and the ratio of retired to active participants shown in column two are held constant while the size of the fund hypothetically grows from $3 billion to $6 billion in assets, as shown in column three. Column four shows how total costs would rise under this scenario. Whereas total costs rise, column six shows that costs per $100,000 of assets (the average amount of assets per participant at the beginning of the scenario) falls slightly due to economies of scale in managing money.

In the second scenario presented in Table 7.1, the asset size of our hypothetical CPF remains constant at $3 billion and the ratio of retirees to active remain constant at 30 percent but the participating membership grows from 30,000 to 60,000. Again, total costs rise in column four, but costs per participant fall due to economies of scale in administering participant accounts. Also notice that more savings come from early growth in participants and that the economies of scale are smaller as the Fund's participation level hypothetically grows. Because the CPF has over 100,000 participants, actual future savings from further growth will continue to encounter these diminishing benefits at the margin.

A study of several hundred multiemployer pension funds in 1975 by Mitchell and Andrews found that there were economies of scale in both money management and participant administration. However, most of these scale economies had been played out at relatively low levels of asset holdings and fund participation.[1] In general, the fact that economies of scale are greatest when growth is jumping from a small starting point helps explain the history of mergers with the CPF. Small funds experience significant economies of scale when they grow. Thus, small funds have a strong incentive to merge with large funds such as the CPF. Larger funds experience diminishing returns from further increases in either their asset holdings or participation. Thus, larger funds do not have the same incentive to merge for the sake of growth. As Chapter 3 showed, the CPF in the 1960s and 1970s tended to enroll smaller local unions within the IUOE rather than the larger local unions within the IUOE. This partly reflects the fact that smaller locals had more to gain from the size advantages offered by the CPF. In the following, we consider whether union membership contraction and aging, the traditional calculations regarding pension fund mergers within the IUOE, remain the same during the present period.

In our third scenario in Table 7.1, both fund asset size and the number of participants are held constant, but the fund is hypothetically allowed to age as the ratio of retired to total participants rises from 30 percent to 60 percent. Again total costs rise because, as we shall show in detail later, retiree accounts are more expensive to administer than the accounts of actively working participants. In this case of shifting participant mix, however, *there are no economies of scale* simply because total costs are rising while the scale of the fund, measured either in number of participants or value of assets, remains constant. Thus, in scenario three average administrative costs per participant rise as the participant mix ages. Again in scenario three, the effect is greatest for earlier changes in the ratio of retirees to total participants. The effect does not diminish much, however, with subsequent increases in the ratio of retirees to total participants. In the future, new computer technologies may narrow the cost differential between the processing of retiree accounts and active accounts, but because our model is based on the historical cost data for the CPF, our model cannot anticipate changing relative costs of processing participant records due to future technology.

These hypothetical results based on actual administrative cost data from the CPF outline a problem and a challenge faced by the CPF in the last fifteen years. Unionization among operating engineers has been declining since the late 1970s. This has affected the CPF in two ways. Because union membership is declining, the number of total Fund participants has stopped growing and has shown some signs of a slow decline. Because the number of new participants has been declining, the mix of Fund participants has been shifting from active to retired workers fairly rapidly. In contrast, the total assets of the CPF have continued to rise despite the decline in participation and consequent aging of CPF participants. As Table 7.1 indicates, when the number of participants within the Fund falls, the CPF experiences diseconomies of scale. Costs per participant rise. Furthermore, as Table 7.1 shows, when the ratio of retirees to active participants rises, average cost per participant rises. Thus, the CPF has recently faced the dual problems of small-scale diseconomies associated with a small decrease in Fund participation and increasing costs associated with a more expensive mix of participants. The second effect has been greater than the first because since the early 1980s, fund participation has declined slightly, whereas the ratio of retirees to active workers has doubled. These upward pressures on administrative costs are offset somewhat by the continued growth in real assets and the money management economies of scale illustrated in scenario one. We now turn to a more detailed examination of the administration of each of the three basic operations of the CPF: collecting contributions, investing assets, and servicing participants.

COLLECTING AND AUDITING CONTRIBUTIONS

The CPF serves more than seventy local unions and almost 8,000 employers from essentially two distinct industries across most of the United States. This complicates the process of tracking the hours of service performed by Fund participants and recording in the correct amount of contributions required from employers. The process is made more difficult by the fact that each collectively bargained contract has its own agreed-on level of pension contributions. Because these are generally hourly contributions, the amount due for each participant will vary based on the number of hours worked. For construction workers, these hours will vary considerably with the season and over the business cycle. The problem of accurately auditing contribution collections becomes even more complex for construction workers who travel from local to local and therefore work under the terms of different contracts with different contribution rates. The Fund must accurately collect the correct amount of contributions for each participant despite variations in contribution rates, hours worked, and employers. If the Fund is unable to collect the correct contributions required for a participant, the Fund is nonetheless legally responsible to pay that participant the benefits owed for the hours worked. Therefore, the Fund has a strong interest, and fiduciary duty, in ensuring that employers correctly contribute for each hour a participant works.

e collection of contributions can be divided into the routine aspects of sending reporting forms, banking contributions, tracking contributions, and the potentially more complicated tasks of identifying and handling delinquent employers. Delinquent employers are identified by auditing their payroll records. There are three types of auditing systems used directly or indirectly by the CPF:

targeted audits, random audits and routine audits. Targeted audits, which the CPF operates from its central offices in Washington, focus on employers who are suspected of being delinquent in their contributions. Routine audits are frequently used at the local level within the CPF and are designed to have every employer audited within a particular time frame, such as three years. A third group of employers are subject to a random audit program in which a group of employers are selected at random for examination.

Audits can be costly. The CPF must pay for the audit and the employer must suffer the inconvenience. Targeted audits tend to promise a high net return because the audits are focusing on the employers who are most likely to be out of compliance. Under the terms of the trust these audit costs can be assessed against, and recovered from, the employer. However, targeted audits are only as efficient as the technical and informal information that identifies the targets. The CPF relies on its computer system to identify some targets. A list of all active employers who are contract signatories is kept. When an active employer fails to report contributions regularly and fails to adequately explain that failure in reply to delinquency notices, that employer is flagged for a possible audit. Although this system can catch gross changes in employer behavior, it is not as effective at identifying employers who are shaving on their contributions. Local union officials often become familiar with the business practices and prospects of unionized employers in their area and consequently these officials are in a position to estimate the employers who are likely to shave on their pension contributions. Furthermore, because active workers receive a semiannual statement, they are in a position to assess whether contributions from employers on their behalf have been appropriate. The CPF uses information generated by local union officials and active Fund participants to help target potential cheaters. Frank Gould states: "We're primary target auditors. We're going after somebody we know we can audit because somebody's complained. Our position is by sending out a semi-annual statement, every participant gets a statement twice a year that says who's paid on it and who hasn't. They [the participants] do the audit. If you look at it that way, every employer is being audited every six months."[2] Mike Crabtree, Fund council and the individual who oversees the targeted audit system, points out that: "You get a higher net return on dollars recovered to dollars expended with a targeted audit program. Since we are a nationwide pension, I am of the opinion that targeted auditing, coupled with routine and random audit programs at our branch administrators, is the best route. But targeted audits do run the risk of the Central Pension Fund getting sucked into a labor-management dispute."[3]

Local union officials or even local employees may be tempted to have an employer targeted for an audit in order to put pressure on that employer for bargaining reasons or other grievances. On the other hand, it is also possible that local union officials might temporarily try to protect an economically distressed employer from being audited. Even if a shaky employer is being protected by local union officials, however, workers may inform the Fund if less than appropriate contributions are being made on their behalf. Even if local union officials are not motivated by these bargaining issues when they identify employers to target, employers may believe that there were illegitimate reasons why they were targeted or why someone else was not targeted. Thus, targeted audits carry potential for some political baggage. Routine audits in which every employer's name comes up in a lottery every few years avoid this political baggage, but at the cost of a more expensive auditing procedure. Thus, the direct revenue payoff from routine audits are typically less. Both audit procedures, however, are also designed to deter cheating as well as catch delinquent employers. Mike Crabtree believes that routine audits are better deterrents: "The routine audit does a better job of generating a deterrent effect. People know when their number is going to come up in the draft and they also know that if they are playing games they are going to get hit hard because they will not only have to pay the delinquent contributions but also the loss of interest on that money, liquidated damages, and possibly the audit fee."[4] In short, with a targeted audit you might get caught but with a routine audit you will eventually get caught. Thus, routine audit systems may generate returns simply by preventing cheating in the first place, whereas targeted audits typically generate greater visible returns if analyzed on the basis of per dollar spent on per dollar recovered. At the national level, the CPF has decided that the costs of a routine audit override the benefits of its stronger deterrent effect. Only 60 percent of all locals within the CPF, however, use locally managed audits. The CPF encourages these local audits because it is more cost effective.

Unionized employers typically pay hourly contributions into more than one fund. A union employer's collective bargaining agreement can call for contributions to health and welfare, pension, apprenticeship training, vacation, or annuity funds for the bargaining unit members. All of these obligations must be audited, so there are local economies of scale associated with jointly collecting and monitoring these contributions together pursuant to a cost-sharing arrangement. In the construction industry, there are possible economies of scale associated with cooperation between the various crafts within a local labor market. Having one collection system within a particular area with the various crafts sharing the costs of that system has been tried in a variety of regions and has succeeded in some.

Frank Stupar, a bricklayer who once helped collect delinquent contributions for a local bricklayers pension fund in Detroit, describes some of the collection advantages of cross-craft cooperation in a strong union city:

I worked for the pension fund in Detroit for seven years. I was a—well the kind word for it is "trust investigator." I used to go after delinquent contractors and late payers. Stuff like that. Audit them. Take them to court. Sue them. Clean them up. When I was a collector in Detroit, the carpenters had a collector, the operating engineers had one, the laborers—everybody, you know. In fact, we had a committee. We would get together once a month. The AGC [the Association of General Contractors] asked me to do it. The chairman was Bill Staley from the Operating Engineers and I was the secretary. He was bigger, but I was smarter. And we'd go over all the bad guys in the three counties around Detroit with a lot more muscle. If somebody had a big job going I would just call the employer [the general contractor] up and say that so and so owes X to all of the following trades. And comes Monday morning, the following people won't be working for you anymore. So instead of just being able to say you're not going to have any bricklayers, I would then tell him you're not going to have any carpenters, no plumbers, no pipefitters, and miraculously he would pay up.[5]

Thus, these local pension funds could share information and costs, piggyback on each other's audits, and enforce payments through bargaining as well as legal means. Leo Majich, pension administrator for the Southern California IUOE construction Local 12, however, states that piggybacking was discussed in his area about twenty years ago but never implemented:

We do not piggyback on the audits of other crafts. There was an attempt to start that type of activity in our area about twenty years ago using a single audit and collection group for all of the trades. After reviewing all of the details, everyone realized that there were too many differences between the various trust funds and piggybacking simply would not work. Consequently, all of the Funds in this area have their own auditing group. We occasionally exchange information with each other but that's about as far as it goes. We have good cooperation with IUOE, Local 3, because contractors in our area move back and forth between the two union areas.[6]

The benefits of auditing an employer are numerous. Obviously, contribution shortages that result in a delinquency are frequently discovered and must be resolved. The audits quite often discover attempts to cheat the Funds and that results in additional monies being collected. More importantly, a good auditing program has a deterrent effect by discouraging employers from attempting to minimize their reporting or from avoiding their full obligation to the Funds. Because of varying trustee policies regarding audits, it is difficult to create cross-craft cooperation. One of the major issues concerning auditing programs is the attempt to use the auditing program as a device to harass employers. Most of the Funds that Majich knows about make a concerted effort to avoid being accused of harassment tactics.

In most cases, locals participating in the CPF who conduct joint pension and health and welfare audits do targeted audits. These audits exploit the economies of scale associated with piggybacking pension audits on the auditing of contributions to health and welfare and other funds within the local. These audits utilize the information local unions have on local employers. This strategy assumes that the high direct payoff of targeted audits based on good local information and the economies of piggybacking on other local audits outweigh the weaker deterrent effect and the possible political costs of targeting.

Mike Crabtree believes there is a third auditing system that may reduce the disadvantages of auditing from a central pension administration. He would con-

Table 7.2
The CPF's money management fees compared with its peer group and the universe of pension funds

	Total Universe Median	$2-5 Billion Universe Median	CPF
Investment Management Fees			
Active Large Capital Equity	44.5	43.0	68.4
Active Small Capital Equity	69.5	69.0	89.5
Active Fixed Income	25.0	24.0	33.2
Active Cash	15.0	15.5	15.4
Active Real Estate	100.2	97.7	15.4
Passive Large Capital Equity	7.0	6.0	2.6
Passive Small Capital Equity	10.5	4.5	4.0
Passive Cash	15.0	NA	3.2

* All numbers are in basis points: one basis point = 1/100 of a percent.

sider a random audit. This plan would share with targeted audits the economizing feature that only a subset of all employers in an area would be audited within a specified time period. Random audits would share with routine audits the depoliticizing feature that no employer would be purposely selected based on worker or union complaints. Random audits would hopefully be seen as less political. Therefore, random audits would be less expensive than routine audits and less political than targeted audits. Whether random audits would have a sufficient deterrent effect would probably depend on what percentage of all employers were audited in any time period. As more employers are audited, the deterrent effect increases but also does the cost. A well-designed random audit might lessen the disadvantages of running a target audit program from a centralized administration.

MONEY MANAGEMENT AND INSURANCE FEES

Currently, the CPF has relatively low administrative costs associated with money management when compared with corporate and other funds of similar size. Table 7.2[7] compares the 1992 money management administrative costs of the CPF to eighty-three other pension funds, including seventy-eight corporate funds, three public funds, and two other multiemployer funds. The total assets held by these eighty-four funds in 1992 was $298 billion. Thus, the average fund held $3.8 billion in assets, a level comparable to the CPF's. Still, some funds in this group had considerably more assets than the CPF and some had considerably less. Consequently, Table 7.2 presents two sets of comparisons with the money management costs paid by the CPF. The first set is an average for all of the eighty-four funds, and the second is an average for those funds with asset holdings similar to those of the CPF ($2 to $5 billion). Various categories of money management costs are presented as a percentage of assets held. In 1992, the Central Pension Fund spent 18 percent of a penny for every dollar it held in order to manage those assets. In contrast, the average spent by all of these funds on asset management was three times higher, at 57 percent of a penny. These small percentages are typically called basis points, and the CPF's eighteen basis points are few compared not only with the fifty-seven paid by these other largely corporate funds, but also compared with the many stock and bond mutual funds that vie for individual savings.

The main reason that asset management is done so cheaply at the CPF is that the fund places a higher percentage of its money in passively managed stocks and bonds. This lowers costs in two ways. First, because passively managed assets are cheaper to manage than actively traded assets, the CPF's average money management costs are lower. Second, because the CPF pours almost 80 percent of its non–real estate funds into passive assets (and there are economies of scale in managing most kinds of assets), the CPF's management costs per dollar passive asset owned are lower. Table 7.2 shows the money management fee paid by the CPF per dollar of asset owned for passively held funds, compared to the fees paid by other funds. Systematically, the CPF pays less per dollar held in passively held assets. In contrast, Table 7.2 shows that the CPF does not systematically pay lower fees to its managers of actively traded assets. The CPF's actively traded real estate holdings obtain lower per dollar fees but that is not true of their actively traded large capital equity assets nor of their actively traded fixed income or cash assets.

Because the CPF pours more of its money into passive assets, the fees it pays to manage these passive assets are lower, but conversely, because the Fund pours less of its money into actively traded assets, the money management fees it pays to manage actively traded assets tends to be at a higher rate. Thus, the CPF pays one third to one half of the investment management fees of these comparison funds overall because it allocates its money disproportionately into passively held assets. If the CPF can get as good a return on its passive holdings (subject to risk) as it can on actively traded assets, then this passive strategy will ultimately provide more benefits for CPF participants because the Fund's investment management fees are lower.

The second most important reason that the CPF has lower overall costs is because its premiums paid to the Pension Benefit Guarantee Corporation (PBGC) are substantially lower per dollar of fund asset compared to the other eighty-three funds whose investment and management fees are reflected in Table 7.2. The CPF's insurance premiums are low because the CPF pays the multiemployer premium of $2.60 per participant rather than the $19 per participant required by corporate plans. Quite often corporate funds do not accumulate assets sufficient to cover their benefit commitments and presume that any short-falls in benefits can be covered by current corporate revenues. Furthermore, unlike a union-management trusteed fund, if the corporation in a single corporate fund goes bankrupt, the pension fund is likely to suffer greatly. Thus, because they skate on thinner ice and put all their eggs in one basket, corporate plans typically pay higher PBGC premiums. Thus, the CPF has kept its money management costs down because it has invested a relatively high percentage of its funds in passively traded assets and because it has minimized its insurance costs by keeping its benefit commitments in line with the assets it has accumulated.

There is, however, a third way the CPF has limited its administrative costs. The CPF's money management and operation costs are lower per dollar of asset and per participant served simply because the CPF is large. The effects of size on money management costs were estimated in Table 7.1. There we saw that at the size of the CPF, additional growth in its $3 billion in assets by itself will not generate substantial new economies in money management. Although movement of assets from active to passive management can significantly lower money management costs, the CPF has 20 percent of its funds remaining in actively managed accounts. Therefore, the CPF has already achieved most of the savings in money management coming from economies of scale or passive investment.

SERVICING PARTICIPANTS

Servicing participants includes a wide range of administrative tasks. The CPF provides counseling services to the participants, processes claims, and pays benefits. The CPF must also perform background tasks, such as actuarial evaluations of what the Fund can afford to pay in benefits and support costs such as legal fees, travel, and trustees' expenses. These aspects of fund administration offer significant possibilities for economies of scale. Computer purchases, actuarial studies, building costs, brochure printing, and similar administrative costs typically involve some fixed costs that do not rise with increased participation. Consequently, when these fixed costs are spread over larger numbers of participants, the cost per participant goes down. This is the source of economies of scale in operating expenses relative to participation. Retired participants, however, are more costly to service than active members. Therefore, economies associated with increased participation must be adjusted for changes in the mix of retired and active participants.

Frank Gould points out that "The bulk of our administrative expenses are in handling our retirees. There is a direct correlation between the amount of people going on retirement and our administrative costs."[8] The single most expensive participant to administer is an IUOE member moving from active to retired status. Our analysis suggests that the next most expensive participant to serve is the retiree, and the least expensive is the actively working Fund participant.

Servicing the needs of the participants involves (1) maintaining records or credited service, (2) processing new retirees, and (3) paying benefits to the retirees. There are no direct data that allocate all administrative expenses among these three groups. This is partly because it is difficult to know how to allocate background expenses such as audits and legal fees among these three groups. Nonetheless, we can get a general sense of the relative costs of these three groups by looking at how total operating expenses have varied over the years as the number and mix of active and retired workers within the Fund have varied. Using a linear regression analysis of total administrative expenses over the lifetime of the CPF, we estimate that in real 1992 dollars, active participants typically cost $26 per year to administer, whereas retired participants cost $123 to service annually and new retirees cost $451 to process during the year of their retirement.[9] This wide variation in costs associated with differing status among participants is based on the differing tasks required to administer the accounts of active, retired and newly retired participants.

Active participants require the least administrative oversight because the required tasks are easiest to standardize and computerize. The participating employers make contributions to the CPF on behalf of their employees. These contributions are received in the Employer Records Department, where they are key punched into an active member's record.[10] After the contributions are entered, an audit is run to make sure the employers are contributing in accord with the collective bargaining agreements. The electronic auditing procedure has removed most of the labor from the audit process. Once entered and audited, the contribution records are sent to the Participant Records Department, where an active participant's record is updated. The collective bargaining agreements between each participating local and the participating employers are updated once per year on the computer system. Active participants communicate questions and requests to the Fund less often than do retirees. Thus, most work for active participants is standard. Much of it is computer automated. Consequently, active participants cost relatively little to service.

Although active participants and their employers are the least expensive to administer, this segment of the CPF is in relative decline. In 1964, there were approximately 8,000 active participants in the CPF (Figure 7.1). By 1971, that number had risen to 93,000, and it peaked at 100,000 in 1980. Since 1980, however, the number of active participants has steadily declined and currently stands at 69,000.

In relative terms, the active segment of the CPF has been in steady decline since the beginning of the Fund (Figure 7.2). This is partly a natural result of the Fund maturing. New funds have relatively few retirees, but over time active members graduate to retired status. This process of a rising percentage of retirees, however, should come to a standstill in a mature, steady state. The CPF has experienced a decline in the proportion of active participants to retirees. The rise and fall in participating employers is one measure of this decline in union membership and active participants. In 1964, 1,335 employers participated in the CPF. The number of employers peaked in 1980 at 12,546 and currently stands at 7,618. With the decline in union membership and consequently new

Figure 7.1

The CPF's operating expenses and the participants it serves

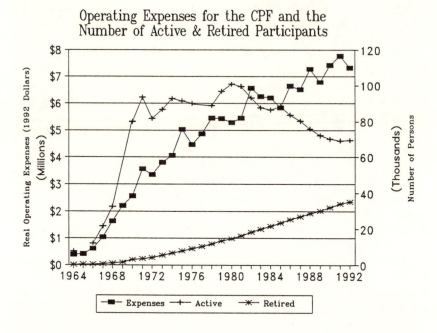

Operating Expenses for the CPF and the
Number of Active & Retired Participants

entrants into the CPF, the relative importance of active participants has fallen below the mature, steady-state equilibrium in participation. This declining state puts added pressure on administrative costs. Trustees of union-management trusteed pension funds generally assume that their pension fund will exist forever and make prudent decisions accordingly. This has led some persons to assume that a mature pension fund must reach a steady state, that is, participants and their contributions *to* the fund must equal the cost of retirees and benefits *out* of the fund to assure perpetuity of the fund. An alternative view of a steady state assumes that a pension fund is mature when it has sufficient funds to pay all of its obligations.

The participation of retirees in the Fund has risen both in absolute numbers and in their relative importance among all Fund participants. In 1964, the CPF had 174 retirees. Since that time, the number of retirees has steadily increased and currently stands at 35,000. In relative terms, retirees in 1964 accounted for 2 percent of all Fund participants, and by 1992 retirees had come to represent one third of all Fund participants (Figure 7.2). Because retirees are roughly five times more expensive than active participants, and because they now represent one third of all participants, these retirees account for the strongest upward pull on per capita administrative costs.

However, new retirees during the year of their retirement cost almost eighteen

Figure 7.2
The ratio of retired to active participants

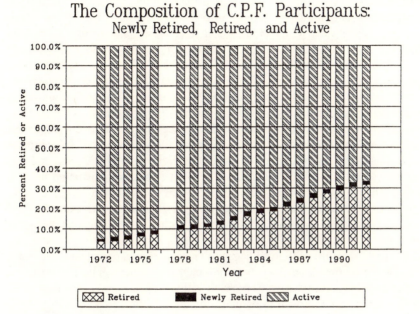

The Composition of C.P.F. Participants:
Newly Retired, Retired, and Active

times more to administer than active participants. New retirees represent only about 2 percent of all participants, but this percentage is slowly rising (Figure 7.2). When an operating engineer is ready to retire, he or she sends the CPF an application for benefits. Processing this application is the most labor-intensive part of CPF operations. The benefit examiners (the highest ranking clerical employees of the CPF) scrutinize the application to make sure that everything is in accord and then calculate the benefit amount. The process of scrutinizing and establishing a new retiree's pension is the most difficult to standardize and thus remains the most expensive. Once on pension, communication with the retiree and the payment of his or her benefit is more routine but nonetheless remains more capital- and labor-intensive than an active member's record. Reflecting this, the Employer Records Department, which handles contributions on behalf of active fund participants has ten employees and one supervisor, whereas the Participant Records Department, which handles all retirees, has twenty-two employees and two supervisors.

The number of participants within the CPF grew very rapidly in the 1960s (Figure 7.2), yet operating costs per participant surprisingly did not fall, as one would have expected, from economies of scale in participation. Real average operating costs per participant did hold constant in the 1960s, but after a big one-year drop in 1970, average operating costs per participant have risen in all later periods. This suggests that the economies of scale associated with increased participation in the 1960s might have been just offsetting the upward cost pressure associated with a rapid percentage increase in the ratio of retired to active participants. This ratio rose rapidly in percentage terms in the 1960s, simply because in the early years of the Fund there were quite naturally very few retirees, and retiree numbers grew thereafter with the maturation of the Fund.

Still, the tremendous growth of CPF participants in the 1960s would lead us to expect that average administrative costs would have fallen, but they did not. The only time in the history of the CPF that the average costs of administering participants' accounts fell in real terms was in 1970, the year the CPF switched to self-administration of participants. It may be that the CPF did experience significant economies of scale throughout the 1960s, but that these economies were captured in the profits of third-party administrators of the Fund and only accrued to the Fund itself when the CPF went to self-administration in 1970. Alternatively, the third-party administrators may have done a poor job in administrating accounts and simply failed to capture the economies associated with a rapidly growing fund. The CPF trustees did believe at the time that they could do a much more efficient job if they went to self-administration. In any case, in 1970, the year the CPF itself began to manage its own participants' accounts, the Fund experienced a dramatic, one-time drop in per capita administrative expenses. This one-time savings probably reflects a realization of the scale economies won through growth in participation through the 1960s.

When looking at the average administrative cost data in Figure 7.1, one may wonder whether the CPF has done a good job administering participants. In every year since 1970, average administrative costs have risen in real terms, adjusting for inflation. The third-party administrators of the 1960s at least held real average administrative costs constant. The CPF administrators, however, faced a very different world after 1970. The rapid participant growth of the 1960s was largely over. Thus, the savings from economies of scale would no longer mask the effect of a rising ratio of retired to active participants.

Thus, we may divide the history of CPF expenses administrating participants' accounts into three eras. In the 1960s, average costs held constant as the costs associated with a rise in the ratio of retirees to active participants was offset by the economies associated with the rapid increase in the number of participants. Average costs, however, should have fallen and third-party administrators either insufficiently captured the economies of scale offered by the rapid growth of the period or they pocketed the savings themselves. At the beginning of the second era in 1970, the CPF's own administrators did capture the economies of scale gained in the 1960s, but this was a one-time savings. The period of rapid growth in percentage terms was over, and what little additional growth occurred did not offset the upward pressure on costs associated with a continued shift from active to retired participants within the Fund. The third period began in 1980. That year the number of participating employers within the Fund peaked and declined thereafter. With union decline has come a decline in participation, while the ratio of retirees to active members continues to rise. In this last period, the CPF has been faced with the double problem of an increasingly expensive mix of participants *and* small diseconomies of scale from declining total partic- ipation. Surprisingly, the rise in average administrative costs during this period has not accelerated.

The explosion of costs that did not occur in the 1980s is probably due to changing information-processing technology and an extension of traditional CPF organizational strategies. The CPF fortuitously began computerizing its opera- tions just as Fund participation peaked in 1980, and the expanded use of com- puters has apparently offset the diseconomies of scale associated with decline in participation. In contrast with many other pension funds that have chosen to out-source their computer services in recent years, the CPF has followed a strat- egy of bringing almost all of their computer-based administrative process in- house. This is following up on the lesson the Fund trustees learned in 1970 when they discovered significant savings by taking over third-party administra- tion.

Given that other pension funds within the IUOE face similar problems with loss of scale economies, there may be emerging pressure to merge many of the various local pension funds with the CPF. A more fundamental solution, of course, would be to rejuvenate local union membership in order to bring re- newed economies of both scale and mix. Many local pension trustees resist merging with more centralized funds because they see their local pension funds as a crucial ingredient in rebuilding local union membership.

ECONOMIES OF SCALE AND MERGERS

Chapter 3 showed that the CPF was built in a twofold process. Many small- and middle-sized locals, along with a few large locals without pension funds joined the CPF, while stationary Locals 501, 94, and 1 brought money they were holding in escrow while they explored various pension options. The large IUOE locals that had pension funds at the time remained outside of the CPF. Leo Majich, current administrator for the large IUOE construction Local 12's pension fund expresses the outlook of those viewing the CPF from the per- spective of a large local fund: "Locals like us and Northern California construc- tion Local 3 and Chicago construction Local 150 are really big and can afford to do a lot of things. Really the CPF is a collection center for all those engineers who can't afford to have their own pension fund."[11] In more technical terms, Majich is arguing that large locals have the economies of scale that allow them to operate their own pension funds, whereas smaller locals must band together to enjoy those same administrative economies. Table 7.3 shows the size and administrative costs of a variety of pension funds within the IUOE for the year 1991. For instance, Majich's Local 12 had 24,569 participants with a retired to total participant ratio of 45 percent. Local 12's operating costs per participant, including benefit-receiving survivors of participants, were $129. Local 12 had

Table 7.3
Comparison of the CPF with IUOE local pension funds

Local	Total Participants	% Who Are Retired	Assets	$ Manger Expense	Operating Expenses	Funded/ Vested	Cost Per $100,000	Cost Per Per Part.
CPF	111,372	31.2%	$2,213,949,424	$2,176,000	$5,150,945	104.0%	$98	$63
3	25,410	35.7%	$1,420,493,900	$2,693,880	$4,462,153	117.4%	$190	$151
12	24,569	45.0%	$1,178,557,900	$1,388,860	$4,598,913	91.0%	$118	$129
150	14,608	23.1%	$779,679,976	$2,059,560	$1,488,017	138.9%	$264	$86
17	6,423	46.3%	$183,028,406	$819,230	$834,214	79.4%	$448	$104
66	6,116	44.4%	$212,348,337	$226,030	$619,124	121.0%	$106	$79
701	4,556	46.3%	$157,187,767	$806,270	$484,815	121.3%	$513	$84
39	4,489	23.0%	$145,423,000	NA	NA	104.9%	NA	NA
478	4,300	24.5%	$185,492,200	$748,330	$777,797	116.9%	$403	$155
15	3,987	29.1%	NA	NA	NA	69.4%	NA	NA
101	3,708	32.7%	NA	$571,620	$307,473	0.0%	NA	$68
132	1,758	43.6%	$70,918,204	$303,190	$259,337	147.3%	$428	$61
428	3,027	42.5%	$111,137,000	$701,690	$530,171	93.7%	$631	$133
4	2,642	55.5%	$71,831,300	$359,420	$1,861,784	94.9%	$500	$491
800	1,556	16.6%	$26,663,397	$78,870	$159,805	128.1%	$296	$86
675	1,336	19.6%	NA	$596,660	NA	0.0%	NA	NA
14	1,312	35.8%	NA	$141,590	$302,461	85.0%	NA	$222

over $1 billion in assets and its money management costs were twelve basis points or 0.12 percent of assets. Local 12's cost structure in 1992 was higher than the CPF's. Local 12 was paying $129 per participant (including survivors) for operating costs compared to the CPF's $63 per participant. Local 12 was paying twelve basis points to manage its money compared to the CPF's ten basis points. But are these cost differentials enough to attract Local 12 into considering a merger with the CPF? The answer is a fairly clear no. In terms of money management costs, the difference between ten and twelve basis points is not great, and Local 12 may believe that for its added money management costs it could be getting a better return on its capital. Leo Majich states:

Our money management expenses are low because for approximately 20 years we had a single investment advisor working for a flat fee that we renegotiated periodically. We did not have multiple money managers during that time. Approximately one year ago the Trustees retained the services of an independent investment manager with full discretion to manage a part of the assets and the fee is a percentage of assets at market value. During the last 20 years the Fund had an average net return to the Fund of 9.5 percent.[12]

Majich is pleased with the Fund's performance and believes the strategy of a single fixed fee money manager was a good one. In terms of operating costs, Local 12's per capita costs are twice that of the CPF. Majich believes that these higher costs come from the greater service that he believes a local fund provides:

It is necessary for our Fund and for Local 3 as well to provide a higher level of service to its membership than is required of CPF. That is due to the fact that the local union officials are directly responsible to their membership and they are required to pass a test every three years, which is the union election process. Consequently, service to the membership becomes very important in the overall operation of the union. In our case we publish monthly and quarterly bulletins to the participants and we conduct Trust Fund area meetings for the benefit of our participants. We make sure that the membership gets the answer to two questions—what do I have coming and how do I get it? We also handle any and all problems that develop regarding benefits. The CPF doesn't compare to us or to Local 3 because they don't have the same relationship to the membership and they really act as a clearinghouse for the other locals that do not have their own Funds.[13]

In fact, most of the union trustees on the CPF are local business managers, but it still may be true that union trustees on locally based pension funds feel more heat from local union politics. In the cases of Local 3, Local 12, and several other locals, the retirees vote for union officers. That puts added pressure on union trustees to provide local pension services. Setting aside the question of retiree voting, however, there may be greater pressure on local funds to provide pension related services. On a local fund, all of the union trustees will be subject to that local's political issues, whereas on a national fund, each union trustee will come from a different local with its own distinct economic and political conditions. In a centralized pension fund, union elections may not be synchronized and economic conditions will differ. Thus, in a national fund, union trustees as a group may feel more insulated from the press of immediate political concerns within one local. In any case, Tom Stapleton, business manager for Northern California's Local 3, agrees that large, locally based pension funds provide a lot of services:

We give the members of our pension fund a lot of services. We have retiree associations and hold meetings all around the district. We also have a fringe benefit center in our local office with one guy assigned just to help our members with fringe benefits. We just kind of take care of them, help them with Social Security, any problem. Some really need the help. Ever since I remember, we have done it that way because even though they're retired, they're our members. We treat them just like the actives, even though we get a lot more calls from the retirees. Our pension services and our health and welfare services are all married together.[14]

Local 3's operating costs in 1991 were $151 per participant, almost three times the costs of the CPF. Although the CPF may offer some economies of scale because of a higher participation base, large locals such as Locals 3 and 12 have chosen a higher level of service than the CPF provides. This accounts for much of the cost differential between these funds. Differences in philosophy about money management and participant services account for most of the difference between the lower CPF costs and the costs of large local funds. Economies of scale account for a smaller portion of the difference and consequently, there is little current attraction to induce large locals to merge with the CPF.

Smaller locals, on the other hand, have a great deal to gain from merging with a large fund such as the CPF. Many IUOE funds with assets below $500,000,000 are paying thirty to sixty basis points to manage their money. Most are paying somewhat higher operating costs per participant without offering significantly greater local services than the CPF. By merging their funds into the CPF, they could cut their administrative costs substantially. However, the CPF itself would not benefit much from such mergers. If, hypothetically, the CPF merged with all the IUOE funds represented in Table 7.3, the CPF would more than double in both participant size and assets, and the ratio of retired to total participants would rise somewhat. Under this scenario and our regression model of CPF costs, CPF money management costs would fall by about two basis points and CPF operating costs would fall by about $6 per participant. These are not major cost savings for the CPF and would have to be balanced against the problems associated with merging with funds that vary widely in their financial health. For instance, five of the eleven smaller funds in Table 7.3 have funded vested ratios less than the CPF's. Such disparities in funded benefits would have to be harmonized in any merger. Thus, no wave of fund mergers is on the horizon because of economies of scale and trends in administrative costs. The larger local funds do not need to merge and the CPF will be selective in deciding with which smaller funds to merge. In relatively good financial situations the CPF will continue on occasion to merge with smaller funds needing the economies of scale the CPF can offer and the larger local funds will continue on their own.

CONCLUSION

Pension fund administrative costs typically enjoy economies of scale. The more money managed, the cheaper it is to manage each dollar, and the more participants involved, the cheaper it is to serve each participant. The CPF has provided economies of scale to a host of IUOE locals. The recent period of union decline has put pressure on administrative costs because fund participation in the CPF and in other local funds has stopped growing, and in many cases participation has been falling. Shrinking participation has meant diseconomies of scale, although these have been small. Favorable new computer technologies could well offset the diseconomies of gradually falling participation. The rising number of retired participants is also a worry, to the extent that retired participants cost more to service than active participants. This is clearly the case for local funds, such as Locals 3 and 12, which provide a lot of retirement counseling. Our regression analysis of the CPF indicates that its retirees cost relatively more as well. A rising ratio of retired to active workers means, among other things, an administratively more expensive mix of participants. By themselves, the pressures of shrinking and aging participation are pressures for the various funds within the IUOE to merge and recapture various economies of scale.

There is, however, more than one way to manage money and more than one way to serve participants. Local unions develop preferred means to audit their employers, to serve their members, and to manage their money. Merging with the CPF would mean harmonizing these policies. For large locals with large funds, the economies offered by the CPF are too small and the differences in policies too great to currently make such a merger attractive. Among smaller funds, however, where the CPF can offer greater administrative economies, the prospect for mergers is more likely.

NOTES

1. Olivia Mitchell and Emily Andrews, "Scale Economies in Private Multiemployer Pension Systems," *Industrial and Labor Relations Review* (July 1981): 522–30.

2. Frank Gould, telephone interview by Peter Philips, tape recording, 17 July 1994.

3. Mike Crabtree, telephone interview by Peter Philips, tape recording, 19 July 1994.

4. Ibid.

5. Frank Stupar, interview by author, tape recording, Washington, D.C., 17 September 1992.

6. Leo Majich, telephone interview by Peter Philips, tape recording, 19 July 1994.

7. CPF.

8. Frank Gould, interview by author, tape recording, Washington, D.C., 11 August 1993.

9. In generating these estimates we have made total operating expenses a function of fixed costs plus variations in costs due to changing numbers of active, retired, and just retiring participants. This method will allocate indirect as well as direct costs to these three categories. Jack Johnson agrees that the just retiring participant is the most expensive to administer but believes that the routinely active and routinely retired participants are roughly equal in their administrative costs. Based on our assumption that routinely retired workers are more expensive to administer, we will argue that the increasing percentage of retired members within the CPF puts a strain on operational costs. If Johnson is correct, then the shifting mix of participants should have no effect on trends in operational costs.

10. During this process the CPF also key punches the contributions to the Health and Welfare Fund of the Pipeline Workers, which is housed in the CPF.

11. Majich, 19 July 1994.

12. Ibid.

13. Ibid.

14. Tom Stapleton, interview by Jeff Petersen, tape recording, Alameda, Calif., 17 November 1993.

Chapter 8

Pensions for the New U.S. Labor Market: Lessons from the CPF

The pension literature is replete with examples from large-scale industry. Sixty-two percent of employers with more than 1,000 employees provide a pension. As employer size dwindles, however, so does pension coverage. Only 30 percent of workers who work for an employer with fewer than 100 employees have coverage. If these are to be supported in retirement by the traditional three-legged stool of public and private pensions and personal savings, viable mechanisms must be found for small-scale and sporadic employment. But pensions do more than support workers in their advanced years. They influence the occupational choices of younger workers and their industry commitments. They have also become the largest single source of investment capital for the American economy, influencing the long-run direction of the entire society.

This chapter draws useful lessons from our case study of the CPF. It explores how multiemployer pension plans may help reshape the future of the new American workforce by achieving the paramount objective of accommodating small and dynamic firms without sacrificing retirement income, skill acquisition, and workers' attachment to the labor force. We also spend some time emphasizing the innovation and promise of a defined-contribution, defined-benefit hybrid. Union-management trusteed plans are tied to the U.S. economy's need for skilled workers, but not in an obvious or direct way. That relationship is explored as well.

The second part of this concluding chapter looks at the investment side of pensions with regard to worker control of pension investments. It asks whether corporate plans could benefit from worker representation in the selection of investments. We also examine issues of centralization and decentralization. What is the trade-off between local control and administrative efficiency? And what of social issues? Is malfeasance more likely in unilateral or jointly trusteed plans? What are the trade-offs between economically targeted investments and shareholder activism, on the one hand, and retirement income security, on the other? We conclude with policy recommendations.

PENSION FUNDS AND THE FUTURE OF THE AMERICAN WORK FORCE

Saving the Future: Training and Pension Funds

Under the press of competition and the lure of consumerism, ours is a society that finds it difficult to set money aside for tomorrow. This is true of both companies and people.

Faced with the growing turbulence and uncertainty of competition on a global scale, many American companies have been downsizing or, as some executives prefer, "rightsizing" their workforces. They have cut employment, reduced long-term commitments to workers, and shortened their planning horizons, hoping to become lean, mean, and ready for anything that competition in the globalized economy has in store. In an effort to become flexible, U.S. companies have increasingly followed a strategy of transforming long-term employment relationships into short-term commitments contingent on the shifting currents of market demand. As long-term employment commitments fade, companies are becoming increasingly reluctant to invest in the skills of their own employees, simply because the workers they train may not be around long. Preparing to cut their workers loose, companies are also cutting back on benefit payments designed to retain workers. Thus, companies are less interested in setting money aside for pensions, simply because deferred wages are not the inducement of choice for contingent workers.

Partly because the world is growing increasingly uncertain for the corporation, consumer advertising is becoming a more important part of corporate strategies. From the corporation's perspective, consumer advertising can be seen as an effort to create loyal, predictable, and growing demand for consumer products to help offset the uncertainty of competition. From the individual's perspective, however, the culture of consumerism and the institutions of consumer credit make setting money aside for tomorrow very difficult. There is too much to be bought now, too much that seems needed now to make saving from today's paycheck attractive. Even when families are able to save, the growing turbulence of labor markets often wipes out those savings as workers are laid off and contingent employment relationships are terminated.

Almost all advertising exhorts us to spend, to buy, to purchase. Even when banks advertise, they usually promote borrowing to buy a home or a car, rather than saving for the sake of future purchases. An exception to this pattern is mutual funds, which do extol the virtues of savings. But even here, the target groups are the well-to-do, the middle and upper middle classes. This highlights an additional problem with retirement savings. With the globalizing economy and the increased turbulence in labor markets has come a marked worsening of income distribution. Over the last twenty-five years in the United States, the rich have been getting richer and the poor have been getting poorer. For the bottom two thirds of the income distribution, saving for retirement has become very difficult.

Globalized competition, turbulent labor markets, the pressure to consume, the abundance of consumer credit, and falling real wages make it very difficult for either the employee or the employer to set money aside for something as distant as retirement. It is only somewhat less difficult for employers or workers to invest in human capital for the more close-at-hand goal of raising someone's skills and productivity. Ironically, these new and emerging problems of setting money aside for training and retirement in the context of market turbulence and contingent employment relationships are old and familiar issues within the construction industry.

Construction has always been a highly cyclical and very competitive sector of the American economy. Construction workers have endured feast and famine income streams that have made it very difficult to save for the future. Construction unions solved the riddle of training in turbulent labor markets having casual connections between workers and contractors by tying the worker to the union, and consequently to the industry rather than to the individual employer. The worker, in his or her craft an entire lifetime, felt more comfortable committing time and money to training knowing that he or she would be learning skills that would lead to employment throughout that lifetime. Construction unions overcame the reluctance of contractors to pay the up-front costs of training by assuring the employer that if a worker left, a call to the union-operated hiring hall could bring a similarly trained worker to replace him. The unions overcame both individual employer and worker reluctance to set money aside for training by collectively bargaining for training funds, making that a cost of doing business uniform to all. Thus, collective action overcame the failures of turbulent markets and the pressures on individual workers and employers.

Stationary engineers do not share that casual employer-employee relationship, but they are typically hired in small numbers by employers unable to generate the economies of scale and spread the risks implicit in a single-employer pension scheme. Although their employees may remain with the firm over long periods of time, the employers usually lack the infrastructure of training departments and professional instructors for on-the-job training.

Just as unions have overcome the problem of how to generate the savings needed to train workers in casual construction labor markets, so have they solved the problem of saving for retirement. As recalled by union leader Peter Babin, Jr., describing construction engineers in Louisiana, "the only pension we had at this time (the 1950s) was a hat," which was passed around the union hall to help retired members of the local who were destitute. Babin relates that "the membership had a kind of bitterness about a pension plan because ... they wanted the money in their pockets. I had to convince them that they had to think about the time when they were old.''[1] In the construction labor market, unions served as the institution that counterbalanced all the pressures to consume.

In industries with large companies and stable employment relationships, corporations and their unions often provided the means and the pressure to save for retirement. But in the construction labor market, the unions acted alone. Construction contractors are typically small employers, the vast majority employing fewer than twenty-five employees. Very few non-union construction workers have pensions as almost all unionized construction workers do. A similar statement can be made for stationary engineers. Whereas 62 percent of workers in companies with more than 1,000 employees have pensions, only 12 percent of workers in companies with fewer than 25 employees have such benefits. Nevertheless despite the small size of their employing units unionized construction workers do have pensions, and in the IUOE, so do their stationary engineer brothers.

In this case study, we have seen that creating pensions for operating engineers was a process of institution building. It was a political and economic process in which first various large locals and subsequently the IUOE created the vehicles for pension savings. The union bargained for pension contributions and created the mechanisms for investing those contributions, eventually distributing benefits to retirees. In the context of volatile blue-collar construction jobs and isolated blue-collar stationary jobs, the creation of pensions was not and could not have been a simple decision on the part of individuals to save. Institutions had to be created that essentially pried money loose from the clutches of current consumption. Reese Hammond recalls that the early goal was to get just anything for a pension contribution. A nickel an hour was fine. Once the institution was in place to collectively bargain for pension contributions, it could be negotiated upward.

Setting up an institution of delayed gratification was not an easy process. Benefit formulas that made sense had to be devised within a union of disparate locals, some with strong bargaining power and some without, some with stable, year-round stationary engineer jobs and others with seasonal construction work. Locals had to agree to come on board. This meant that the younger members had to be convinced this was something that they should do for themselves and for the older members who had built up the local. Older members had to be convinced they would get a meaningful pension even though they would receive contributions for only a few years before they actually retired. Local union leaders had to be convinced that joining a central pension fund was better than starting their own local fund.

The CPF's early leadership had tough decisions to make. How much should the CPF redistribute away from younger members and toward retirees in order to jump-start the CPF? What made sense both in terms of fairness and in terms of cost? Should and could the CPF induce larger locals with their own pension funds to join the new fund? What should the relationship be between the CPF and the IUOE? What forms of insurance and spousal benefits should the CPF provide, and how early could engineers be allowed to retire? With these and many other formative decisions, the founders of the CPF were creating a savings institution in the middle of a society that discouraged savings, and among workers whose income instability made savings difficult.

In addition to a savings institution, the CPF was an insurance institution. In a union tradition of mutual help and insurance that goes back almost 200 years, the CPF followed the pattern of most other union-management trusteed funds in being a defined-benefit pension fund that insured its participants against the economic pitfalls of longevity. Those participants who lived shorter lives would essentially underwrite those who lived unexpectedly long. This made the CPF more than an individual savings program, even more than a tax-favored one such as a 401K. We will examine the hybrid nature of the CPF's contribution and benefit formula here. The point to be made is this: In a society where institutions, culture, and circumstance typically conspire against savings for retirement, IUOE union leaders, with the agreement and help of unionized employers, created an institution and a process for collectively bargained savings and investment for the future, as well as for mutual insurance against the privations of disability and old age.

The importance of this achievement resides not only in the decent pensions now received by CPF participants. This case study provides a model for retirement savings and mutual insurance in moderately paid jobs among smaller firms with contingent employment relationships in the service sector and elsewhere. Many kinds of workers are more attached to their occupations or crafts than to any particular employer. These workers are usually employed by firms in industries that have small firms and sporadic employment relationships. Increasing proportions of workers will likely work only a short time for numerous employers in their working lifetimes. Few of their employers have the economies of scale and probabilities of survival to dependably promise a job in the next year, not to mention a pension on retirement. The problem is how, in those settings, can the contributions of many small employers be combined to ensure an adequate retirement income. Some employees of such firms may have long-term commitments to an industry, such as construction. Others may be employed in a variety of industries, as are stationary engineers. The corollary problem is how to ensure a pool of skilled labor to firms who may be new, undercapitalized, competitive, and small.

One route would be government-sponsored training and retirement. President Clinton's labor secretary, Robert B. Reich, has argued that the new U.S. labor force does not have the institutions available to get the skills needed to make globally competitive products. He blames the market for failing to give employers incentives to train their workers. Reich argues that firms, especially small- and medium-sized firms, fear self-defeat if they invest in training. It is a rational fear that the investing firm's trained workers could be bid away by competitors who would reap the advantage of the first firm's investment. In addition to this "free-rider" problem, downsizing has fractured whatever long-term labor commitment had existed in the American workforce. Previously, these informal long-term contracts had helped firms feel comfortable enough to invest in training. Reich points favorably to many German industries that have established industry training funds into which employers contribute equally. Workers move from competitor to competitor, augmenting their skills as they move around. It is a salubrious arrangement for the German workers, firms, and economy. Employers pay a fair share to produce a valuable pool of skilled labor. Productivity is higher and German competitiveness is enhanced. Candidate Clinton had proposed a mandatory 1 percent training tax to create a pool along the lines of the German example. However, the concerted effort from the employer community and the press kept the proposal from surviving President Clinton's first budget.

Meanwhile, Social Security faces a long-term crisis. A pay-as-you-go retirement system, Social Security is being squeezed by both demographic and economic pressures. Americans are living longer and having fewer babies. Consequently, with the passage of each successive generation, there are fewer younger people to support a growing population of older Americans. Because it is a pay-as-you-go system, Social Security is not directing funds into capital-building savings that would enhance the capacity of the future young to make the goods and services needed to support the future old. All the while, the federal budget is in deficit for other reasons, which constrain the possibilities for either increased Social Security taxes or the redirecting of funds toward investment. Thus, although it is conceivable for government to provide the collective institution needed to save for training and retirement, the politics of such reforms are doubtful.

Ironically, we do not need to look to Germany to inspire American labor market rehabilitation, nor are increased Social Security taxes the only road to a secure working-class retirement. This case study of the CPF, and multiemployer contracts in general, offers examples of how unions can operate within sporadic and competitive markets to create skilled and mobile workers who are reasonably cared for in their old age.

Workers in unions in the construction, maritime, and trucking industries, and to a lesser extent in the mining and textile industries, created union-management trusteed plans in the context of and in response to the pressures of casual labor markets. These multiemployer plans provide a significant lesson for today's labor market because they were established in situations where the union members worked for many different small employers in competitive industries. They created retirement security from careers of inherent employment insecurity. Restaurant workers, dental hygienists, home-health workers, and even janitors are examples of occupations that could benefit from "occupational unionism" and its attendant social insurance plans.[2]

Setting aside for the moment defined-contribution pension plans, there are three kinds of U.S. defined-benefit pension plans, distinguished by their sponsors and by their governance rules: government, corporate, and multiemployer. The smallest group are the multiemployer pension plans, sometimes called union plans or union-management trusteed plans as we have chosen to title them, because they are all collectively bargained. Taken together, union-management trusteed plans hold about $800 billion in assets. Public plans have over $1 trillion in assets, and private corporate plans own approximately $1.2 trillion. Union-management trusteed plans also account for about 20 percent of all defined-benefit plan participants. Thus, the smallest type of defined-benefit pension, union-management trusteed funds, are still quite important. These multiemployer plans provide defined-benefit pension plan coverage without tying workers to a particular employer. This fact stands in remarkable contrast to the conventional view that defined-benefit plans are devised to discourage worker mobility among firms. The CPF hybrid benefit formula is especially important in understanding how a union-management trusteed plan can allow mobility across firms, yet hold workers to occupations in the context of mixed occupations such as stationary and construction engineers.

THE DEFINED-BENEFIT/DEFINED-CONTRIBUTION HYBRID

Most defined-benefit pension rules reward those who are attached to the firm and acquire the skills that come about with experience and training. These skills are often specific to a firm and workplace. Yet the changing structure of the American economy needs an employer-based pension system that enables people to acquire occupational skills and retirement income security in a labor market where people are moving around, typically among smaller firms. A union-management trusteed fund can provide that model.

By summarizing how longevity is rewarded in a defined-benefit pension plan, we will see how labor force attachment to the firm, the occupation, or the industry is manipulated and molded by the benefits of the plan. Vesting rules specify how many creditable years qualify a worker for a pension. By law, corporate plans must vest participants in five years; multiemployer plans can require ten (the CPF, nonetheless, has chosen a five-year vesting rule). Crediting rules, which define a certain number of hours worked per year as a creditable year toward vesting, tend to disqualify many part-time or sporadic workers. If mobile workers leave covered employment, they stop earning pension credit. Break-in-service rules require people who have left the company, industry, or trade to work a certain number of hours connected to their length of absence before they can be credited with additional service and avoid forfeiture of accrued service.

With vesting, crediting, and break-in-service rules, pension benefits influence and discipline labor mobility. Just as corporations use these rules to strengthen the tie between a worker and the company, unions in the multiemployer context use these rules to strengthen the tie between a worker and the union. By implication, ties to craft unions also tie a worker to an occupation. Pension plans become linked to training plans when they present the worker with both the carrot and the stick to stay with a company or an occupation. With reasons to stay, the worker will find reasons to be trained and employers will find reasons to train the worker. This helps the formation of human capital stocks, which are foundational in supporting future generations of retirees.

Of course, benefit rules can be abused by special interests, as well as used for the global good. Vesting rules have been shortened by law to prevent bait-and-switch tactics in which an attractive twenty-year pension is available, but few, if any, ever qualify. Conventional wisdom believes that multiemployer union-management trusteed plans, which by law now require no more than ten-year vesting rules, will provide fewer eventual vested participants than corporate plans with five-year vesting. However, the ratio of non-vested participants to all active participants is actually lower for the ten-year vesting of union-management trusteed plans than for the five-year vesting of corporate plans. This is probably because workers are more likely to leave a company within five years than an occupation within ten. Well-designed defined-benefit plans develop benefit rules that mold the labor supply to encourage human capital formation, but at the same time avoid either the temptation to play bait-and-switch games or to rob Peter simply to pay Paul.

Comparing Defined-Benefit and Defined-Contribution Formulas

Defined-contribution plans define the contribution paid into a pension plan by or on behalf of a worker, but defined-contribution plans do not specify the benefits eventually to be received by that worker. In short, in a defined-contribution plan the worker knows what is being paid into a retirement fund on his or her behalf, but must be uncertain about what pension benefits will be available on retirement. Defined-contribution plans are best thought of as individual savings plans to which the employer contributes. The worker is immediately vested and owns all the contributions paid into the plan on his or her behalf. When the worker-employer relationship is terminated, the contributions go with the worker.

The defined-contribution plan is distinct from individual savings, in that the contributions and income generated from the investment of those contributions are tax-deferred. Clear individual ownership is an attractive aspect of defined contribution plans. You cannot lose your pension savings when you move about within the labor market or out of it entirely. Also, as the safety of corporate pension plans comes into question, the individual ownership of defined-contribution plans becomes more attractive.

Defined contribution plans are not, however, without risk. They may not provide insurance against living too long, and the eventual worth of an individually owned pension is more sensitive to the exact timing of when an individual happens to retire. This will be explained later. Also, defined-contribution plans typically allow for savings withdrawals subject to penalties but prior to retirement. Thus, they are induced savings but not the forced savings of defined-benefit plans. This may appear to be an advantage in the short run, but it is a subsequently regretted option in old age. Obviously, defined-contribution plans have less of an effect on individual mobility across industries, occupations, and firms.

This last point may account for the fact that whereas 52 percent of all corporate pension plan participants are in defined-contribution plans, only 6 percent of all collectively bargained plans' participants are in defined-contribution plans. The proximate institutional reason for this disparity is that unions in both corporate and multiemployer contexts tend to remain devoted to the maintenance of an industry or occupation, whereas companies are seeking greater flexibility and less commitment. Thus, it is in the union context that pension benefits become disproportionately tied to labor market behavior. Part of the consequence of this pattern is that pension benefits rules in the union environment promote greater retirement income security by prohibiting early withdrawals, and greater human capital formation by allowing for long-run planning of labor market movements.

The CPF: A Promising Hybrid

The CPF began in 1960, which was later than many union plans. In 1993, it was the sixth largest union-management trusteed fund, and it ranks 148th of all U.S. pension funds. The CPF's benefit formula is typical of multiemployer plans and is a fascinating hybrid between a defined-contribution and a defined-benefit plan. With its provisions for portability and making benefits a percentage of contributions, the CPF formula offers the mobility of a defined-contribution plan, as well as, the social insurance aspects of a defined-benefit plan. More than 8,000 employers contribute to the plan, in amounts determined by the collectively bargained contracts between each employer and over eighty-five participating IUOE locals. The contributions range from $0.11 to over $3.00 per hour. At retirement, the monthly benefit is currently defined as 3.3 percent of the worker's recorded balance—the contributions made on his or her behalf—for the rest of that worker's life (the CPF also has standard provisions for survivors' benefits).

Consistent with a protection motive, the disability benefits are actuarially favorable in the CPF. After age forty, one receives full benefits if fully disabled, which means a redistribution away from other participants and toward the disabled. The CPF gave four ad hoc increases to retirees in the 1980s, an era during which corporate plans greatly reduced COLA payments.[3] These kinds of disability and retiree COLA policies reflect an institution that has a perceived loyalty to a craft.

In contrast, a defined-contribution pension is, in effect, an annuity purchased at the time of retirement with the contributions and interest in an individual's account. There are no COLAs, unless purchased through a lower set of early annuity payments, nor are there actuarially favorable benefits to the disabled.

How does this hybrid affect labor supply? Vesting, crediting, break-in-service, reciprocity, portability, and return to work rules are ways to micro-manage labor supply. Multiemployer pensions are also a tool in the union's strategy to improve conditions, and they pay in two ways: by eliminating low-productivity employers who can only compete by sweating labor, and by improving their own labor skills by increasing workers' attachment to the craft and union.

Multiemployer pension funds can tie a worker to an occupation, as well as a firm. In the CPF, people are long-stayers and get more out of the fund if they remain in the occupation of operating engineer when they change employers. The members of the CPF acquire skills in their occupation and are not dependent on a capital-intensive employer, although they are dependent on a capital-intensive industry. Thus, the CPF combines the flexibility of a defined-contribution plan with the rewards of longevity and skill acquisition imbedded in a defined-benefit plan.

In sum, this union-sponsored hybrid model regulates labor supply and provides good retirement to mobile workers. The hybrid reduces many of the disadvantages of defined-benefit and defined-contribution plans while retaining most of the advantages. Like defined-contribution plans, the hybrid is easily understood and the minimal breakage increases benefits and encourages loyalty to the craft. In addition, the hybrid defines the benefit so the timing risk—the risk that finance markets are bad at retirement—borne by the defined-contribution participant does not exist. Defined-contribution plans create timing risk and increase the absolute amount of market risk. Timing risk does not exist in defined-benefit plans because the actuary smooths the interest rate assumptions across participants and over time. Although market risks exist in defined-benefit plans and are borne by the sponsor, they are lower than if individual workers bear them because employers are less risk-adverse than any one worker, and the employer is able to spread the risk across all the participants and into the future. Lower risk makes for better benefits. The hybrid, like the defined-benefit plans, can provide disability and cost-of-living increases to retirees. At the same time, the hybrid prevents workers from using the account for non-retirement needs, which defined-contribution participants are able to do.

A union-management trusteed plan is something like a fully funded mini-Social Security Administration, picking off the bits and pieces of employer contribution and assembling a coherent pension benefit. Workers, especially when real wages grow slowly and consumer debt is widespread, need forced savings. That is best achieved in paternalistic and centralized institutions. A retired officer of a major local of the International Union of Operating Engineers said that in "the old days" when the pension fund was started, the officers "did the thinking for the men." Unions are shelter-builders against the fluctuations in a capitalist economy.[4] Old-age income insecurity is a risk from which the union-management trusteed plan shelters workers. The economics enable the union to centralize the pension plan; the politics motivate them.

Multiemployer plans have been the subject of few studies. Hybrid formulas were developed to meet goals of labor supply regulation and retirement income security. For this reason, they may be a model for occupation-based pension plans, especially where workers are quite mobile. Hybrid formulas have the insurance aspect of defined-benefit plans, but the mobility benefits of defined-contribution plans.

MANAGEMENT AND INVESTMENT: PENSION FUND GOVERNANCE

We move now to the governance of the CPF and what this case study can tell us about how collectively bargained pension funds should be managed. Should union and management trustees jointly oversee the operations of a fund as they do in the multiemployer context? Or is it appropriate for corporate trustees to shoulder the entire responsibility for governance, as is the practice in the single-employer context? What should be the role of professional pension fund managers, financial consultants, actuaries, and lawyers? What are the advantages and disadvantages of a centrally run pension fund compared with local funds? At what size do local funds become efficient, and what should be the role of a national pension fund in providing a home for established funds too small to capture the various economies of scale associated with pension fund operations?

Joint Trusteeship

The Taft-Hartley Act of 1947 required that all collectively bargained, multiemployer pension funds be jointly overseen by an equal number of union and management trustees. In keeping with this regulation, the CPF, originally conceived as a union initiative, was jointly trusteed from its inception. Because the IUOE represents both stationary and hoisting and portable engineers, management trustees come from two distinct industries, one in construction and one primarily in the service sector. Actually, more than two industries are involved. Stationary engineers may work in government or in a variety of manufacturing sub-sectors, such as hotels or office buildings. Even in construction, hoisting and portable engineers may work in a variety of sectors, such as heavy and highway construction, or commercial or industrial building construction. Furthermore, regional differences in construction are important, with some contractors active nationwide and many contractors doing business within only one region. Thus, there is an inherent asymmetry of organization at the CPF trustees' table.

Union trustees come from locals of a national organization. Although the IUOE has a relatively decentralized political structure, it also has a national, institutional coherence reflected in its structure of local, regional, and national meetings. The CPF management trustees do not meet with each other on a regular and systematic basis in any context other than the three annual meetings of the Fund itself. When a new management trustee is to be appointed to replace an outgoing management trustee, the remaining management trustees caucus to select the successor. They consider the important economic sectors represented by the CPF and attempt to ensure that each sector is represented by a management voice. This informal procedure helps give the management side of the table a coherence that the union side naturally derives from the overall national structure of the union.

Culture is as important as structure in ensuring equity and openness among CPF trustees. Union and management trustees, both past and present, have testified to the non-adversarial character of CPF trustee meetings. Indeed, they all claim that management and union identities fade into the background as they assume the roles of fiduciarily responsible trustees of a pension fund. The culture of governance within the CPF is one of consensus, and the overwhelming majority of votes taken by the trustees are unanimous. Areas of conflict are typically resolved prior to a vote, and votes are often delayed if consensus cannot be reached. Trustees believe that one reason for this culture of consensus may be the centralized structure of the pension fund. Trustees rarely confront each other at the bargaining table in other roles as union and management trustees of a local fund commonly do. Union trustees come from disparate locals, and this may diffuse non–pension fund concerns that officials from the same local may all share. Still, in our observations of trustee meetings and in conversations with trustees after meetings, it was clear that union trustees and management trustees represented distinct interests and viewpoints, although softened by a culture of cooperation. These distinct perspectives enriched the collective decision-making powers of the board as a whole.

The CPF has a culture of professionalism, as well as one of cooperation. Professional managers and advisors are in attendance at every board meeting. Some of these professionals are permanent employees of the CPF, whereas others are outside consultants. Most of the consultants have long-standing relationships with the CPF and return on a regular basis to make reports and give advice. None of these professionals has a vote on the board, but their advice is very influential. Professionals educate the trustees as well as advise them. Significant time at board meetings is devoted to financial and actuarial reports, which attempt to provide a long view of the CPF's investment prospects and benefit commitments. Between board meetings, the actual daily operations of the CPF are in the hands of the permanent employees in consultation with one or two designated trustees. The advice and work of professionals circumscribe the range of choices the trustees consider and consequently help shape the overall policies of the CPF.

The CPF has obviously been strengthened by its joint union-management decision making. Should single-employer funds be jointly trusteed just as multiemployer funds are? The traditional industrial model of labor relations has been that management directed the enterprise and unions bargained over wages and working conditions. Management hired, fired, trained, and supervised production. Workers followed orders and unions sought to protect workers by contractually circumscribing those orders. In construction, the traditions have been different. Unions do the recruitment, selection, and referral of employees. They play a substantial role in training workers, and workers singularly and in groups are often responsible for self-direction on the job. In many ways, the old-fashioned construction industry had been practicing worker self-management long before its recent vogue in other industries. Partly because unions initiated and organized pension funds in the multiemployer context and partly because in the construction industry there was a culture of worker self-management, it only seemed natural that union members should trustee pension funds. The Taft-Hartley Act required that management trustees join with union trustees in that control.

Recent managerial innovations have sought greater worker input for management decisions and, in the union context, a relaxation of work rules in exchange for greater direct involvement in production. Putting union trustees on corporate defined-benefit pension plans would be an extension of union involvement in the direction of production. A union voice at pension board meetings would be biased in favor of benefit rules that encouraged human capital formation. Industrial unions might well favor rules that permitted portability across firms in that union's industrial jurisdiction. It would be a step away from the notion that the control and direction of jobs were solely the prerogative of management. In the multiemployer context, the union is seen as a joint custodian over the direction of human capital formation. If union trustees were required on corporate pension plans, the collective voice of workers would begin to speak regarding the direction of overall human capital formation within the firm and industry. The CPF is an example of non-conflictual, union-management cooperation that single-employer pension funds should consider.

Should third-party professionals be trustees on pension fund boards? It is clear from our interviews that in the case of the CPF, financial, managerial, legal, and actuarial professionals have a distinct perspective. As a group, they tend to view the CPF as an institution separate from the union and industry from which it emerged. To a surprising extent, both union and management trustees set aside their daily roles to become fiduciarily responsible pension fund trustees at their meetings. But the professional staff have no direct link to either industry or unions. As permanently employed professionals, their primary constituency are the currently enrolled participants of the CPF.

This is both a strength and a weakness. It is a voice for careful, conservative management, but it also tends to see the pension funds as having emerged *deus ex machina* rather than from the larger picture of economic events and labor relations. We believe that the voice of the professional in the CPF is strong enough without a third-party trustee. We also wonder how third-party trustees would be selected. However, we also believe that a strong professional voice is essential to the good operations of collectively bargained pension funds. Where those voices are absent, a fund is weakened.

Centralization versus Decentralization

In Chapter 7, we examined the economies of scale associated with both the operational and financial management of pension funds. Roughly one out of every five active members of the IUOE are in the CPF. Should the other pension funds within the IUOE merge with the CPF? Because economies of scale peter out as pension funds become larger, the large pension funds within the IUOE have no solid financial reason for joining the CPF. Smaller funds could benefit from the economies of scale offered by the CPF. However, the CPF must carefully pick and choose among the smaller funds that would like to merge with it. The CPF has little to gain from the additional growth provided by the addition of smaller funds, and the CPF has much to lose by taking on smaller pension funds if these funds have become financially troubled. The CPF was established to create an institutional home for smaller locals that could not obtain the economies of scale that made a pension fund affordable. The CPF grew primarily by adding locals that did not yet have pension funds. Now, practically all IUOE locals have pension funds of one sort or another. Although the CPF occasionally still merges with some of these smaller funds, smaller financially troubled funds are more or less on their own. Although the CPF might suffer from absorbing weak local funds, those potential pension beneficiaries are also IUOE members. What are the obligations of union brotherhood?

Among construction unions, the IUOE has some of the largest locals. Thus, this union is well-positioned to have strong local pension funds. Other construction unions with smaller locals need to find ways to capture various economies of scale. This may best be done through third-party administrators, which provide many of the advantages of size by administering a host of small pension funds. This provides some economies of scale without the complexities of formal mergers. Similar arrangements can be made to pool investment monies. Collectively bargained multiemployer pension funds, by their nature and history, tend to be relatively small and stem from a heritage that emphasized local control. It remains for another comparison study of a small pension fund to tease out the various advantages and disadvantages of central and local pension fund administration. Yet it is evident that through the development of third-party administration companies and mutually invested funds, the market has already provided to these smaller funds many if not all of the economies of scale available to the CPF.

Conflicts of Interest

Because pension funds accumulate a lot of money, all involve potential personal and institutional conflicts of interest. Our case study has helped us learn about some of the structural causes of conflicts of interest. The underlying potential conflicts in collectively bargained multiemployer pension funds are quite different from those in single-employer pension funds. In a single-employer fund, the financial commitments of the pension fund are backed by the financial health of the corporate treasury. This is one justification for excluding union trustees from the pension fund board because the trustees are seen as spending the money of the corporation. But because pension assets and corporate assets are seen as essentially coming from the same pot, corporations are sometimes tempted not to put money into the pension fund in order to allocate it to a promising corporate investment. This might not only be in the interest of the corporation. If the corporate expansion is profitable, it could benefit the pension fund by improving the health of the corporate treasury that ultimately backs the pension fund. It could even add new employees to both the corporation and the pension fund, thus strengthening the fund and spreading its risks. Thus, by targeting money for self-investment rather than pooling it in the general investments of the pension fund, a corporation may improve both its prospects and those of the pension fund. This is, however, also a primary source of malfeasance in a corporate fund. We will explain this momentarily. It is not to be forgotten that 16,000 corporate plans were reported by the PBGC to be underfunded by a total of $53.4 billion in 1994.[5]

There are no corporate treasuries backing the collectively bargained multiemployer pension funds. That is an advantage rather than a disadvantage. This is one reason the benefit commitments of multiemployer pensions tend to be better funded than corporate pensions. There is no safety net, so multiemployer funds are more conservative. Because there is no corporate backing, individual employers in a multiemployer fund are required to pay a portion of any unfunded liability if and when they choose to withdraw from a pension fund, even if that employer did not create the liability. Therefore, employer trustees in multiemployer pension funds tend to be wary of underfunding. Multiemployer pension funds, however, do face an investment choice similar to the one faced by single-employer funds. Once money has been contributed to a multiemployer fund, the trustees may see an opportunity to invest that money in a way that not only reaps returns to the pension fund but also creates jobs for the fund's participating employers and workers. This may work to the advantage of the pension fund by increasing contributions and participation, just like a good self-targeted investment by a corporation might be in the interest of a single-employer pension. Economically targeted investments aiming at greater corporate profit in the single-employer case, and greater union employment in the multiemployer case, however, open the possibility for chicanery and malfeasance in both cases.

One pension fund manager told us that if he wanted to steal from a single-employer pension fund, he would never put the needed money in. If he wanted to steal from a multiemployer fund, he would put money in and then steal it. This aptly captures the structural differences in the temptations to malfeasance in the single-employer and multiemployer cases. In the single-employer or corporate pension plan, money that does not go into the pension capital investment fund can be used by the corporation that controls the pension. So corporate decision makers are constantly faced with the decision whether to put monies into the pension plan or retain that money for corporate purposes. In a multiemployer pension, the pension trustees or administrators cannot treat or mistreat monies until they come under the pension fund's control. Thus, the aphorism, to steal from a corporate plan, you never put the money into it but to steal from a multiemployer plan, the money has to first be deposited into the fund. In both cases, stupidity is probably a greater source of problems than greed. The corporation may retain monies due the corporate pension fund in the pious hope that by investing these retained earnings in corporate expansion, the corporation will prosper and expand. This prosperity and expansion would then finance future pension obligations. The corporate decision makers think or hope that the corporate self-targeted investment will go well and that both the corporation and the pension fund will prosper. But this opens the door to malfeasance when the corporation starts throwing good money after bad in doubtful or disparate self-investment schemes rather than allocating that money to a judicious and diversified pension investment fund. In short, what is good for the corporation may not always be what is good for the corporation's pension fund. The multiemployer board of trustees faces as analogous temptation once monies are deposited with the pension fund. The multiemployer board of union and management trustees may identify an investment that will both reap a good return to the pension fund and create work for union members and/or business for union contractors. The prospects for double benefits do not always work out and a bad guess can sometimes be fostered by the hopes that what is good for the industry is good for the pension fund. There are also occasionally cases of greed. Corporate takeovers financed by raids on single-employer pension funds are notorious. In the multiemployer pension fund case, "brother-in-law" investments occasionally occur, where the fund invests in venture that some board member or fund manager has a direct or indirect interest. The CPF has been cautious in exploring economically targeted investments, not because greed never entered its board rooms, but simply because the trustees did not want to wind up with egg on their collective face when something that seemed too good to be true turned out to be just that.

Economically Targeted Investments

It is not easy to target investments in ways that create jobs for operating engineers. If the money finances a building, most of the construction workers will come from other trades, not operating engineers. When the building is completed, no more than a handful of stationary engineers might be permanently employed. Hoisting and portable engineers work in concentrated numbers building highways and dams. These public works are difficult to invest in directly, although some thought has recently gone into creating a financial instrument that would facilitate this. There are also some current experiments in privately financed highways. Local operating engineer pension funds have cooperated with other local construction pension funds in jointly financing local construction. The biggest danger in targeting pension fund investments in ways that have favorable spillover effects on participating employers and workers are the risks associated with lack of diversification or putting too many eggs in one basket. Thus, financial instruments that spread risks across projects and regions must be created. But the temptation to engage in targeted investments can often have a large, localized effect.

One reason the CPF has been wary of many economically targeted investments is because it is a central rather than a local fund. Like many collectively bargained multiemployer pension funds, the assets of the CPF grew significantly in the 1970s and particularly the 1980s. Ironically, the same pro-business climate that sparked rapid growth in stock market values created hard times for labor unions. The globalization of markets, falling domestic real wages, and pro-business federal administrations helped capital and hurt labor. But at the same time, those forces helped labor's capital—pension fund assets. As circumstances got tough in various regions among various unions and unionized contractors, union and management trustees saw these growing pension assets as a possible tool to stem the crisis. Because the CPF draws from many regions and across the construction and service sectors, however, the crisis may not have been felt as sharply at any one time as it was by local unions in some regions, particularly in construction.

Another reason why the CPF is conservative with respect to economically targeted investments may be due to the role of professionals as permanent employees of the fund. These professionals have a heightened concern for the financial health of the fund and are not as attuned to the economic health of local unions and their contractors. They serve as a caution to the "governor" of possible double benefits from targeted investments. Symbolically, the CPF has always been housed separately from the IUOE Washington headquarters. This physical separation is emblematic of a tradition of relative autonomy between the CPF and the IUOE, an independence that both sides have wanted and respected. This probably lessens the pressure for targeting investments to create jobs as well as to create profits. In general, the trend within the building trades, however, is to continue to explore financial instruments that would provide the secondary benefit of creating union jobs while serving the primary benefit of generating solid, safe returns.

Although the building trades are reputed to be the conservative wing of the U.S. labor movement, they have creatively explored the prospects of strategic investments. In the 1970s, the building trades started counteracting their precipitous drop in membership by creating a demand for their own labor. Union funds can legally make investments to provide "ancillary" or additional benefits (aside from a maximum risk-adjusted rate of return) without violating ERISA. Union participation in mortgage pools that fund union-built construction is the most popular way to invest to create union jobs. For instance, the AFL-CIO Housing Investment Trust (HIT) is funded by contributions from pension funds (80 percent from union plans) and provides pooled loans to housing projects around the nation. The Clinton administration supports the use of federal grants, loans, and guarantees to leverage the AFL-CIO money to meet U.S. policy goals for rehabilitating the inner city. The CPF has participated in these initiatives and has its own policies for investing the real estate portion of its portfolio in union buildings within the regions occupied by its participating locals.

As the building trades and government develop vehicles for investment that allow for the spreading of risk, the CPF is likely to increase its participation in economically targeted investments. Indeed, because it is a national rather than a local pension fund, it is well placed to influence the development of these financial instruments. Because it is large, it can have a significant impact without risking a large percentage of its assets, and because it has a broad, almost national constituency, these national investment instruments are probably most germane to the CPF's self-interest.

POLICY LESSONS FROM THE CPF

Although multiemployer pension funds are fundamentally institutions for mutual protection and self-help, they effect society at large and are an integral part of an overall system committed to generating decent jobs, productive workers, and secure retirees. Consequently, government should continue a reasonable regulation of these funds to ensure their financial health. The favorable tax treatment for multiemployer funds should continue because it helps promote plans that are useful to workers and their industries and has positive side effects on society through increased human capital formation and enhanced investment. Defined-contribution plans, if portable and used as retirement assets as opposed to current consumption, should be tax-favored.

Our case study shows that joint trusteeship provides incentives for good management. Congress should consider mandating joint trusteeship for corporate plans as proposed by Rep. Visclosky in 1990. Our case study does not support the idea that third-party administrators should be mandated. In the case of the CPF, professional voices are now being heard on a continuous and appropriate basis, and there is no reason to think they are not so heard in other union-management trusteed plans.

The commonplace wisdom that large funds make sense because they are less costly to manage is only partly true. Smaller funds can use third-party administrators and jointly invested funds to capture some of the economies of scale available to the CPF. Consolidating existing pension funds is much more complicated than creating a centralized pension fund for small locals without pension funds. Thus, the process of capturing economies of scale should be left to the market and the political dynamics within unions.

Trustees of union-management trusteed funds experience needless contradiction. Both management and union trustees want to invest in productive job-creating projects. They also want the highest financial return. When these goals are in seeming contradiction, they are given little guidance. The Departments of Labor and Housing and Urban Development can help promote investments in U.S. economic development by subsidizing information and brokerage costs. That means the highest priority of retirement can remain uncompromised at the same time societal needs are balanced.

CONCLUSION

The originators and perpetuators of the Central Pension Fund of the International Union of Operating Engineers and Participating Employers confronted a formidable challenge: how to provide adequate retirement income to workers who would throughout their working lifetimes be sporadically employed by numerous employers or more steadily employed in employing units too small to generate viable pension schemes. Those pioneers responded to that challenge admirably and built a system that has gone on to confront and so far surmount a rising retirement burden during a period of declining union membership. Other challenges are undoubtedly out there still to be met, but the past augurs well for the future.

In meeting its own challenges, the CPF has provided lessons and inspiration for those employees, their representatives, and their employers in other industries and settings equally and increasingly confronted by casualization and fragmentation throughout American labor markets. To those who have lived through the CPF experience, these pages should offer a sense of satisfaction; to those still searching for answers, a sense of direction.

NOTES

1. See section in Chapter 3 entitled "Local 406 Enters the CFP in 1966."
2. Dorothy Sue Cobble, "Organizing the Post-Industrial Workforce: Lessons from the History of Waitress Unions," *Industrial Relations and Research Review* 44 (1992), 419–436.
3. Allen, "Post-Retirement Benefit Increases."
4. Jill Rubery, "Structured Labour Markets, Worker Organization and Low Pay," *Cambridge Journal of Economics* 2 (1978): 17–36.
5. *Business Week*, 19 September 1994, 91.

Appendix: Board of Trustees for the Central Pension Fund

UNION TRUSTEES

Appointed by:	Trustee Name	Year
Joe Delaney	S. A. Boston, IUOE	1960
	John Possehl, Local 18	1960
	R. W. Tucker, Local 501	1960
	Reese Hammond, IUOE	1961
Hunter Wharton	Forrest Bugher, IUOE	1962
	R. H. Fox, Jr., Local 501	1965
	Gilbert Bosworth, Local 841	1966
	Lawrence Gough, Local 49	1967
	J. A. McMahon, Local 450	1970
	Richard T. Wren, Local 399	1972
J. C. Turner	Russel T. Conlon, IUOE	1977
	Frank Hanley, IUOE	1978
	R. H. Fox, Local 501	1980
	Earl A. Erwin, IUOE	1982
	Larry Dugan, Jr., IUOE	1984
Larry Dugan, Jr.	Fred Dereshuk, Local 49	1986
	Richard Griffin, IUOE	1986
Frank Hanley	Dan Smart, Local 103	1990
	John R. Bowen, Local 94	1991
	Jim McLaughlin, Local 501	1993

EMPLOYER TRUSTEES

Trustee Name	Company	Year
James F. Egan	Ward Baking Company	1960
Richard E. Dennis	Dennis Trucking Co., Inc.	1960
David J. Martin	General Contractors Assn.	1961
George Kall	Beatrice Foods Co.	1961
Louis Moses	Meat Packers, Inc.	1961
Richard Gump	Pipe Line Contractors Assn.	1962
Hailey Roberts	Pipe Line Contractors Assn.	1966
A. W. McIntyre	S. Birch, Inc.	1966
John E. Cullerton	Hilton Hotel Corp.	1976
Bob McCormick	National Constructors Assn.	1982
Noel Borck	National Erectors Assn.	1986
Paul Gehl	Lunda Construction Co.	1991

Selected Bibliography

Allen, Steven. "Declining Unionization in Construction: The Facts and the Reasons." *Industrial and Labor Relations Review* 41 (April 1988): 343–59.

Applebaum, Eileen, and Rosemary Batt. *The New American Workplace.* Armonk, N.Y.: M.E. Sharpe, 1994.

Babin, Peter III. Interview by authors, tape recording, New Orleans, 17 December 1992.

Babin, Peter, Jr. Interview by authors, tape recording, New Orleans, 30 October 1992.

Barber, Randy, and Teresa Ghilarducci. "Pension Funds and the Economy." *Transforming the Financial System.* Edited by Gary Dymski, Gerry Epstein, and Robert Pollin. Armonk, N.Y.: M.E. Sharpe, 1993, 287–316.

Bartell, Robert. *Pension Funds of Multiemployer Industrial Groups, Unions and Nonprofit Organizations.* New York: National Bureau of Economic Research, 1968.

Baum, Bernie. Interview by Peter Philips, tape recording, Chicago, 28 August 1992.

Bernstein, Peter. *Capital Ideas: The Improbable Origins of Modern Wall Street.* New York: Free Press, 1992.

Blodgett, Richard. *Conflict of Interest: Union Pension Funds Asset Management.* New York: Twentieth Century Fund, 1977.

Carlough, Walter. Interview by authors, tape recording, Alexandria, Va., 17 September 1992.

Clark, Robert, and Joseph J. Spenger. *The Economics of Individual and Population Aging.* Cambridge: Cambridge University Press, 1980.

Cobble, Dorothy Sue. "Labor Law Reform." *Dissent* (Summer 1994).

Crabtree, Mike. Telephone interview by Peter Philips, tape recording, 19 July 1994.

Cullen, Donald, and Louis Feinberg. *The Bargaining Structure in Construction: Problems and Prospects Labor-Management Services Administration.* Washington, D.C.: Government Printing Office, 1980.

Cullerton, Jack. Interview by authors, tape recording, New Orleans, 29 October 1992.

Dorsey, Stuart, and John A. Turner. "Union and Nonunion Differences in Pension Fund

Investments and Earnings.'' *Industrial and Labor Relations Review* (July 1990): 543–55.

Employee Benefit Research Institute (EBRI). *Tabulations of the March 1993 Current Population Survey*. Washington, D.C.: EBRI, 1993.

Ennis, Richard. Interview by authors, tape recording, Chicago, 27 August 1992.

Fox, Robert. Interviews by Jeff Petersen and Peter Philips, tape recording, Los Angeles, 30 December 1992 and 2 August 1993.

Ghilarducci, Teresa. *Labor's Capital: The Economics and Politics of Private Pensions*. Cambridge, Mass.: MIT Press, 1992.

Goodpastor, Dan. Interview by Jeff Petersen and Andrew McDiarmid, tape recording, Compton, California, 2 August 1993.

Gould, Frank. Interview by authors, tape recording, Washington, D.C., 19 September 1992; and telephone interview by Peter Philips, tape recording, 17 July 1994.

Hammond, Reese. Interview by Peter Philips, tape recording, Washington, D.C., 28 April 1993.

Ierley, Merrit. *With Charity for All: Welfare and Society, Ancient Times to the Present*. New York: Praeger, 1984.

The International Operating Engineer. Washington, D.C.: Operating Engineer Press. Various issues.

James, Ralph and Estelle. *Hoffa and the Teamsters: A Study of Union Power*. Princeton, N.J.: D. Van Nostrand Company, 1965.

Johnson, Jack. Interviews by Jeff Petersen and Teresa Ghilarducci, tape recording, Washington, D.C., 27 August 1993 and 20 June 1994.

Kennedy, James B. *Beneficiary Features of American Trade Unions*. Baltimore: Johns Hopkins Press, 1908.

Kohler, Peter. *The Evolution of Social Insurance 1881–1981: Studies of Germany, France, Great Britain, Austria, and Switzerland*. London: Frances Pinter, 1982.

Lakonishok, Josef, Andrei Shleifer, and Robert Vishney, ''The Structure and Performance of the Money Management Industry,'' Preliminary Draft, University of Chicago, November 1991.

Lescohier, Don D. ''Old Age Pensions, Private Plans.'' *History of Labor in the United States, 1896–1932*. New York: The Macmillan Company, 1935.

Majich, Leo. Telephone interview by Peter Philips, tape recording, 19 July 1994.

Mangum, Garth L., and John Walsh. *Union Resilience in Troubled Times: The Story of the Operating Engineers, AFL-CIO, 1960–1993*. New York: M.E. Sharpe, 1994.

McCormick, Bob. Interview by authors, tape recording, New Orleans, 29 November 1992.

Mittelstaedt, Fred H. ''An Empirical Analysis of the Factors Underlying the Decision to Remove Excess Assets from Overfunded Pension Plans.'' *Journal of Accounting and Economics* 11 (November 1989): 399–418.

Morris, Robert. *Rethinking Social Welfare: Why Care for the Stranger?* New York and London: Longman, Inc., 1986.

Munnell, Alicia. ''Pension Contributions and the Stock Market.'' *New England Economic Review* (November/December 1987): 3–14.

Nash, Gerald D. *Social Security: The First Half Century*. Albuquerque: University of New Mexico Press, 1988.

Ogden, Warren, and Gerard Gasperini. ''Avoiding MPPAA Liability via Continued Participation or Total Participation.'' *Labor Law Journal* (April 1985): 239.

Petersen, Mitchell. "Pension Reversions and Worker-Shareholder Wealth Transfers." *Quarterly Journal of Economics* 107 (3) (August 1992): 1033–56.

Polanyi, Karl. *The Great Transformation: The Political and Economic Origins of Our Time.* Boston: Beacon Press, 1944.

Ricardo, David. *The Principles of Political Economy and Taxation.* London: Dent, 1962.

Riehl, Bill. Interview by Peter Philips, tape recording, New Orleans, 29 November 1992.

Rimlinger, Gaston. *Welfare Policy and Industrialization in Europe, America, and Russia.* New York: John Wiley & Sons, Inc., 1971.

Rizzuto, Paul. Interview by Teresa Ghilarducci, tape recording, date unknown.

Ross, Arthur, "The New Industrial Pensions." *The Review of Economics and Statistics* (May 1950): 133–38.

Sass, Steven. "Pension Bargains: The Heyday of U.S. Collectively Bargained Pension Arrangements." *Workers Versus Pensioners: Intergenerational Justice in an Ageing World.* Manchester: Manchester University Press, 1989.

Smart, Dan. Interview by Teresa Ghilarducci, tape recording, Indianapolis, 13 January 1994.

Somers, Norman A., and Louis Schwartz. "Pension and Welfare Plans: Gratuities or Compensation?" *Industrial and Labor Relations Review* (October 1950).

Stapleton, Tom. Interview by Jeff Petersen, tape recording, Alameda, Calif., 17 November 1993.

Steinberg, Richard, et al. *Pensions and Other Employee Benefits: A Financial Reporting and ERISA Compliance Guide.* New York: John Wiley & Sons, 1993.

Stupar, Frank. Interview by authors, tape recording, Washington, D.C., 17 September 1992.

Sweeny, John. Interview by Jeff Petersen, tape recording, San Francisco, Calif., 17 November 1993.

Tischler, Hace. *Self Reliance and Social Security: 1870–1917.* Port Washington, N.Y.: National University Publications, 1971.

Tucker, Ray. Interview by Jeff Petersen, tape recording, Redlands, Calif., 2 August 1993.

Turner, John A., and Daniel J. Beller. *Trends in Pensions.* Washington, D.C.: Government Printing Office, 1992.

U.S. Bureau of the Census. *Historical Statistics of the United States: Colonial Times to the Present.* New York: Basic Book Publishers, 1975.

U.S. Bureau of Labor Statistics. *Multiemployer Pension Plans Under Collective Bargaining.* Washington, D.C.: Government Printing Office, 1960.

U.S. Committee on Economic Security. *Social Security in America: The Factual Background of the Social Security Act as Summarized from Staff Reports to the Committee on Economic Security.* Washington, D.C.: Government Printing Office, 1937.

U.S. Congressional Research Service. *Joint Pension Trusteeship: An Analysis of the Visclosky Proposal,* Hearings Before the Subcommittee of Labor Management on H.R. 2664, Washington, D.C., Feb. 21–28, 1990.

U.S. Council of Economics Advisors. *Economic Report of the President.* Washington, D.C.: Government Printing Office, January 1993.

U.S. Department of Commerce. *Business and Statistics: 1963–1992.* Washington, D.C.: Government Printing Office, 1993.

U.S. Department of Labor. *Pension Plans Under Collective Bargaining.* Washington, D.C.: Government Printing Office, 1953.

U.S. Department of Labor. *Monthly Labor Review*. Washington, D.C.: Government Printing Office, January 1954.

U.S. Department of Labor. *National Union Benefit Plans 1947–1967*. Washington, D.C.: Government Printing Office, 1970.

U.S. Department of Labor. *Employment, Hours, and Earnings, United States, 1909–1990, Volume I*. Washington, D.C.: Government Printing Office, 1991.

U.S. Department of Labor. *High Performance Firms*. Washington, D.C.: Government Printing Office, 1994.

Viat, Art. Interview by Jeff Petersen, tape recording, San Francisco, Calif., 22 November 1993.

Warshawsky, Mark J. "Pension Plans: Funding, Assets, and Regulatory Environment." *Federal Reserve Bulletin* (November 1988): 717–30.

Wial, Howard. "Labor Law Reform and Secondary Workers." *Yale Law Review* 1993.

Williamson, John, and Frederick Pampel. *Old Age Income Security in Comparative Perspective*. Oxford: Oxford University Press, 1993.

Wolfson, Martin. *Financial Crises*. Armonk, N.Y.: M.E. Sharpe, 1994.

Index

About the Authors

TERESA GHILARDUCCI is an economist and Associate Professor at the University of Notre Dame. She is the author of *Labor's Capital, The Economics and Politics of Private Pensions.* She works on the pension policies of innovative firms and the effect of pension funds on capital markets.

GARTH MANGUM, economist and Professor at the University of Utah, is a well-known author in the history and economics of American labor relations. Mangum has in-depth knowledge of the unions and a sophisticated institutional perspective. He has published many scholarly case studies on unions.

JEFFREY S. PETERSEN specializes in political economy and labor economics.

PETER PHILIPS, labor economist and historian, is a Professor at the University of Utah, where he heads the Labor Center. He is best known for his detailed case studies in labor and industrial relations. His field of expertise is segmented labor markets and the construction industry.

ISBN 0-89930-995-X

90000>

EAN

9 780899 309958

HARDCOVER BAR CODE

WTIHDRAWN from
Monroe College Library

620
Por

Ref

Portable pension
plans for casual
labor markets.

23,514

DATE			

MONROE COLLEGE LIBRARY
2468 Jerome Ave.
Bronx, NY 10468

BAKER & TAYLOR

WTIHDRAWN from
Monroe College Library